REVISED & EXPANDED

MARY KATHLEEN GLAVICH, SND

WEEKDAY LITURGIES

 FOR

CHILDREN

Creative

WAYS TO CELEBRATE
YEAR-ROUND

TWENTY
THIRD *23rd*
PUBLICATIONS
NEW LONDON, CT 06320
WWW.23RDPUBLICATIONS.COM

To my colleague and friend Michael McKeefery,
whose enthusiasm and dedication to the work of the Church
has benefited thousands, including me

My gratitude to Reverend Ronald F. Krisman, Mary Agnes O'Malley, SND, and Mary Nanette Herman, SND, for their assistance with this project, and to the personnel at Twenty-Third Publications for their support, patience, and friendly collaboration that make work a joy.

TWENTY-THIRD PUBLICATIONS
A Division of Bayard; One Montauk Avenue, Suite 200; P.O. Box 6015; New London, CT 06320
(860) 536-2611 or (800) 321-0411; www.23rdpublications.com

Library of Congress Cataloging-in-Publication Data

Glavich, Mary Kathleen.
    Weekday liturgies for children : creative ways to celebrate year-round / Mary Kathleen Glavich.
        p. cm.
    ISBN 978-1-58595-882-5
    1. Children's liturgies.   2. Catholic Church—Liturgy—Texts. I. Title.
    BX2045.C553G53 2012
        264'.020083--dc23
                    2012017910

ISBN 978-1-58595-882-5
Printed in the U.S.A.

Currie

CONTENTS

Season of Easter

Ordinary Time

Last Weeks in Ordinary Time

Proper of Saints

[**Note:** *Numbers followed by "a" or "b" note celebrations found in the* New Roman Missal *but not in the* Lectionary for Masses with Children.]

January

Commons

Sacraments

Masses for Various Needs and Occasions

Appendix

Introduction

"A fully Christian life cannot be conceived without participation in the liturgical services in which the faithful, gathered into a single assembly, celebrate the paschal mystery."
DIRECTORY FOR MASSES WITH CHILDREN, #8

The Mass is innately fascinating for children. How many of us played Mass when we were young, using candy wafers for communion? One young man I know even wore vestments his mother made for his "home" Masses. Even though my childhood Masses were in Latin, I knew that when I was there, I was giving glory to God. I remember how proud I was when I was able to chime in with "two-two-O" at certain times in the liturgy. I also recall my joy in swinging on a tire my father hung from a tree and singing away with gusto a majestic, "*Et in terra pax hominibus.*"

Understanding and Appreciation

Young Catholics today are fortunate that our liturgies are in English and not a foreign language. However, children still need to be helped to understand and appreciate the Eucharist. It has to be translated for their lives. Why should we take pains to do this for them? Because the Eucharist is the heart and center of the Christian life. It is our most important prayer, our greatest act of worship, the highest point of contact with the incarnate Christ.

During the Eucharist we offer our almighty and loving God thanksgiving and praise. We remember and make present the sacrifice of Jesus Christ, which saved us. We participate in the paschal mystery of Jesus: his death and resurrection. We are nourished by God's word and then by God's very self in communion. As a community, the body of Christ, we are united in faith and love as we celebrate the sacred meal that is a forerunner of the eternal banquet of love.

More Than Good Feelings

Children can enjoy Mass because of its repetition, its various forms of human expression, and the experience of sharing an event in community. It is important, however, that they derive more than good feelings from the Eucharist. Granted, liturgy is basically an adult ritual and a mystery; yet, if adaptations are made and children are introduced to its riches on their own level, they will find it has meaning for them and their lives. Moreover, they will be better prepared to participate in the Eucharist when they are adult members of the community.

Teaching children about the liturgy does not mean catechizing them during Mass. Instruction about the significance, parts, and history of the Mass, its prayers, vestments, and vessels should take place outside of liturgy. This can be done in the classroom or during a class or family church tour. Likewise, individual Masses with their particular symbols and rituals should be prepared for prior to the actual celebration.

Liturgy Teaches

The liturgy is its own teacher; it needs no other. Participating in it can teach children in the way they learn best: through their senses and actions. The experience of a good liturgy can have a powerful impact on children, just as it does for adults. A woman even told me that she began inquiring about the Catholic faith because of a Catholic funeral she attended. She said she was drawn to share the faith, hope, and love of the community that she witnessed worshiping at the Mass.

Of course, one of the most effective ways to teach children about liturgy is through example. I once saw a father at Mass with his daughter, who was about four years old. He stood her on the railing of the pew in front of him so that she leaned against him. When it was time to cross himself before the gospel, he crossed her forehead, lips, and heart. That child was learning worship rituals from her parent, who is her primary teacher in the eyes of the Church.

Recently I saw a young boy returning from communion behind his grandfather. Both had a rosary in their hands. They were even on the same decade. I'm not advocating praying the rosary during Mass, but the example illustrates the influence of adult models on children.

I highly recommend having adults participate in school Masses. Invite parents, grandparents, school staff members, and other significant adults to the children's liturgies, and encourage them to take active roles. Ask the school librarian to do the reading, a parent to read the Universal Prayer (Prayer of the Faithful), the custodian to take up the gifts, and the school secretary to be an extraordinary minister of the Eucharist.

Older children can serve as role models for the younger children. Pair the children in the lower grades with children in the upper grades, and have them sit together at Mass. This also motivates the older children to behave better.

Lively Celebrations

Sadly, all too often children are subjected to dry, unfathomable liturgies. Not only is the celebration over their heads, but it doesn't resemble a celebration at all. No wonder they are bored. No wonder they don't care to go to Mass. With a little creativity and effort, Masses can be more appealing to children. We can involve them in the preparation and as active participants. We can use symbols, actions, and words that speak to their hearts.

What liturgies stand out in your mind? Probably those that were a little different. I recall a Mass where I was the only member of the congregation. Each time the priest prayed "you," he looked at me and nodded. Imagine the impact of the words, "This is my body which will be given up for you." Another Mass that is particularly memorable for me was a celebration at SS. Paul and Augustine Parish in Washington. The music and singing of this predominantly Black community sent my heart soaring.

At another parish Mass on the feast of the Holy Family, we each drew a Scripture verse from a basket. Mine was tailor-made for my family situation at that time. By providing weekday Masses for children that are just a little different, we can make the experience of liturgy more interesting. By exercising creativity and ingenuity and by allowing the children to exercise theirs, we can bring about liturgical experiences that make a lasting impression.

Our aim, of course, is not to make every Mass extraordinary. That will not prepare children for the liturgies they will experience as adults. Most of children's Masses should be recognizable as the rituals that are the tradition and heritage of our Church. For example, certain responses should stay the same. But something special every now and then in the children's liturgies will make them more meaningful.

What's in This Book

The first part of this book gives general suggestions for how to vary liturgies. The second and major part contains ideas for weekday Masses based on the readings in the *Lectionary for Masses with Children*. This lectionary is no longer in print. If you do not have one available, you will still find this book helpful. The Scripture references are provided for the readings on which each plan is based. This enables you to use them and the suggestions related to them for a Mass. On the other hand, if you prefer to stay with the readings given in the adult lectionary, you will find all of the readings used in this book listed in the back. Planners and homilists can easily see if the day's readings given in the adult lectionary are included in this book.

It's helpful to know that the 1973 *Directory for Masses with Children* states: "If all the readings assigned to the day seem to be unsuited to the capacity of the children, it is permissible to choose readings or a reading either from the Lectionary of the Roman Missal or directly from the Bible, but taking into account the liturgical seasons" (43).

Plans for the Masses comprise an introduction, universal prayer, special features to appeal to the children, suggested songs, and ideas for homilies. Not every priest has the ability to speak to children. The presider may be unable to express thoughts in the simple language of children and be unfamiliar with stories and examples that are geared to them. As a result, he may be uncomfortable and ineffective in addressing children. In this case, the *Directory for Masses with Children* allows the presider to permit another adult participating in the Mass to speak to the children after the gospel reading (DMC, 24). The suggested stories, illustrations, and themes provided here will facilitate this ministry for the presider or the person he designates to speak to the children.

The ideas in this book can also be incorporated into paraliturgical celebrations in classrooms and homes. These celebrations usually include readings, prayers, rituals, and songs and are similar to our eucharistic celebration. Thus they help foster children's understanding of liturgy.

Suggestions are also given for the proper of saints for the entire year, not only the school months, so that this book is a resource for teachers of vacation Bible schools and other summer religion programs.

Who It's For

This book is for catechists, DREs, priests, ministers of the liturgy, and anyone else responsible for planning liturgies for children. Many of the ideas draw on the imagination and talents of the participants. Sometimes a minor change will color the whole liturgy for children, just as a small adjustment in a kaleidoscope changes the whole scene.

To those so in awe of the liturgy that they hesitate to make such adjustments, I quote what Aidan Kavanagh warned in his book *Elements of Rite: A Handbook of Liturgical Style*: "To be consumed with worry over making liturgical mistakes is the greatest mistake of all. Reverence is a virtue, not a neurosis, and God can take care of Himself."

By making Masses meaningful to young hearts and minds, we enable children to be more open to their power and lead them to love and prize the Eucharist. Most important, we comply with the request of Jesus, "Let the children come to me" (Luke 18:16).

General Guidelines

Over the years many people have asked for a resource that they could use for children's liturgies, and this book is a response to that plea. The titles, numbers, and page numbers referred to in this book correlate with the readings in the Liturgical Press edition of the *Lectionary for Masses with Children* (Weekdays). If you do not have this lectionary, ignore these references.

The order of readings in the lectionary and also in this book is as follows:

Proper of Seasons
The Season of Advent
The Season of Lent
The Season of Easter
Ordinary Time

Proper of Saints
Feasts, Memorials, Solemnities

Commons
Apostles
Martyrs
Doctors, etc.

Sacraments
Baptism
Confirmation
Holy Eucharist
Reconciliation

For Various Needs and Occasions
Beginning of School Year
End of School Year
In Thanksgiving
For Vocations, etc.

The Table of Contents lists all of these topics in detail.

Variations in the Liturgy

1. Planning a Mass

Good liturgies are planned and practiced. They usually just don't happen spontaneously. The efforts that go into the eucharistic celebration are part of the gift. So, in planning children's Masses, always involve the children. If time allows, let the children work together to plan a liturgy. Depending on the age of the children, make decisions as a whole class, or divide the class into small groups and assign separate tasks for the following parts of the Mass:

- Entrance Procession
- Readings
- Universal Prayer
- Preparation of Gifts
- Thanksgiving after Communion
- Music

In the Appendix of this book you will find worksheets that can be duplicated and filled in by the planning groups. Once these are completed, make copies of them for the presider, the music director, and other participants who may need them.

Choose people for roles in the Mass according to their gifts. Poor readers who stumble through passages detract from the beauty and flow of the Mass and make others uncomfortable. They can better serve as ushers or members of a procession. Practice with the children who will take special roles in the Mass. This will make them more confi-dent and at ease and also insure that the worshipers are inspired to prayer and not distracted from it. Let the readers practice with the microphone if that is what they will be using. Coach them to project, enunciate, pronounce words correctly, and use expression.

Involve as many children as possible in the planning and celebrating. Let them set up the chalice, paten, and cruets. Children can even function as hosts and hostesses, greeting others at the door, providing them with programs or music sheets, and seating them. Servers should be chosen from the particular class or classes celebrating the Eucharist.

For a very special Mass, a program or sheet listing the songs and special prayers should be prepared for the participants. Have a student design the art for it. In adapting the liturgy for children, always preserve the structure of the Eucharist: Introductory Rites, Liturgy of the Word, Liturgy of the Eucharist, and Concluding Rite.

Some schools find it beneficial to organize a liturgy team composed of faculty, staff, and children representing various grade levels. This group can be responsible for planning Masses or for helping a particular grade level plan Masses. They can think of ways to prepare the entire school for participation in a special liturgy.

For example, a liturgy team at St. Leo the Great in Cleveland, Ohio, planned a Mass for the feast of Francis of Assisi. In the various classes, children read stories about Francis and reflected on people in their lives who were like him. Then the younger children cut out pictures of creation, which were put together to form a world, while the older children cut out articles from newspapers and magazines that revealed a lack of peace. The articles and the world were placed on a large banner, which the presider used in the homily.

2. Variations of Elements

When you plan children's Masses, keep in mind that there are many ways to vary elements like themes, environment, vestments, symbols, music, and so on. Consider the following suggestions.

The Theme of the Mass

The underlying themes of each Mass are thanksgiving and praise. Each particular liturgy, however, may flow out of another chosen theme. It is good to choose a theme based on the readings for the Mass. The theme can be in keeping with the season of the liturgical year or the feast or person commemorated at the Mass. Sometimes the celebration of a special secular event or occasion or even a topic being studied in school may suggest a theme.

Once the theme is identified, you might plan the songs, rituals, and decorations for the Mass around it. The Mass then unfolds as one unified movement. Remember, though, that the readings and prayers are rich in themselves. Through them God speaks to our hearts whether or not the Mass is planned around a theme.

Liturgy has an uncanny way of providentially fitting occasions. One day someone complimented Sister Joela for planning our community Mass centered on the birthday of our "nonagenerian." Someone else commented that she thought the Mass was intended to focus on our discernment for a new provincial superior. It turned out that Sister Joela had simply planned a Mass based on the readings of the day. Similarly, liturgies can speak to each

of us individually, meeting our needs, supporting our thoughts and immediate feelings. Liturgies can also speak to children in this way.

Possible themes you might use include God's goodness, the gift of life, listening to God's word, creation, prayer, God's mercy, love of others, the good shepherd, peace, vocations, helping the poor, justice, trust, courage, sharing the Good News, reconciliation, the cross, eternal life, patience, discipleship, growth, choices, beginnings, saints, the Holy Spirit, Mary as mother of the Church, perseverance, service, friends, and animals.

Whatever your theme, keep in mind that the purpose of the Mass is not to develop a theme or to teach people a lesson. It is always primarily a celebration of the paschal mystery of Jesus: his life, death, and rising that saved us.

The Environment

Occasionally hold the eucharistic celebration somewhere other than a church. Whether the space is a classroom, the school library, a home, or even outdoors, prepare and decorate it suitably for the sacred mysteries. Small children will be more comfortable seated on the floor, perhaps on rugs or pillows.

When the liturgy is in the church, decorate a bulletin board in the vestibule according to the season or the theme of the celebration.

Enhance the altar with an antependium (a large cloth that hangs in front of the altar). This cloth can contain a colorful display of symbols pertaining to the liturgy to be celebrated. Children, even families, may help to make the antependium. For example, for a Mass with the theme "God's Family," each family could provide a family photo to be fastened to the antependium.

Near the altar, display objects or pictures related to the theme of the celebration, for example, an arrangement of candles to carry out the theme of light or a photo or statue of the saint who is honored at the liturgy.

Decorate the lectern with a banner. Banners can also be displayed behind or near the altar. A banner or banners that change or have additions throughout a season like Advent or Lent are very effective. Banners can be composed of words, symbols, or both. They may be purchased or made by teachers, parents, or students out of burlap and felt, or even construction paper taped together. Banners can be hung on poles, affixed to walls, or draped over furniture. They can also be hung at the ends of pews.

Arrange flowers on or near the altar to beautify the space and create a festive atmosphere. These can be placed on a gracefully draped cloth. Garlands of flowers can be strung around columns. (Note that during Lent, flowers should not be part of the decorations except on the Feast of the Annunciation and St. Joseph's feast.)

Put a burning candle near the lectern to represent the light of the word of God. Display the children's creations: a mural, posters, collages, mobiles, cardboard boxes decorated on all sides. Use colors coordinated with the season or theme: green for ordinary time, purple for Advent, blue for Marian liturgies. Add special lighting effects, such as a spotlight on the lectionary or the crucifix.

Keep in mind the artistic principle "less is more." In all cases the decorations should not hide or distract from the central items of the Eucharist: the altar, the lectern, and the presider's chair.

Outside the Place of Worship

Decorate the outside of the church or chapel so as to proclaim the celebration taking place inside. During the Christmas season a large wreath and a manger scene are in order. During Easter white and gold banners may be hung. Children could use chalk to decorate the sidewalk with pictures related to the season. In places where there is ice and snow, they may make ice sculptures outside.

Vestments for the Presider

Help the children design a chasuble or stole for the priest. A parent could make a simple chasuble or stole from cotton cloth, and children could cut symbols out of material and sew them on. Or children could draw pictures with iron-on crayons, which could then be transferred onto the material.

Symbols Used at Mass

Objects convey messages and evoke feelings. They feed our senses and speak to our hearts. Incorporate simple, basic symbols into the liturgy to make an impact on your students. Primary symbols convey their meaning at once; they need not be explained. Fire, water, bread, wine, and oil, for example, are eloquent in themselves.

The two main symbols used in the Eucharist are bread and wine. To emphasize these, try the following. Occasionally use a very large host. Use a glass flagon so that the wine is visible. Help a class bake the unleavened bread that will be used at Mass. Display symbols in the sanctuary or have them carried to the sanctuary in the entrance procession. Give participants symbols as a memento of the Mass: a wooden cross, a piece of material, a small vial of oil, or a clay pendant strung on yarn or ribbon.

Incense, holy water, and candles are also significant symbols. The priest may incense the altar, the congregation, and the lectionary. Incense may be part of the display. Use a variety of scents. Mass may begin with the sprinkling rite using holy water.

Candles can enhance the sanctuary. They can be carried in procession and lit at appropriate times during the Mass. Practice with the children who will be carrying candles. Use caution. In some cases electric candles might be preferred.

Music for Liturgy

Music is integral to all human celebrations. It expresses and causes a range of emotions. Liturgical music is prayer. It creates unity in a group and deepens our response to God. Take advantage of children's affinity for music by using it liberally during the Eucharist.

When planning music for Mass, choose hymns that suit the particular part of the Mass, that focus on the season or theme, and that are meaningful to the children. The music should be of good quality and geared to the children's developmental levels. Hold a short singing practice before the Mass.

The four acclamations of the Mass are meant to be sung. They are the Gospel Acclamation; the Holy, holy; the Mystery of Faith acclamation; and the Great Amen. Have a person, even a child with a good singing voice, serve as a song leader for the community.

Try some of the following ideas for implementing music at Mass:

- Vary the parts of the Mass where music is used.
- Sing the Lord, Have Mercy; the Glory to God; the Eucharistic Acclamations; the Lord's Prayer; and the Lamb of God.
- Use different types of music, including popular songs, folk songs, classical pieces, and Latin songs.
- Play background music.
- Use various instruments: organ, piano, guitar, flute, trumpet, drum, tambourine, handbells, autoharp.
- Have small children play rhythm instruments like woodblocks and triangles.
- Vary the place in church where a group play the instruments.
- Have the instruments played in different parts of the church. For instance, children may ring handbells in each corner.
- Sing without any instrumental accompaniment.
- Alternate singing with a cantor.
- Have solo singers, duets, trios, and small groups.
- Add harmony to songs.
- Teach songs that are rounds.
- Use recordings of songs to support the singing, but only if necessary.
- Invite the children to sway, clap to the rhythm, or tap their feet.
- Add gestures to songs. Sign language is particularly good.

- Form a children's choir.
- Show slides during a song.

Times for Silence

Include space for prayerful silence during Mass so that children can absorb what is being said and pray in their hearts. The following times are conducive to silence: after the words "Let us pray," after the readings, after the homily, during the preparation of gifts, and after communion.

Commentary during Mass

The priest may make brief comments to introduce certain parts of the Mass. These comments can reinforce the theme and link particular parts of the Mass to the life of the children. They can also serve to guide the periods of silent prayer. The following are the times when comments may be added: Penitential Rite, Preface, Lord's Prayer, Sign of Peace, Communion, Final Blessing.

Gestures and Movement

The more the children participate in the Mass, the more they will enjoy and remember it. Gestures have meaning that children understand. Once at a school Mass, after the sign of peace, I noticed that five-year-old Michael was crying. When I went to him and asked what was wrong, he whispered, "Nobody shook my hand." Michael knew the meaning of that sign. I promptly shook his hand and hugged him.

The following ideas are additional ways to use gestures at Mass:

- Let a small group of children or the entire congregation add gestures to songs.
- Different groups of children may contribute a gesture to each line of a song.
- Have the children who do the gestures stand before the altar and face the congregation.
- Let a leader or small group of children lead the congregation in adding gestures to a song or prayer.
- Incorporate genuflections and deep bows into the rituals.

- Use sign language for songs or for responses such as Alleluia.

One final note: The priest, deacon, or persons who do the readings can make the Scripture come alive with gestures. For example, when the gospel says, "He stretched out his hand," the priest or deacon could extend his hand.

Postures during Mass

Most children learn the appropriate postures at Mass by repeating them. They thus learn when to stand, sit, or kneel. For a good reason postures may be changed in certain seasons.

For example, at a Lenten Mass, kneeling would be suitable for the Penitential Rite. At an Easter Mass, standing during the Eucharistic Prayer would express our status as redeemed people who look forward to a life of glory. A deep bow and a genuflection, such as the one made during the Creed on the feast of the Annunciation, are also meaningful options.

Liturgical Dancing

Dance adds much to the celebration. Invent or learn movements to favorite religious songs yourself or let the children choreograph dances. The dance, just as a liturgical song, should not be done as a performance, but as an act of worship. Naturally it should be in good taste. Here are some ways to incorporate dance in a liturgy:

- Use dance as part of the entrance procession, communion reflection, or recessional.
- Accompany the gospel reading with interpretative dance.
- Have dancers use colorful streamers, tambourines, or scarves as they dance.
- Let the dancers wear special clothes; for instance, the girls can wear long skirts; boys can wear vests or ties.

Special Attire

For special-occasion liturgies, let the children wear crowns, hats, arm bands, belts, banners, badges, or pendants. They might make these items as part of their Mass preparation.

Mementos to Distribute

Distribute mementos to all the participants at liturgies. These objects should be related to the theme of the Mass. The class who plans the Mass might make or provide these. Possible mementos are holy cards, prayers, placards, poems, medals, pins, buttons, or symbolic objects such as candles, flowers, materials, vials of oil, small clay pots, hearts, wooden crosses, shards, and stones.

Pass out the mementos before or after Mass or after communion as part of the reflection time. Suggest possible uses for these items: keep them in Bibles, give them to someone else, hold them in their hands when they pray, or set them on their desks or dressers at home as reminders of God's love for them.

3. Variations for Parts of the Mass

When you plan children's Masses, also keep in mind that there are many ways to add variation to parts of the Mass, such as processions, prayers, readings, and so on. Here are some suggestions for these:

The Entrance Procession

The procession is a form of prayer. All members should walk with dignity. The procession could include all the ministers of the Mass: the presider, lector, extraordinary ministers of the Eucharist, musicians, and servers. The reader carries the lectionary and should raise it high, holding it with two hands. The procession is usually led by the processional cross. You may also want to have children in it carry candles, banners, incense, and bells.

Occasionally invite the entire congregation to be part of the entrance procession, or plan for children in the procession to carry something to the sanctuary to add to a display there. Add dancers to the procession. Periodically in their dance, they might pause and look to the altar. Instead of singing a song, chant or recite the entrance antiphon, or play only instrumental music.

Introductory Comments

If the group is small, the presider may want to greet everyone individually, or he may just want to give a one-sentence introduction to focus on the theme of the Mass. Let a participant read a short paragraph linked to the day's Mass that serves to remind everyone what they are about to do.

The Penitential Rite

Make use of all three options given in the Roman Missal.

When using option C, you can add more invocations. You might also incorporate one or more of the following:

- Show slides as you recite a penitential meditation.
- Exchange a sign of peace (reconciliation) here instead of later.
- Substitute the Rite of Blessing and Sprinkling of Holy Water (the *aspergus*). After the priest has blessed the water, let faculty, staff, or children sprinkle the assembly using pine branches.
- Insert text in the Lord, Have Mercy. For example, "Jesus, who loved little children, we ask forgiveness…"
- Substitute a brief examination of conscience. Ask a question, pause for reflection, and then have the congregation make a response such as "Jesus, we are sorry" or "Lord, forgive us."

The Glory to God

Substitute another prayer of praise such as the Glory Be. Or use a child's or class's original prayer praising the Father, Son, and Holy Spirit.

The Collect (opening prayer)

The priest can sing or recite this prayer. Adapt the words for children but preserve the ideas of the prayer. Ask the priest to guide the children's thoughts for the silent pause after "Let us pray" by referring to the theme. For example: "Let us pray that we use God's gifts in the best way possible."

The Readings

The introduction to the *Lectionary for Masses with Children* states, "The proclamation of the word transcends the mere communication of information and becomes a community-building celebration of God's saving mystery especially when candles, incense, banners, and processions magnify the word's impact on eyes and ears, in hearts and minds" (50).

Use the *Lectionary for Masses with Children* (or the regular lectionary) and follow the guidelines in its introduction. The readings should be done from the lectionary or an attractive book, not from a sheet of paper or a missalette.

The readings may be preceded by a line or two of introduction. One reading may be sufficient, and if so, it should be the gospel. The reader should check the pronunciation of unfamiliar words, and read in a loud and clear voice so that all can hear and understand the reading. Remind the reader to look up at the assembly periodically. Other ways to enhance the readings include:

- Instruct the reader to hold the lectionary high in the entrance procession.
- Have the reader carry the lectionary to the lectern with other children in procession.
- Have servers hold candles and stand near the lectionary during the reading.
- Help the reader memorize the reading and deliver it by heart.
- Encourage the reader to add gestures to the reading.
- Plan for two or more children to each read a part of the first reading.
- If there is dialogue in the reading, have children take the parts.
- Allow a few moments of silence after the reading and before the responsorial psalm.

Responsorial Psalm

Teach those who read the responsorial psalm to look up or lift their hand as a clue to the congregation when to respond. If there is only one reading, the responsorial psalm may be sung after the homily.

If the psalm is sung, the chosen song could be the psalm for the day in the lectionary or one that has a similar theme. The song should be the psalm itself, not just a song that is like the psalm. *We Are God's People: Psalms for the Family of God* by Jeanne Cotter (GIA) is one collection that is based on the *Lectionary for Masses with Children*. See "Resources" on page 210 for other options.

A cantor can sing or recite the verses, and the congregation can respond in song. Or have the congregation sing the entire psalm and response. Other alternatives include:

- Sing the psalm on a psalm tone.
- As the psalm is recited, have music played in the background.
- Include a visual response.
- Ask individuals or small groups to add gestures to the psalm as it is read.
- Replace the psalm with a reflective silence.

Alleluia or Gospel Acclamation

The Alleluia should be sung or omitted. Have the children raise their hands as they sing "alleluia," or use American Sign Language for it. Occasionally invite them to clap to the Alleluia.

The Gospel

Have children take narrative parts for the gospel whenever possible and shorten or lengthen the text when appropriate. Other ways to vary the proclamation of the gospel include the following:

- Use a child's poem or composition as an introduction to the gospel or as a meditation afterward.
- Add a reference to a saint or other readings as an introduction to or reflection on Scripture.

- If the gospel is a story, have a group of children pantomime it, add gestures, or dramatize it. The introduction to the *Lectionary for Masses with Children* cautions, however, against presenting the word as a major production with costumes and props (52).
- Tell the gospel story as an echo pantomime. Read one line at a time, making a gesture to represent its meaning. After each line, the assembly repeats it, imitating the gesture.
- As the gospel is read, have the children hold up pictures they have made.
- Use appropriate slides as the gospel is read, including scenes of the children themselves.
- Sing an antiphon or a line from an appropriate song periodically during the gospel reading.

The Homily

In place of the priest presider, another adult participant may speak to the children about the readings. Keep the following pointers in mind.

- Stand close to the children to speak. If the group is small, gather them around and let them sit on the floor.
- Draw the children into the homily through questioning.
- Use a puppet or other visual aids, like an object or a poster, to attract and keep the children's attention. Pull the object out of a bag or an apron.
- Include a song, story, poem, or other creative additions that enhance your points.
- Incorporate a cheer like the following:

  Give me a J!   (J)
  Give me an E!   (E)
  Give me an S!   (S)
  Give me a U!   (U)
  Give me an S!   (S)
  Who loves us? (Jesus)

- On a saint's feast day have someone pose as the saint and talk about his or her life or be interviewed by the homilist.

Universal Prayer

The best petitions will flow from the readings, come from the heart of the participants, and are expressed in the children's own words. The presider begins them with an invitation to prayer and concludes them with a prayer addressed to God. Consider these suggestions.

- Use a folder or a sheet of heavy paper to back the paper from which the prayers are read.
- Have one person read all of the petitions, or individuals each read one.
- Vary the responses to them, for example, sing or chant them and the response. Also allow for spontaneous petitions.
- Occasionally accompany each petition with a visual image, such as a slide or a picture a child has made.

Presentation of Gifts

The presentation of gifts may be preceded by the dressing of the altar. Children may spread the altar cloth and linens on the altar and set in place the Roman Missal and flowers. The focus should be on the offering of the gifts of bread and wine. Gifts for the poor or for the Church may also be brought up in procession. Gifts other than the bread and wine should not be placed on the altar. Those in the procession should walk reverently. Accompany the procession with a song, prayer, instrumental music, or an audiovisual. The procession may be omitted.

The Eucharistic Prayer

Here are some guidelines to consider:

- Use one of the three Eucharistic Prayers for Children (they are not printed in the new Roman Missal, but they may still be used), or use one of the Eucharistic Prayers for Reconciliation. Vary the Eucharistic Prayer that is used.
- Have the children sing the responses. Occasionally invite them to gather around the altar.

- Have a burst of sound, such as a trumpet fanfare, accompany the great amen, one of the most important responses of the Mass.

The Our Father

Introduce the prayer, linking it to the theme of the Mass. Invite children to do one of the following during it: hold hands, raise hands, or add gestures.

The Sign of Peace

This can be done in several ways. For example: give a handshake; give a hug; place hands on one another's heads in blessing; sign one another's palms with a cross; vary the words; sing a song of peace; bow to one another (especially when colds and the flu are prevalent); say "Shalom"; exchange a paper heart made before the Mass.

In a small group, hold hands and pass a squeeze of the hand from one to another initiated by the presider.

Communion

On special occasions offer the cup as well as the bread to the children. Also, invite parents to be extraordinary ministers of the Eucharist.

Thanksgiving after Communion

Offer thanks in the following ways: sing a song; have an individual pray a prayer; have the entire congregation pray a prayer from the program, a prayer book, or an overhead transparency; show slides; have dancers dance; allow for a time of silence.

The Final Blessing

Before this final blessing, the presider may want to refer to the theme, possibly in the form of a prayer.

The Recessional

Sign the forehead or hands of the participants with perfume or oil as they go out, or have dancers lead the procession. Invite the entire congregation to process out behind the celebrant.

How to Choose Weekday Readings

Use an ordo (the Church's liturgical calendar that is published annually), to help you determine the title, rank, and season of the year for the day you are celebrating. Use the *Lectionary for Masses with Children* table of contents to locate the sections mentioned here.

1. For a solemnity, a feast, or November 2, use the readings in the Proper of Saints.
2. For a day that is a memorial or unmarked, choose any of the readings suggested in
   - the Proper of Saints,
   - Ordinary Time or (during Advent, Lent, or Eastertime) readings from the respective seasonal section, or
   - the section "For Various Needs and Occasions." (One reading may be from the Proper of Saints and the other from the seasonal section.)
3. For any other day, if it is Advent, Lent, or Eastertime, choose from the readings for the respective season. Otherwise, choose readings from Ordinary Time or from the section "For Various Needs and Occasions."
4. In Christmastime for a solemnity or feast use the readings in the Sunday Lectionary or in the Proper of Saints. On other weekdays use readings from the Season of Christmas in the Sunday Lectionary.

How to Use the Suggestions in This Book

The introductions and intercessions may be copied and personalized for the celebrating community.

Introduction: A suggested introduction is given. You may want to adapt it to reflect your particular group of children at the particular time you are celebrating the Eucharist. A participant in the Mass may read it before the entrance procession.

Universal Prayer: The petitions should be adapted and added to in order to suit your particular celebration, group of children, and current needs. The petitions begin with prayers for the whole Church and world and then include the needs of specific groups. You may want to invite participants to mention other intentions. You may also add a final petition: "For all the prayer requests we hold in our hearts."

Special Features: These are many ways to make a particular liturgy special. Refer to the first part of this book for suggestions for enhancing a eucharistic celebration.

Songs: The songs suggested here are found in parish or school hymnals. If possible, the Mass songs should reflect the liturgical season. Keep in mind the purpose of each song. The entrance song is a joyful song of gathering that sets the tone for the Mass. The presentation song reflects the idea of giving the gifts of bread and wine. The communion song has to do with sharing the Body and Blood of Jesus and best accompanies the communion procession when it is a mantra (a short repeated song) or a song with an easy refrain. The recessional song should motivate participants to go out and spread the Good News through Christlike lives.

Musical settings for the responsorial psalms in the *Lectionary for Masses with Children* are available. Otherwise, you may prefer to use those that the children hear at the Sunday liturgies when they worship with their families.

Homily Ideas: The visuals suggested here are only options. Keep in mind though that concrete visuals capture the attention of children and help them remember concepts.

I offer ideas in point form, but feel free to rearrange or expand them. They may be "borrowed" from another Mass plan. The homilist can choose those ideas that best fit the group, the situation, and the chosen readings. If my suggested ideas give rise to entirely new and more creative ideas, all the better.

Proper of Saints: Summaries and Themes

In the section Proper of Saints (beginning on page 105) I have provided a paragraph summarizing the life of each saint or explaining the feast. The information there could be used in the homily or as an introduction to the readings.

After the summary paragraph, several themes are proposed in case the homilist wishes to add to or depart from the homily plan suggested in the common of the Mass.

PROPER *of* SEASONS

WEEKDAY READINGS

Once again, note that numbers before and under each title refer to sections and pages, respectively, in the *Lectionary for Masses with Children*.

Season of Advent

172 Prepare for the Coming of the Lord

(*PAGE W5*) ISAIAH 30:19B-21 • LUKE 12:35-38

We are in Advent, the season when we prepare for the coming of Christ. During this eucharistic celebration, Christ will come to us in word, under the forms of bread and wine, and through one another. Let us be prepared to welcome him. Let our bodies and our voices show our thanks, our praise, and our joy that Jesus is Emmanuel, God with us.

Universal Prayer

The response is *"Lord, hear our prayer."*

That during Advent the Church may become more ready for Jesus' coming in glory at the end of the world, let us pray to the Lord.

That our government leaders may see Christ in others and serve them well, let us pray to the Lord.

That the poor and the sick may have the grace to know God's goodness through the help of others during Advent, let us pray to the Lord.

That our hearts will be ready to welcome Christ in all the ways he comes to us, let us pray to the Lord.

Special Features

- Hold an Advent wreath ceremony and explain the symbolism of the Advent wreath.
- Distribute cards that say "Prepare" or purple ribbons to wear as reminders to pray, listen, and obey all during Advent.
- Play a recording of an Advent song as the children assemble for Mass.

Songs

Alleluia; Hurry, the Lord Is Near; Come, Lord Jesus; Do Not Delay; The King of Glory; The King Shall Come; O Come, O Come, Emmanuel; Prepare the Way; Let the Valleys Be Raised; Soon and Very Soon; We Long for You, O Lord

Homily Ideas

Visual: A clock

Show a clock and ask the children to recall an experience of expecting someone to come at a certain time. Perhaps a parent was supposed to come home, or a friend or relative was coming to visit.

Ask the children to remember how they felt as the time drew near and how they prepared for the hour.

. . . .

Ask how the children would have felt if they had missed seeing the person because they were not prepared. Maybe they had the wrong time or were not home on time or fell asleep.

. . . .

Remind the children that we must be ready and waiting for Jesus or we will miss him. In the gospel Jesus tells us about a master whose servants wait for him and welcome him. These servants are models for us. They are awake and prepared for their master's return at night. They have their lamps burning and open the door for him. The master was pleased with these good servants and rewarded them.

. . . .

Tell the children that the first reading says that the Lord comes to help us and to show us the road to follow. Jesus comes to us in many ways. In Advent we remember how the chosen people waited for him until he came on Christmas night in Bethlehem. Every day he comes to us in spiritual ways in other people and in the gift of the Eucharist. Someday at the end of the world he will come again, this time in glory and majesty.

. . . .

Suggest three ways to be ready for Jesus: pray, listen, and obey. Explain: Pray extra during Advent. Listen to what God is saying through your parents and in the Bible. Try harder to obey God's laws. These three ways will make our hearts ready to recognize and welcome Jesus when he comes. Mary, the Mother of Jesus, got ready for him in these ways.

. . . .

Tell the Russian legend of Babushka. It is about an old woman who is told one night that there is a young couple with a newborn baby in a barn. Babushka plans to take gifts to the family, but since she is busy about the house and it is night, she decides to sleep first and go the next day. The next morning when she goes with her gifts to the barn, the family is gone. Babushka missed the savior!

173 The Kingdom of Heaven Is Near

(PAGE W8) ISAIAH 30:19, 23-24, 26 • MATTHEW 9:35—10:1, 5A, 6-7

God is kind to us. God wants to heal us from all that keeps us from being as well and happy as we should be. For this reason God sent Jesus into the world to save us. During this Mass we pray that Jesus will come to bring us health. We pray for the coming of God's kingdom, in which there will be no sorrow, no sickness, and no tears.

Universal Prayer

The response is *"Lord, come heal us."*

That our church leaders may heal and be healed especially through the sacrament of reconciliation, we pray to the Lord.

That our world leaders may be instruments of healing for all people, we pray to the Lord.

That those who are sick in mind or body may be comforted and healed, we pray to the Lord.

That sinners may come to know the healing touch of God in their lives, we pray to the Lord.

That we may be people who heal and soothe others, we pray to the Lord.

Special Features

- At the sign of peace, invite participants to greet one another with "May Jesus heal you."

- Make "prescriptions" for a happy life on slips of paper. These can be particular virtues or Scripture quotations. After communion pass a box or boxes around and let each person draw out a paper and spend time quietly reflecting on how to develop the virtue or take to heart the Scripture message.
- Give each person a bandaid as a reminder to be a healer like Jesus, or give out cards with a purple chi rho drawn on them as an Advent reminder.

Songs

Because of Jesus; Come, Thou Long-Expected Jesus; Every Valley; Lay Your Hands; Mighty Lord; Mine Eyes Have Seen the Glory; My Soul in Stillness Waits; Wake, Awake

Homily Ideas

Visuals: A bandage, a globe

Tell about a time when you were sick and a doctor helped you get well. Ask the children how many of them have been sick. Comment how wonderful it is to feel better again after doing what the doctor says.

• • •

Explain that Jesus is called the divine physician because he brought healing to the whole world. After original sin had brought sin, suffering, and death into the world, Jesus gave us a chance for new life again. (Put the bandage on the globe.) Jesus gave us salvation. The word "salvation" is like the word "salve," which heals us and soothes us.

• • • •

Explain that Jesus' power over sickness and death shown in his miracles was a sign of his power to give us new life. Give or ask the children to give examples of times when Jesus healed people.

• • • •

Name some "diseases" we might have: the crabbies, the gimmies, the lazies, big heads, sharp tongues, itching fingers. Comment that the power of Jesus can heal us and make us better persons, the ones we were meant to be. We need Jesus.

• • • •

Name some "diseases" the world has today: poverty, violence, racism, and so on. Give examples from the news that all is not well. The world needs the peace and love that Jesus brings.

• • • •

Comment that the chi rho, which stands for Christ, resembles the symbol on a prescription. (You might show cards with the symbols.) Christ is what the world needs to be healed. During Advent we pray that Jesus will come to save us.

• • • •

Recall that Isaiah said that as soon as God hears us crying, God comes to help and "binds up his people's injuries." We can pray during Mass for a particular healing we would like for ourselves or someone else.

• • • •

Point out that in the gospel Jesus gave his disciples power to heal too. (Ask how we can "heal" others by being kind, by loving them, by praying for them.)

174 The Kingdom of God Is Within You

(PAGE W11) ISAIAH 40:25-26, 29-31 • LUKE 7:17-26

Our God who comes to save us is mighty. Those who trust in God are also strong. They are like John the Baptist, who wasn't afraid to be tough on himself and to stand up for what was right. During this Mass let us pray that Jesus, whom John preached about, will make us strong witnesses like John.

Universal Prayer

The response is *"God, give us strength!"*

That the pope, bishops, and other church leaders look to God for strength and wisdom, we pray to the Lord.

That our country's leaders realize that those who are in power have a responsibility to help the weak, we pray to the Lord.

That those who suffer in prisons or on the streets or in hospitals may find hope and strength in Jesus, we pray to the Lord.

That all of us may be renewed during Advent to live as followers of Jesus and to spread the Good News of his love, we pray to the Lord.

Special Features

- As a communion reflection, show slides that demonstrate the power of God: mountains, stars, canyons, oceans, an eagle. During the presentation, play one of the songs listed under "Songs" or pray a prayer about God as our strength.
- For the responsorial psalm, have the children fold their hands for "let your mercy be on us" and raise them for "as we place our trust in you."

Songs

God Gives His People Strength; If God Is for Us; The King of Glory Comes; The King Shall Come; Mighty Lord; O Come, Divine Messiah; On Eagle's Wings; On Jordan's Bank

Homily Ideas

Visual: Vitamin pills

Ask the children if they have ever felt so tired that they couldn't keep their eyes open or couldn't stand. They had no energy left. Tell them that one Christmas song has the line "The weary world rejoices." In Advent we look forward to Christ's coming to wake us up and fill us with new life and energy. Jesus the Messiah gave new life and hope to the blind, the lame, the deaf, the crippled, and the poor. He was strong enough to do this then, and he can fill us now with life.

• • •

Recall that the reading from Isaiah promises us that if we trust in God we will be as strong as eagles that soar in the sky. An eagle that weighs from eight to twelve pounds is capable of carrying away an animal of seven and a half pounds. Ask what kind of strength Isaiah is talking about (strength to do good, to suffer, to love). God is almighty. We can see that from the billions of gigantic stars God has created. God will give power to those who ask for it.

• • •

Remind the children that Jesus said that John the Baptist was strong and not like tall grass blown by the wind. John did not live a comfortable, easy life. He called people to repent, and he prepared the way for Jesus and God's kingdom. In the end John was killed for it. Ask the children if they are strong enough to be a follower of Jesus, to witness to Jesus, to be a Christian. Give examples of strength, perhaps examples shown by the children themselves.

• • •

Show the bottle of vitamins and name the vitamins a Christian life requires: Vitamin A—Action: Do what Jesus says and you will have energy to do even more. Your muscles will be built up. Vitamin B—Belief: Believe in Jesus and his promises. Pray to believe even more. Vitamin C—Confidence: Trust that God loves you. God within you will help you make the right decisions. Vitamin D—Daring:

Dare to love the way Jesus did. Love God with all your heart. Love the people in your life. This may sometimes take a lot of courage.

• • •

Tell the children the quotation: God and I are the majority. Ask what it means (with God on our side, no one can overpower us).

175 My Heart Praises the Lord

(PAGE W14) 2 CORINTHIANS 1:3–4 • LUKE 1:46–56

Mary, the Mother of God, is a key figure during Advent. We look to her, the first and best Christian, as our model. As Mary cooperated with God in saving the world, we, too, offer ourselves as God's servants, willing to do what God asks. With Mary we praise and thank God. The word "Eucharist" means thanksgiving. We offer this Mass to praise and thank God for the great work of our salvation.

Universal Prayer

The response is *"Lord, hear our prayer."*

That the Church may always be open to the coming of God as Mary was, let us pray to the Lord.

That world leaders may remember that their role is to serve others, let us pray to the Lord.

That pregnant women may be helped to anticipate the birth of their children with joy, let us pray to the Lord.

That we may long for God, let us pray to the Lord.

That we might all be generous in letting God use us for spreading the kingdom of justice and peace, let us pray to the Lord.

Special Features

- Have an Advent Mary candle displayed in the sanctuary. Explain it before Mass.
- Distribute holy cards, medals of Mary, or blue ribbons.
- Make up gestures for the first reading so that it can be read as an echo pantomime with the children repeating each line and gesture.
- As a communion reflection, play a recording of Mary's canticle, the Magnificat, such as John Michael Talbot's "Holy Is His Name." Liturgical dancers might perform a dance of praise to the music.

Songs

Behold a Virgin Bearing Him; Come, My Children; Come, O Long-Awaited Savior; Do Not Delay; Hail Mary: Gentle Woman; I Have Loved You; Lo, How a Rose E'er Blooming; Magnificat; Mary's Joy; Mary's Song; May We Praise You; My Soul Rejoices; See How the Virgin Waits; Sing Alleluia, Sing; Sing of Mary; We Praise You

Homily Ideas

Visual: A flute or other wind instrument
Begin the homily with a song about Mary, such as "Hail Mary: Gentle Woman."

. . . .

Show the wind instrument and ask how it works (someone blows air through it). Explain that someone once compared Mary to a reed or a flute because she let God's breath work through her.

She said yes to God's messenger, the angel Gabriel, and she agreed to be the Mother of God. She was puzzled about how this would be, and she probably knew there would be suffering involved. Still she said yes. God was able to do great things through Mary, just as a musician is able to make beautiful music through a flute.

. . . .

Explain that Mary was not proud and puffed up about her important role. As the one who would give birth to the Messiah everyone was waiting for, she could have been self-centered. Instead, she reached out to others. One of the first things Mary did was to give service to an older relative named Elizabeth who was pregnant. Mary, carrying Christ within her, went to help someone. She did what Paul in the first reading tells us to do: she comforted someone in great need.

. . . .

Tell the children that when Elizabeth told Mary she knew she was God's mother, Mary broke out in a song of praise to God that the Church prays every day in its official evening prayer. This song of praise is called the Magnificat.

. . . .

Point out that in her song Mary predicted that God was about to overturn the old way of doing things. The weak would become powerful, and the powerful would be made weak. Mary foretold that because of God's goodness to her, everyone would call her blessed. Ask: When do we call Mary blessed? (in the Hail Mary). You might have the children pray the Hail Mary now and raise their hands when they reach the part that calls Mary blessed.

. . . .

Comment that in her song, Mary praised God for the good things God did, especially for keeping the promise to send a savior. She praised God for being just and merciful. Ask: What are some things we could praise God for? How can we praise God? Mention that the angels praised God the night Jesus was born. Ask what they said (glory to God in the highest).

. . . .

Mention to the children that as they prepare their hearts during Advent, they should be making them into hearts full of praise.

Season of Lent

176 Pray, Fast, and Share

(PAGE W19) ISAIAH 58:6-9 • MATTHEW 6:1-6, 16-18 or
MATTHEW 6:1-4 or MATTHEW 6:1, 5-6 or MATTHEW 6:1, 16-18

[***Note:*** There is a choice of gospel readings here. Selection A is about giving to the poor, praying, and fasting in secret. B is only about giving to the poor, C is only about praying, and D is only about fasting.]

It is good to be gathered together here today to celebrate Mass. For we are in Lent, the season of the Church year when we remember how Jesus offered himself on the cross for us. Each Mass re-presents Jesus' sacrifice so we can offer him to the Father, too, and offer ourselves with him. Let us praise and thank God today with full hearts and full voices and ask for the grace to love God more and more.

Universal Prayer

The response is *"Create in us a new spirit, O Lord."*

For the whole people of God, that we may become holier through our acts of love this Lent, let us pray to the Lord.

For leaders of nations, that they may work for peace and justice for all people, let us pray to the Lord.

For those who are hungry or homeless or who are suffering because of injustice, that they may be helped, let us pray to the Lord.

For each of us here, that we may be strong enough to keep our Lenten resolutions, let us pray to the Lord.

Special Features

- Have a large wooden cross displayed and a banner with the words "pray," "fast," "share." Or have each word written on a puzzle piece, which when put together form a cross. These may be given to three children who bring them up and place them together during the homily.
- Give each child a penny as a reminder to repent during Lent.
- After the gospel have the children renew their baptismal promises.
- If the group is small, invite them to come and stand around the altar after the Holy, Holy.

Songs

All That We Have; Ashes; Pardon Your People; Seek the Lord; Take Up Your Cross; Throughout These Forty Days; Turn to Me

Homily Ideas

Visuals: An old penny and a soup bowl or an alms box (as used with Operation Rice Bowl)

Remind the children that the gospel acclamation was "Repent, says the Lord; the kingdom of heaven is at hand." Tell them that Lent is a time to repent. Ask what it means to repent (to be sorry for sins). Inform the children that their Lenten resolutions will help them repent, be sorry for their sins.

• • •

Show the children the old penny. Tell them that the penny was once shiny copper, but with years of handling, it has become dirty and dull. Ask how it could be made to look like new again (by shining it with copper cleaner). You might shine the penny.

• • •

Compare the penny to us. Explain that at baptism we received God's life of grace. We were beautiful and holy. The white garment we wore then was a sign of our bright new life. As time went on, we did things that made us less beautiful. We hurt others and failed to show love for God. During Lent we can polish ourselves, until we are like new again.

• • •

Explain that the gospel reading told us three ways to repent and become like new. They are three Lenten practices. We are to pray, to fast (which means not to eat as much as we usually do), and to share what we have with the poor. Show a soup bowl, alms box, or any other symbol related to a Lenten practice that your parish may be carrying out.

• • •

Give examples of how the children can pray extra prayers during Lent or pray extra well, fast from sweets or extra helpings of what they like, and share with those who are not as fortunate as they are.

• • •

Hold your hand to your mouth and pretend to blow a trumpet to announce something. Say, "This morning I said extra morning prayers. Everyone applaud me please." Let the children applaud. Continue, "And I only drank one cup of coffee instead of two. Applaud please." (*Pause.*) "Besides that, I gave away some of the clothes I don't use. Applaud please. What's wrong with what I'm doing?" (You are doing good things to be praised.)

• • •

Comment that we pray, fast, and share during Lent because we love God, not because we want other people to admire us. Jesus told us to do our acts of penance in secret. If we truly repent, then when the kingdom comes, we will enter it and all the angels and saints will applaud us.

---

177 What We Do for Others, We Do for Jesus

(*PAGE W24*) ACTS 11:27-30 • MATTHEW 25:31-40

The Church, like its founder Jesus Christ, has always had a heart for the poor. From its earliest days its members have shared with those who have less. Lent *is a time to renew ourselves in the love shown by sharing (or almsgiving). Today at our celebration let us pray for those in need, aware that Jesus considers anything done for others as done for himself. In addition to our prayers, we will offer donations for (name of organization).*

Universal Prayer

The response is *"Lord, hear our prayer."*

For members of the Church who do not have enough to eat or a place to sleep, let us pray to the Lord.

For government leaders, that they may make laws to protect and help the poor, let us pray to the Lord.

For children in certain countries who have to work instead of going to school or playing, let us pray to the Lord.

For ourselves, that we may learn to respond to people as we would respond to Jesus, let us pray to the Lord.

Special Features

- Before the gospel is read, tell the children to listen carefully to see if they would rather be a sheep or a goat.
- Take up an offertory collection to help a particular group in need. Let two children carry up the donations at the presentation of gifts. Let the children know what organization will receive their money. Later share with them any letters of acknowledgment and gratitude.
- Before the homily, tell the story of a saint who was known for caring for the needy, such as Vincent de Paul, Martin de Porres, Elizabeth of Hungary, or perhaps the patron of your parish.

Songs

Bread for the World; Each Time That We Love; From the Depths We Cry to Thee; God of the Hungry; Send Us Forth; Service; Whatsoever You Do

Homily Ideas

Visual: A large paper heart or Valentine candy box

Recall that the gospel is a story about judgment day at the end of the world. Ask the children how many would want to be a sheep on that day and how many would want to be a goat. Ask why most would like to be sheep (the sheep go to heaven). Ask the children what things the sheep did in order to be rewarded.

. . .

Show the heart and state that one word describes all the acts that the king rewarded. Ask what it is (love). Tell the children that a great saint, John of the Cross, once said that at the end of the world we will all be judged on love. We won't be judged on how much money we made, or how much we learned, or how famous we were, but on how much we loved.

. . .

Tell the children that the things Jesus named we now call works of mercy. There are seven corporal works of mercy that have to do with the body and seven spiritual works of mercy that have to do with the soul. Name these. (*Corporal:* Feed the hungry. Give drink to the thirsty. Clothe the naked. Visit the sick. Shelter the homeless. Visit the imprisoned. Bury the dead. *Spiritual:* Warn the sinner. Instruct the ignorant. Counsel the doubtful. Comfort the sorrowing. Bear wrongs patiently. Forgive all injuries. Pray for the living and the dead.)

. . .

Explain that the king in the story stands for Jesus. Ask how Jesus regards things we do for other people (as if done to himself). Ask, "If Jesus were hungry would you feed him? If Jesus needed clothes, would you give him some? If he were sick, would you take care of him?"

. . .

Tell Tolstoy's story of Martin the cobbler who repaired shoes. He had a dream in which Jesus told him he would be coming to his cobbler's shop the next day. All the following day, Martin waited for

Jesus to come. As he waited, several poor people came to the store and Martin took care of them. At the end of the day Martin was disappointed that Jesus hadn't come. He asked Jesus, "Why didn't you come?" Jesus answered, "I did. I was in every person who came to your store."

· · ·

Give or ask the children for examples of how to practice each work of mercy mentioned by Jesus. For example, the children could feed the hungry by sharing a snack with a friend. They could welcome a stranger by being kind to a new student in their class. They could give clothes to the naked by donating to a clothing drive.

· · ·

Mention that the first reading tells us that even at the beginning of the Church the members helped one another. When there was going to be a famine and not enough to eat, the Christians in Antioch sent gifts to the Christians in Jerusalem.

· · ·

If a collection will be taken for a particular need, explain what it is.

178 Forgive One Another

(PAGE W27) COLOSSIANS 3:12–14 • MATTHEW 6:7–15

Lent is a time to make things new. Sometimes our relationship with God and with others is in need of repair. Jesus made us one with God again by his death and resurrection, and that's what we celebrate at this Eucharist. It is up to us to become one with one another by asking pardon and by offering forgiveness. Today let us pray for the grace to be able to do this.

Universal Prayer

The response is *"Lord, hear our prayer."*

That church members be models of forgiveness and of granting pardon, let us pray to the Lord.

That leaders of nations lead in such a way that their countries will not need to ask forgiveness of other peoples, let us pray to the Lord.

That people who have been treated unjustly may have the grace to forgive those who hurt them, let us pray to the Lord.

That the hearts of people who seek revenge and hold grudges may be softened, let us pray to the Lord.

That we may have the humility to ask forgiveness and the love to grant forgiveness, let us pray to the Lord.

Special Features

- Before the penitential rite, the presider could mention that those at the Mass are about to ask and receive pardon from God for their sins.
- At the Our Father have everyone hold hands. Before praying it, the presider could remind the children that they are about to ask God to forgive them in the same way they forgive others.
- For the sign of peace, have the children express sorrow and forgiveness for the times they have hurt God's family, the Church, by their sin. Have them take turns saying "I'm sorry" and "I forgive you" to one another.

Songs

Christians, Let Us Love One Another; Faithful Family; Forgive Our Sins; The Forgiveness Song; Pardon Your People; When Charity and Love Prevail

Homily Ideas

Visuals: A sheet of paper and tape

Tell the children that one of the greatest things we can experience as human beings is friendship. Sometimes, though, we do things that damage our friendship with other people. Tear the sheet of paper in half. Comment that we become separated from each other because of sins like unkind words, mean acts, or thoughtless ways.

. . .

Explain that Lent is a good time to patch up friendships with our parents, brothers and sisters, neighbors, classmates, and friends. Ask the children if they know the words that can put friendships back together again (I'm sorry, I forgive you). Hold up one half of the paper and state that when one person says, "I'm sorry" and the other says, "That's OK. I forgive you" then the friendship is healed. Tape the paper together.

. . .

Point out that the first reading says that love ties everything together. If we love, we will put up with each other and forgive. The reading says we are God's chosen people, so we are to be gentle, kind, humble, meek, and patient. A gentle person forgives, a kind person forgives, a humble person forgives, a person who doesn't get angry forgives, and a patient person forgives.

. . .

Ask the children who has forgiven all of them (Jesus). Ask when (when they are sorry; when they celebrate the sacrament of reconciliation). Remind them that on the cross Jesus forgave those who put him to death. He said, "Father, forgive them. They don't know what they are doing."

. . .

Ask the children if they know how many times Jesus said we should be willing to forgive someone (without end).

. . .

Ask what line of the Lord's Prayer has to do with forgiveness (forgive us our trespasses as we forgive those who trespass against us). Explain that this means whenever we pray this prayer we are asking God to forgive us only as much as we forgive others. What if we hold grudges and never forget when people hurt us? What if we never forgive others? Then we're in trouble because we pray that God will forgive us the way we forgive others.

. . .

Tell a story about someone who has forgiven. For example, St. Jane Frances de Chantal forgave the man who shot her husband and asked him to become the godfather of her child. Pope John Paul II forgave the man who shot him and even visited him in prison. Steve MacDonald, a New York policeman, was shot by a young man and is now confined to a wheelchair. He forgave the man. When the man was later killed in a motorcycle accident, Steve expressed sorrow for his death.

179 Ask and You Will Receive

(PAGE W29) ISAIAH 12:4B-5 • MATTHEW 7:7-11

God is good to us. God showers us with gifts. Everything in the fantastic world we live in is a free gift. God does amazing things for us. Through Jesus, God became one of us and died on a cross so that we could live forever. In the Scripture readings today, we will hear God telling us that whatever we want, we have only to ask. Let us celebrate God's goodness to us during this Mass with hearts full of gratitude.

Universal Prayer

The response is *"Lord, hear our prayer."*

That church members pray for one another's needs, let us pray to the Lord.

That world leaders turn to God for help in carrying out their important work, let us pray to the Lord.

That those who are in most need—the sick, the dying, the homeless, the poor, and sinners—may be helped, let us pray to the Lord.

That we may learn to depend on God for our daily needs as a child depends on its parents, let us pray to the Lord.

That our own requests may be granted (these may be stated aloud or thought about in silence), let us pray to the Lord.

Special Features

- Sing the response to the Universal Prayer.
- Children may come with pictures showing special needs drawn or cut from magazines or newspapers. These may be posted on a church wall or hung from the pews.
- Display a banner with the words "God cares."
- After Mass distribute curved pretzels as a reminder to pray. These originated during Lent and are in the shape of praying hands.

Songs

Glory and Praise to Our God; Happy Those Who Hear the Word of God; May We Praise You; Seek Ye First.

Homily Ideas

Visual: A gift-wrapped box

Show the gift box and ask the children what giving someone a gift shows (love or thanks). Ask: Who loves us more than anyone in the whole world? (God). Invite the children to close their eyes and picture some of the great gifts that God has given them: the sky…lakes…beautiful flowers…someone who takes care of them…their friends…their pets. Point out that God's best gift is Jesus. During Lent we especially remember that Jesus suffered and died for us so that we could live forever in heaven with God.

. . . .

Recall that in the gospel Jesus told us to ask God for things. He said, "Ask, and you will receive. Search, and you will find. Knock, and the door will be opened for you." Repeat, "Ask, search, knock." Then ask, "What do the first letters of those words spell?" (ask). Over and over Jesus assures us that God will give us what we need and want. God wants us to ask for things. Jesus said we are to trust that God will answer us the way a good parent gives good things to a child.

. . . .

Point out that sometimes God says no, because God has a better idea in mind. Tell the story of the young boy who prayed that God would give him the power to do what his uncle could do. Each night the uncle could take out his teeth and put them in a glass of water. When the boy grew older he was glad that God had said no to his prayer.

. . . .

Refer to people in the gospels whose requests Jesus granted, or ask the children to name them (Bartimaeus the blind man, Mary at Cana, Martha and Mary for their brother Lazarus who was sick, Jairus for his daughter, the apostles in the storm).

. . . .

Tell about a time when God answered your prayer or the prayer of someone you know.

. . . .

Encourage the children to pray when they need something, when they are sick, when they are worried or afraid, and when someone they love is in trouble or sick or needs something. Name any current needs in the parish or school. Tell the children that God loves them and listens to them. Ask the children if they have a particular need right now or know of someone who has a particular need. Let them pray for this intention either in their hearts at this point or later in the Universal Prayer.

· · ·

Remind the children that when God answers our prayers we should give thanks. The responsorial psalm says, "the Lord has worked miracles for us" and "the Lord has done great things for us." Invite the children to think of a wonderful deed God has done for them. Tell them to thank God for it especially during this Mass.

180 Be at Peace with Everyone

(PAGE W31) GENESIS 50:15-21 • MATTHEW 5:20-24

Everyone longs for peace: world peace, peace in our neighborhoods, peace in our families, and peace in our hearts. Each person can help make peace. It is Jesus who can give us peace. During this Eucharist we celebrate that Jesus has made peace between God and all human beings by the sacrifice of his life. Let us ask Jesus to bring about peace among all men and women. Let us pray for the grace to be peacemakers ourselves.

Universal Prayer

The response is *"Lord, grant us peace."*

That the efforts of church leaders to promote world peace be successful, let us pray to the Lord.

That public officials make and enforce laws that are just and keep peace, let us pray to the Lord.

That countries in the world that do not have peace *(name some)* may soon be blessed with it, let us pray to the Lord.

That people and nations learn to solve problems through peaceful means, let us pray to the Lord.

That we may be strong enough and big-hearted enough to show the love, cooperation, and forgiveness that bring about peace, let us pray to the Lord.

Special Features

- At the sign of peace greet one another with "Shalom."
- Display a banner with a dove and the word "peace."
- Provide an opportunity for the children to experience the sacrament of peace, reconciliation, during the week before or the week after the Mass.
- After communion, do one of the following:
  » Invite students to do liturgical movements, interpreting a song about peace.
  » Allow a moment of silence during which everyone prays for peace in troubled areas of the world.
  » Have the children alternate (left side, right side) in praying the Peace Prayer of St. Francis of Assisi.
  » Have someone pray aloud the World Peace Prayer (below). Or you might sing or play Marty Haugen's musical setting for it (GIA).

   World Peace Prayer
   Lead me from death to life, / from falsehood to truth. / Lead me from despair to hope, / from fear to trust. / Lead me from hate to love, / from war to peace. / Let peace fill our hearts, / our world, our universe.

Songs

City of God; Christ's Peace; Lay Your Hands; Let There Be Peace on Earth; Make Me a Channel of Your Peace; Peace Is Flowing like a River; Peace Prayer

Homily Ideas

Visual: A newspaper

Refer to news items to illustrate the need for peace in the world today. Ask children what they think peace is.

. . . .

Point out that when Jesus was born, angels proclaimed, "Peace to people of good will," and that after Jesus had died and risen, his first words to the apostles were "Peace be to you." Jesus is called the Prince of Peace.

. . . .

Explain that as followers of Jesus we, too, are to bring peace to the world. The gospel tells us how. We are not to be angry with others, call them names, or make fun of them. We are not to do things that make others angry with us. Jesus said that before we offer our gift to God at the altar we are to make peace with anyone who is angry with us. Ask the children if they know of anyone who is upset with them now: a mother or father, a sister or brother, a friend or teacher. Tell them they will not actually leave the church to make peace, but will have time to think of how they can make peace with that person and resolve to carry out that action after Mass. Then allow time for reflection.

. . . .

Tell the children that sin destroys peace. The sin of Adam and Eve cost them the peace of paradise. After we sin we are not at peace. Encourage the children to celebrate the sacrament of peace: reconciliation.

. . . .

Provide the background for the story of Joseph in the first reading, perhaps before the reading is proclaimed. Explain that Joseph's eleven brothers were jealous of him because their father favored Joseph and had given him a special robe. Joseph also told his brothers about dreams he had in which he was greater than they were. In anger the brothers beat him up and threw him into an empty well. When merchants on the way to Egypt passed by, the brothers sold Joseph to them as a slave. These were the cruel and terrible things Joseph's brothers had done to him. Instead of seeking revenge, Joseph actually helped his brothers and their families. When there was little food to eat in the land, he kept them from starving and took care of them. Joseph was a real peacemaker.

. . . .

Ask the children how they feel when they are not at peace with someone. Explain that living without peace causes bad feelings: anger, worry, fear, and guilt. It can keep people from sleeping and can make them physically sick. Jesus wants us to avoid the things that destroy peace such as hatred, grudges, revenge, and injustice. He wants us to spread peace in the world by being kind and forgiving. Those who do so will be blessed and will enjoy peace forever in heaven.

---

181 Love Everyone

(PAGE W34) ROMANS 12:17-18, 21 • MATTHEW 5:43-48

Jesus' followers are to be known by their love for one another and even for their enemies. The Eucharist

is a Christian love feast. We celebrate God's tremendous love for us. Jesus offers himself to the Father out of love for us. We offer Jesus and ourselves in a sacrifice of love. Then by sharing the one bread and the one cup that are the body and blood of Christ we grow in love and unity.

Universal Prayer

The response is *"Lord, hear our prayer."*

For the Church, that its members may be filled with Christlike love and draw others to it, let us pray to the Lord.

For people everywhere, that their governments may enable them to live in peace and justice, let us pray to the Lord.

For those whose hearts are hard and unloving, that someone may touch their lives with love and change them, let us pray to the Lord.

For all of us, that we may have the grace to love those who do not love us, let us pray to the Lord.

For the poor and hungry, that they may be helped, let us pray to the Lord.

Special Features

- After Mass, at the door pass out cookies made with honey.
- Display a mobile of hearts each with a characteristic of love written in it.
- Distribute bee stickers.

Songs

Bread of Friendship; Faith, Hope, and Love; God Has Made Us a Family; Jesus, You Love Us; Love Is Colored like a Rainbow; A New Commandment; Jesu, Jesu, Fill Us with Your Love; Service; Song of the Body of Christ; They'll Know We Are Christians by Our Love; Walk On

Homily Ideas

Visual: A jar of honey

Show a jar of honey and ask the children if they like honey. Explain that a Christian is supposed to be sweet, like honey, not sour like vinegar. We are to be sweet, kind, and pleasant to all. Our words are supposed to be sweet and soothing. Our deeds are to be loving. Jesus told us that everyone should be able to tell we are his followers because of the way we love. He gave us the golden rule, gold like honey. Ask: Who knows what the golden rule is? (Do to others what you would like them to do to you.)

• • •

Tell the children that Jesus taught us to love by showing us how. Ask how Jesus showed love (by healing, teaching, washing the feet of the disciples, dying on the cross). He told us that we were to love as he loved us. He taught something new. We are to love even our enemies. Then we will be like God. It's easy to love people who love us, but it's not easy to love people who act as though they don't like us or love us.

• • •

Quote Abraham Lincoln who said that the way to get rid of your enemies is to make them your friends. Ask how we can make enemies friends (being kind to them over and over, forgiving them, praying for them).

• • •

Recall the fairy tale "Beauty and the Beast" in which a beast is changed through someone's love for him.

• • •

Tell the story of *Les Miserables* in which a freed prisoner is given food and shelter by a bishop and then steals the bishop's silverware. When the police catch the thief and take him to the bishop, instead of accusing the man, the bishop says that he was glad the man returned, for he had forgotten to give him the silver candlesticks as well. This act of kindness changes the man for life. He becomes someone who in turn does good for others.

• • •

Explain that when someone hurts or offends us and we hurt them back, we multiply the evil. It becomes like a snowball rolling down a hill, growing larger and larger. We also hurt ourselves, for we become a worse person. If, on the other hand, we return good for evil, evil is conquered. It melts away.

. . .

Comment that Lent is in the springtime when bees start making honey again. During this season we should practice kind, loving acts that will sweeten the lives of others and make the world a better, happier place. Ask the children how many "bees" they can think of, such as "be kind, be helpful."

182 Love of God and Love of Neighbor

(PAGE W37) DEUTERONOMY 10:12–14 • MARK 12:28B–31

Only one thing is necessary to get to heaven and that is to love. As we join in the Mass today, we will hear God tell us the two great laws of love. Through the merits of Jesus' sacrifice offered on the altar, we receive the grace we need to follow those laws. Filled with the life of Jesus whom we receive in Holy Communion, we will become known as loving persons.

Universal Prayer

The response is *"Lord, fill us with love."*

That church leaders be good models in showing us the way to love, let us pray to the Lord.

That government leaders practice justice and mercy, let us pray to the Lord.

That people in the Church always put God first in their lives, let us pray to the Lord.

That others in the world come to know God's love through our love for them, let us pray to the Lord.

Special Features

- Distribute crucifixes or holy cards that show a crucifix.
- Before the gospel tell the story of St. Maximilian Kolbe. He showed love for God by becoming a priest and by publishing religious materials to spread the gospel. He showed love for others in an extraordinary way. When he was in prison ten men were chosen to be killed. Because one of the men had a family, Maximilian volunteered to die in his place.
- Display a banner with a heart and the words "Jesus," "Others," "You."
- Have students write special intercessions that all begin with the words "Love is…"

Songs

Center of My Life; The Church of Christ in Every Age; Faith, Hope, and Love; In Perfect Charity; Jesu, Jesu, Fill Us with Your Love; Love Is Colored like a Rainbow; Love, Love; A New Commandment; O How He Loves You and Me; Only in God; Service

Homily Ideas

Visual: The sign language for "I love you." (Hold up your hand, put the middle and ring fingers down. This is a combination of the letters *I*, *L*, and *Y*.)

Ask the children what the three most important words in our language are. Give the clue that they were probably among the first words they learned (I love you). Demonstrate how to say it in sign language. Comment that these words are the key to heaven.

. . .

Explain that when someone asked Jesus how to live forever, Jesus answered that the greatest commandment was to love God and the second greatest was to love your neighbor as you love yourself. The Ten Commandments spell out how to love.

• • •

Tell the children that to love God is the most important thing to do in life. The Jewish people know this. In Scripture God commands, "You shall love the LORD, your God, with all your heart, and with all your soul, and with all your strength." Some Jewish people have this verse in small boxes that they wear on their foreheads and on their arms when they pray (called phylacteries). They also have this verse in boxes (called mezuzahs) that they put at their doorways and touch as they enter the house. These boxes remind them to love God.

• • •

Point out that we Catholics have crucifixes to remind us to love God. When we see how much God loves us, then we want to love God in return.

• • •

Ask the children how they show they love God (by praying, keeping God's name holy, keeping God's day holy, trying to follow God's laws).

• • •

Remind the children that they are to love themselves and take care of themselves because they belong to God who made them. Most people love themselves quite a bit. Jesus tells us to love others as much as we love ourselves. Would we hurt ourselves? Tell lies about ourselves that make us look bad? Damage our things? Of course not. Then we shouldn't treat others that way either.

• • •

Ask the children for examples of how to show love.

• • •

Tell the children that to have our lives in the right order, we should put Jesus first, then others, then ourselves. Ask them what the first letters of these words spell: Jesus, others, you (joy). When we follow God's laws and love God and others, we have joy in this life and the next.

183 Trust in the Lord

(PAGE W39) LAMENTATIONS 3:22–25 • JOHN 4:46–53

We are God's children. We look to God for everything we need. We know we can trust God to care for us, for God has sent us Jesus. Jesus shows us what God is like. Because Jesus was loving and full of compassion for people, we know that God also is. During this Mass we place before God our needs and the needs of those we love. We trust that our loving Father will hear and answer our prayers.

Universal Prayer

The response is *"Hear us, O Lord."*

That the Church may always depend on God's help in spreading the gospel throughout the world, let us pray to the Lord.

That nations may be led to put their trust not in weapons but in living according to God's plan, let us pray to the Lord.

That people who have no hope may come to realize God's love for them, let us pray to the Lord.

That we may remember to trust in God when we meet difficulties in life, let us pray to the Lord.

That our families may live in safety and peace, let us pray to the Lord.

Special Features

- As the children assemble, play a song of faith.
- Let children take the parts in the gospel: the narrator, Jesus, the official, and two servants.

Songs

Be Not Afraid; Don't Be Worried; If God Is for Us; O How He Loves You and Me; Lead Me, Guide Me; On Eagle's Wings; Only in God (Talbot); Though the Mountains May Fall; Trust in the Lord; You Are Mine

Homily Ideas

Visual: A dollar bill

Ask the children if anyone knows what religious words are on the dollar bill (in God we trust). Comment that it is good to be reminded that we trust not in money, not in power, not in armies, not in other people, not in ourselves, but in God. Ask why it is safe to put our trust in God (God loves us. God is all-good. God won't fail us).

· · ·

Point out that the first reading says that God is kind and merciful. We can depend on God. In the gospel we see Jesus, who is God in the flesh, acting in a trustworthy way. The official's son was sick. The father went to the town where Jesus was and asked him to come. He trusted that Jesus could do something and that Jesus would do something. And Jesus did. He worked a miracle for him and healed his boy. Ask the children to give examples of times when we can turn to God for help (in times of sickness, danger, trouble, when we don't know what to do).

· · ·

Tell the story of Scott O'Grady whose plane was shot down in enemy territory. While he was surrounded by enemies in a field, he prayed and trusted that God would save him. He survived this way for six days before being rescued. On television Scott told the world that it was God who had saved him.

· · ·

Remind the children that God sent Jesus to save us from sin and death. Certainly we can trust God to help us in less dangerous situations.

· · ·

State that there is a song that begins "Put your hand in the hand of the man who calmed the water." Ask: Who is the one strong enough to calm storms, winds, and waves? (Jesus) He offers his hand to us to help us. If we put our hand into his, we will be safe.

· · ·

Tell the children that each time they pray they make an act of trust in God. They trust that God hears their prayers and will answer them in the way that is best for them.

· · ·

Comment that God is the best friend the children have. God will never let them down or disappoint them. They can count on God and his love for them.

184 Jesus Brings Together All People

(PAGE W42) EZEKIEL 37:21-22, 24 • JOHN 11:47-52

Jesus is the one who unites all people and makes us one. At this Eucharist we celebrate his saving acts through which he accomplished this: his death and resurrection. We look forward to that eternal banquet in heaven when all people will be united in peace and love. There Jesus, the Son of David and the son of Mary, will reign over all forever.

Universal Prayer

The response is *"Lord, hear our prayer."*

That church members work with all their hearts to make God's kingdom known, let us pray to the Lord.

That the leaders of all nations strive for world unity and peace, let us pray to the Lord.

That people who feel cut off from others experience the hope that comes from the Good News of Jesus, let us pray to the Lord.

That we may someday be numbered among the saints in heaven, let us pray to the Lord.

Special Features

• Display a mural made of pictures of people from many different nations. Place the silhouette of a cross in the middle of it.

• Precede the homily (or the Mass) with a brief talk about the missions.

• Hold a special collection for the missions and bring up the donations during the presentation of gifts.

• During the presentation of gifts, play music that is obviously from another nation, such as Africa or India.

Songs

Bread of Friendship; Bring Forth the Kingdom; Companions on the Journey; In Christ There Is No East or West; God's Holy Family; One Bread, One Body; See Us, Lord, about Your Altar; Song of Gathering; We Are the Church; We Are the Family; We Remember

Homily Ideas

Visual: A globe or world map

Point out on a globe or map some of the nations in the world into which people are grouped. State that there are about 6,900 languages in the world. Explain that sometimes small nations unite and become larger nations. Centuries ago the Jewish people were divided until their great King David united them into one kingdom of Israel.

. . . .

Explain that Jesus, who belongs to David's family, is the ruler who will again unite not only Jewish people, but the people of the whole world. He foretold that if he would be lifted up on the cross, he would draw all people to himself. The death of Jesus brought about the kingdom of God on earth. Our mission as Christians is to spread this kingdom, to invite others to join it until the whole world is part of it. Mention that the shape of the cross points to the four corners of the world: north, south, east, and west.

. . . .

Recall that the chief priests and Pharisees said that if they didn't stop Jesus soon, everyone would believe in him. They tried to stop Jesus by killing him, but they didn't stop his work and message. These go on through his followers, through us.

. . . .

Tell this story someone made up:

> *Jesus went back to heaven after the resurrection. All the angels met him and marveled at the wounds in his hands and feet and side. They asked, "Will all people know how much you suffered for them and how much you loved them?"*
>
> *Jesus said, "My friends the apostles know. They'll tell others, and these others will tell the rest."*
>
> *The angels asked, "But what if down through the years they forget? What if they just don't bother?"*
>
> *Jesus replied, "I'm counting on them."*

Elaborate that Jesus is counting on us to continue his work and spread the news of his Father's love until everyone believes.

* * *

Ask the children what they can do to draw people to believe in Jesus (act with faith themselves, tell people about Jesus, invite friends to religious events, pray that others join Jesus' Church).

* * *

Have the children imagine what the population of heaven will look like: millions and millions of people of every race with different colored skin and different facial features, people from past centuries and future centuries. They will all be one in worshiping and loving God who made them. Comment that all those who are now in heaven are united with you in the celebration of the Eucharist. With you they are praying, "Holy, holy, holy Lord, God of hosts."

Season of Easter

185 Witnesses of the Resurrection

(PAGE W47) ACTS 2:32-33 • JOHN 20:11-18

After the consecration of the Mass we proclaim the great mystery of our faith and say, for example, "We proclaim your Death, O Lord, and profess your Resurrection until you come again." The Easter message is the foundation of our faith, and our response is "Alleluia," which means "praise the Lord." Today in this season of Easter we celebrate this mystery in a special way. Let us rejoice and be glad together.

Universal Prayer

The response is *"Lord of life, save us."*

For the Church, that all the members may be true signs of the resurrection, let us pray to the Lord.

For government officials, that they may remember that there is another world after this one, let us pray to the Lord.

For missionaries and those whom they serve, that the Spirit may enlighten them, let us pray to the Lord.

For ourselves, that we may realize the wonder of the Easter message and desire to share it, let us pray to the Lord.

For the dying, that their belief in the resurrection may comfort them, let us pray to the Lord.

Special Features

- Decorate the church with butterflies.
- Carry in a banner with "Alleluia" on it.
- Have both an entrance procession and a recessional that are especially joyful. They may include dancers and a tambourine. The children may clap to the music. You might play the "Hallelujah Chorus" from Handel's *Messiah*.
- Begin Mass by sprinkling the congregation with holy water. Use a leafy branch and a bowl.
- The children may sing the response to the responsorial psalm.

Songs

Alleluia! Alleluia! Let the Holy Anthem Rise; The Church's One Foundation; Easter People; He Is Lord; Jesus Christ Is Risen Today; Living Is the Word; Resucitó

Homily Ideas

Visual: A rock

Ask the children how they know Jesus was risen (someone told them). Our faith is passed on by word of mouth. Our faith is founded on rock in two ways. Show the rock. Explain that in the first reading we heard the words of Peter, whose name means rock. When the Spirit came to Peter on Pentecost he went out and boldly proclaimed the Easter message that Jesus is risen. Peter had seen the empty tomb himself. He had seen and talked to the risen Lord. He and the apostles were eye-witnesses to the fact that Jesus was alive. Our faith stands on solid rock.

. . .

Explain that in the gospel Mary Magdalene visited Jesus' tomb, which was carved into rock. That empty rock-tomb also was proof that Jesus was risen. Both Peter and Mary Magdalene told the Good News of Jesus' resurrection. We call Mary "the apostle to the apostles," for she was sent by Jesus to bring the Easter message to his apostles. In fact, Mary met the risen Lord before Peter did. In her great love for Jesus she went to his tomb and discovered he was not there. She asked the angels where his body was so she could bring it back, not realizing that she wasn't strong enough to carry it herself.

. . .

Point out that Jesus told Mary he was going to his Father. Later in the Pentecost sermon, Peter stated that Jesus was at the right hand of the Father. Jesus had been sent by the Father to save us from sin and death. When his mission was accomplished, he returned to the Father and is now glorified in heaven. Because he died and was raised up, we can believe his promise that we will someday rise, too.

. . .

Tell the children Peter Marshall's explanation of dying. He said it is like a child who falls asleep and whose Father carries him to his own room. The next morning the child awakes to find himself at home in his own bed.

. . .

Mention that during Easter in the Byzantine liturgy one person says, "Christ is risen," and the other responds, "Christ is truly risen."

. . .

Remind the children that the Spirit who gave Peter courage to go out to tell the Good News came to us at our baptism. We have the same mission as the apostles and the same Spirit within us to carry it out. One way to show that Jesus is risen is to look as if we believe it. We should be happy people full of joy and hope. St. Augustine said we should be an alleluia from head to toe.

. . .

Tell the story of the class that was going to put on a play about Jesus rising from the dead. When the children were choosing parts for the play, one little boy said he wanted to be the rock. The teacher asked why and he replied, "So I could let Jesus out of the tomb." Comment that this is what all Christians are called to do—to let Jesus out of the tomb, to let the power of his new life work through us and change the world.

---

186 The Power of Jesus' Name

(PAGE W50) ACTS 3:1–10 • JOHN 14:12–14

Jesus Christ is risen. We, the people who believe in him and follow him, are named Christians after him.

We can call on his all-powerful name. In our prayers and in particular at the Eucharist, we worship the

Father through Jesus Christ. We ask for our needs in his name, and we can be certain that we will be heard.

Universal Prayer

The response is *"Lord, hear our prayer."*

That the entire Church may be blessed as it works in the name of Jesus, let us pray to the Lord.

That all countries may come to recognize the power of Jesus' name, let us pray to the Lord.

That people who are hopeless, depressed, or suffering may find hope in Jesus' name, let us pray to the Lord.

That we may always remember to call on the name of Jesus in time of need, let us pray to the Lord.

Special Features

- As the first reading is being read, six or seven children could pantomime it: Peter, John, lame man, two friends to "carry" the man, and people going into the Temple.
- Distribute decorated cards that have the name of Jesus printed on them, ones that will help children see that the name is special.
- Sing the response of the responsorial psalm.
- Renew baptismal promises after the homily.
- As the communion reflection, pray part of the litany of the Holy Name of Jesus.

Songs

All Hail the Power of Jesus' Name; All My Days; At the Name of Jesus; Holy God, We Praise Thy Name; Holy Name Communion Song; In Praise of His Name; Lift Up Your Hearts; Praise His Name; Silver and Gold Have I None

Homily Ideas

Visual: Something with a child's name on it

Ask the children if anyone has something there with his or her name on it. Have a child bring it up. (Or have a child prepared ahead of time.) Talk about the importance of our names. We mark things with our name. People can get our attention by calling our name. Our names stand for us.

. . . .

Ask the children to guess what is the most wonderful name of all (Jesus). Ask if they know how Jesus got his name (an angel from God told Mary and Joseph to name him that.) Explain that the name Jesus means "God saves" and that is exactly what happened through Jesus. God saved the entire world from sin and death.

. . . .

Recall that in the gospel Jesus told us to call on his name and to ask for things in his name. The name of Jesus is powerful. In the first reading Peter and John made a lame man walk again in the name of Jesus Christ from Nazareth. In the gospels other people had miracles worked for them when they called on Jesus' name. For example, Bartimaeus, the blind beggar, called out, "Jesus, son of David, have pity on me," and he received his sight.

. . . .

Explain that Jesus in heaven now acts as an intercessor for us, a go-between.

. . . .

Mention that we were baptized in the name of the Father and of the Son and of the Holy Spirit. In the sacrament of reconciliation we are forgiven in the name of Jesus. We belong to Jesus. It is as though we have his name stamped on our foreheads.

. . . .

Encourage the children to listen for the times during the Mass when we end a prayer with the words "We ask this in the name of Jesus," or "We ask this through Christ our Lord."

. . . .

Tell the children that the shortest prayer we can say is the name "Jesus." They can pray it over and over again and focus on Jesus present in their hearts.

. . . .

Point out that the holy name of Jesus has power over evil.

· · · ·

Read Philippians 2:6–11 to the children. It is about the glory and honor that should be given to Jesus at the sound of his name.

· · · ·

Suggest that the children begin the habit of bowing their heads whenever the name Jesus is spoken.

· · · ·

Comment that a letter in the Bible tells us, "What you do, in word or in deed, do everything in the name of the Lord Jesus" (Colossians 3:17).

---

187 One in Christ Jesus

(PAGE W53) ACTS 4:32–35 • JOHN 17:21–23

Sin divides and separates people. Jesus came and healed us from sin. He made us one with God again and with one another. We, his people, are one in faith and one in love. In this holy banquet of the Eucharist, as we share the same bread and wine, Jesus makes us more completely one. May the communion we share draw us into a closer union.

Universal Prayer

The response is *"Lord, hear our prayer."*

For the Church, that we may always show our oneness in faith and in love, let us pray to the Lord.

For civil authorities, that they may govern and serve so that there may be justice for all, let us pray to the Lord.

For those who lack even the bare necessities of life, that they may find help, let us pray to the Lord.

For those who suffer in purgatory, that they may soon be with God in heaven, let us pray to the Lord.

For ourselves, that our hearts may long to be one with others, let us pray to the Lord.

Special Features

· Have everyone present join in the entrance procession. When they reach the front, have them add a drop of water that represents themselves to a large container. Explain the ritual ahead of time.

· Take up a collection for needy people before or during the Mass. Bring up the donations during the presentation of gifts.

· Hold hands during the Our Father.

Songs

As Grains of Wheat; I Am the Vine; One Bread, One Body; One Lord; Lord, Who at Thy First Eucharist; Song of Gathering; There Is One Lord; Walk On; We Are One in the Spirit

Homily Ideas

Visuals: An eyedropper and a clear glass filled with water

Announce that a characteristic of Jesus' Church is unity. Ask what unity means (oneness, togetherness, like-mindedness). Demonstrate by putting a drop of water into the glass of water. Ask the children if they can see the new drop added to the water. Ask them if they can take that drop back out again. Comment that that is unity. The one drop has completely joined with the rest to make the glass of water.

· · · ·

Explain that Jesus said that he and his Father are one. He said he is one with us. He is with us and in us so much so that we are called Christ's body. Jesus prayed that his followers would all be one.

. . .

Ask if anyone remembers how the first reading showed that early church members lived as one (they shared everything; no one was in need). The first Christians pooled all their belongings so that everyone had enough. Comment that if we were one today, we would feel bad when our brothers and sisters do not have what we have. We would try to help them.

. . .

Tell the story of the two Jewish brothers. One brother lived alone on a farm. The other was married and had many children. The brother who lived alone thought, "My brother has a family to care for. I will give him some of my grain." So during the night this man would carry a sack of grain from his barn and add it to his brother's barn. This brother in the meantime thought, "My brother lives alone. He has a hard life. I will give him some of my grain." So during the night he would carry a sack of grain from his barn and add it to his brother's barn. This went on until one night the brothers met in

the field. The town planted a tree to remember the love of the two brothers.

. . .

Give an example of how people function as one and come to the aid of one another. For example, after Hurricane Katrina struck the Gulf Coast, people came from all over the country to help with the rescue efforts.

. . .

Ask for examples of how the children can show that they are one with people in school, with people in their neighborhoods, with people in other countries.

. . .

Explain that at Mass the bread and wine stand for our oneness. Many grains of wheat make the one bread. Many grapes are crushed to make the one wine. When we share the bread and wine that is Jesus, we are celebrating that we are one. Eating the same food makes us one. That is why we call the sacred bread and wine "communion." We are in union with one another then. In Jesus we find the strength to grow in unity and love.

. . .

Remind the children that at Mass we are also one with the saints and those who have died. We are praying with them.

188 Followers of Jesus

(PAGE W55) ACTS 5:17-21 • JOHN 15:18-21

To be a follower of Jesus Christ is a challenge and a risk. It can be unpleasant and even dangerous. Those who accept the challenge and take the risk will be glad they did. Although we Christians may suffer in this life as Jesus did, we will share his glory in the next. The celebration of the Eucharist gives us courage to be Christian. Let us pray that we may be strong, faithful followers of Jesus, who loved us to death.

Universal Prayer

The response is *"Lord, hear our prayer."*

For those in authority in our Church, that they may have the wisdom and courage to lead us to live according to the gospel, let us pray to the Lord.

For leaders of nations, that they may take a stand for justice at all costs, let us pray to the Lord.

For those who are suffering for their faith right now, that the Holy Spirit may be their strength and their guide, let us pray to the Lord.

For us, that we may follow Christ wholeheartedly and be true to our baptismal promises, let us pray to the Lord.

Special Features

- Sing the response to the responsorial psalm.
- Have the children renew their baptismal promises after the homily.
- As a communion reflection pray this prayer of St. Richard of Chichester:

  Thank you, Lord Jesus Christ, for all the benefits and blessings you have given me, for all the pains you have borne for me. Merciful Friend, Brother and Redeemer, may I know you more clearly, love you more dearly, and follow you more nearly, day by day.

Songs

Come, Follow Me; Faith of Our Fathers; He Has Anointed Me; Here I Am, Lord; I Have Decided to Follow Jesus; I, the Lord; If You Belong to Me; Lord, You Have Come; Only This I Want; O Sons and Daughters; Sing Out His Goodness; We Have No Glory; Wherever He Leads, I'll Go

Homily Ideas

Visual: Handcuffs or chains

Recall the first reading in which the apostles were imprisoned for teaching about Jesus. Show the handcuffs or chains. Explain that the apostles were carrying on the work of Jesus. Point out that in the gospel we hear that Jesus warned his followers that people would hate them. Tell the children that this came true. All of the apostles except John were killed for being followers of Jesus.

· · · ·

Define the term "martyr" as one who gives his or her life for the faith. The word also means witness. Martyrs witness to the truth by giving their lives. Usually a person who becomes a martyr is hated because he or she is a follower of Jesus. Sometimes people do not want to hear Jesus' message. They don't believe in him. They do not want to live by his laws of love that mean promoting justice and peace. These people punish, persecute, and even kill those who work for Jesus.

· · · ·

Explain that there are martyrs for Christ today, almost two thousand years later. Tell the story of Archbishop Oscar Romero of El Salvador. He spoke out against the people who were oppressing the poor in his country. He acted to fight against the great injustices there. People in power who wanted to keep their power and their wealth were bothered by him and hated him. One day when Archbishop Romero was celebrating Mass, soldiers came and shot him to death.

· · · ·

Give or ask for examples of times when it may be hard to be a follower of Jesus (when other children call you names for doing the right thing; when you would rather be like other children; when you don't feel like it; when it costs you something). Remind them that "Christian" means like Christ. If we live like Christ, we will not have an easy life. Ask what Christ suffered in carrying out his mission (persecution, tiredness, suffering, the cross).

· · · ·

Tell the children that the Holy Spirit, the Spirit of Jesus, helps them to be Christian and to live up to their baptismal promises. This Holy Spirit lives within them and gives them the gift of courage, or fortitude, to do what is right. Suggest that the children pray to the Holy Spirit for help when they are tempted to be less than they are called to be.

· · · ·

Point out that the apostles were freed from prison by an angel. God will help us, too, when we try our best to spread the Good News by our words and by the way we live. One of the letters in the Bible says, "The word of God is not chained" (2 Timothy 2:9).

.   .   .

Encourage the children to be loyal to Christ.

189 Obedience to God

(PAGE W58) ACTS 5:27–32 • JOHN 14:21–26

Out of deep love for us God tells us what to do to be happy. We who listen to God and obey God's laws find true peace and joy. At this Mass God speaks to us. In the Scripture readings we hear God's word. During the prayers, and especially after communion, God speaks to our hearts. Let our ears be open today to God's message for us.

Universal Prayer

The response is *"Lord, hear our prayer."*

God appointed church leaders to govern us. That they may listen to God and lead us to follow God's way, let us pray to the Lord.

God's laws are good. That officials may make and enforce laws that lead us to happiness, we pray to the Lord.

The Holy Spirit reminds us of what Jesus said. That people who have never heard of Jesus may learn of him and his way of life, let us pray to the Lord.

Jesus was obedient to his Father. That we may be open to God and try to do the things that please God, let us pray to the Lord.

Special Features

• Have a special procession with the gospel book to take it from the altar to the lectern to be read. Accompany it with two candles and incense.

• Distribute Scripture verses to the children after communion as their word of God for the day. Have the verses in a heart-shaped box.

Songs

Christians, Let Us Love One Another; The Good News of God's Salvation; The Lord Is with You; Path of Life; Speak, Lord; That There May Be Bread; We Have Been Told

Homily Ideas

Visual: A Bible

Tell the story of Elijah the prophet. When people were trying to kill him, he took refuge in a cave. God told him to stand outside and God would pass by. Elijah waited for God. A strong wind came, but God wasn't in the wind. An earthquake came, but God wasn't in the earthquake. A fire came, but God wasn't in the fire. Then a tiny whispering sound came, and God spoke to Elijah. God speaks to us in other ways today.

.   .   .

Show the Bible. Explain that God speaks to us in Scripture. God's law, the ten commandments, are in the Old Testament. The words of Jesus, including his new commandment of love, are in the New Testament. God's commandments are words of wisdom. They are the way to life that the Church has been teaching for two thousand years.

.   .   .

Recall that when the apostles were accused of disobeying the Jewish leaders, they stated that they did not obey people, but God. Explain that the word "obey" comes from the Latin word for "hear." To obey is to hear, to listen to. Christians listen to God.

• • •

Tell the children that Mary, the mother of Jesus, is called the listening virgin. She was always ready to hear God's word and obey even when it was difficult.

• • •

Mention that Jesus said that if we love him, we will obey him. If we don't like people, we don't pay attention to them. We turn a deaf ear to them. It is easy to obey someone we love. We say to that person, "Your slightest wish is my command." We try our best to please someone we love. This is how we show our love.

• • •

Recall Jesus' promise in the gospel that if we obeyed him, then he and the Father would come and live in us. Encourage the children to read the gospels to find out what Jesus wants them to do. Ask them if they know some things that Jesus told his followers to do.

• • •

Point out that we also find out what God wants us to do from our parents, our teachers, and others in authority over us. When we obey them, we obey God.

• • •

Tell the children that the responsorial psalm is from the longest psalm in the Bible. It has one hundred seventy-six verses and is a song of thanks and praise to God for giving us the law. This psalm says, "Your laws are my greatest joy!" Give an example of how one of God's commands leads to joy. For example, "Do not steal" is the seventh commandment. If it is obeyed, the children don't have to worry about their belongings. They can relax and enjoy life.

• • •

Comment that Jesus hates sin because it hurts us. The word "evil" spelled backward is "live." Evil keeps us from truly living, and when we avoid it, we are truly alive.

190 There Are Other Sheep Who Belong to Me

(PAGE W61) ACTS 9:1–20 • JOHN 10:14–16

God wants all people to be saved. Jesus sent his apostles to preach to all nations. Everyone is invited to the banquet in God's kingdom. At this Eucharist, let us be thankful that we are among God's people. Let us pray that those who do not yet know God may hear the Good News.

Universal Prayer

The response is *"Lord, hear our prayer."*

That the Church may be enthusiastic in spreading God's word to all people, let us pray to the Lord.

That world leaders do not block the spread of the gospel in their countries, let us pray to the Lord.

That people who have never heard about God and God's love for them may be reached, let us pray to the Lord.

That we may bring others to know about God through the example of our lives, let us pray to the Lord.

Special Features

- Take up a collection for missionaries.
- Post pictures of people from various nations.
- Make paper sheep and on each one write the name of a country. Have the children take a sheep and pray in a special way for the people of that country.

Songs

Lord, You Gave the Great Commission; Send Us Forth; Sing of the Lord's Goodness; Take Christ to the World; Neighbors; Bread of Friendship

Homily Ideas

Visual: Three children

Call three children to stand in front. Point out their differences in physical appearance: size, color of eyes, and so on. Ask their nationalities. State that they are all God's unique creations. God loves each one of them. Mention that there are more than seven billion people in the world. Each one is different. All of them are God's children. Have the children be seated.

• • •

Explain that the Jews were God's chosen people. They were the first to know God and hear God's promises. Jesus the Messiah was Jewish; so were his mother and father and his apostles. Jesus preached to the Jews in Israel. But God wanted all the world to be chosen people. This meant Gentiles, too. A Gentile is someone who is not Jewish. We are Gentiles.

• • •

Tell about Saul. After Jesus died, God called a Jew named Saul to preach to the Gentiles. Saul was a faithful Jew who thought that Christians were wrong. Jesus spoke to him one day and changed his life. Saul became St. Paul. He traveled to many countries to spread the Good News and started many churches. He helped convince the church leaders that God meant for Gentiles to be Christian too. Many of the letters that Paul wrote to the Christians are in the Bible.

• • •

Read from Paul's letter to the Galatians: "Through faith you are all children of God in Christ Jesus" (Galatians 3:26).

• • •

Comment that Jesus died for all people who would ever live. He called himself the good shepherd and all of us his sheep. He said he wanted all people to belong to his one flock. Name different groups of people.

• • •

Ask the children how they can help gather sheep for Jesus' flock (pray for the missions; donate money for missionary work; talk to people about Jesus). Tell the children that St. Thérèse is the patron of missionaries even though she never left her convent. She prayed for them every day.

• • •

Mention that some people have separated themselves from Christ's flock. Suggest that the children invite a parent, relative, or friend who doesn't go to church to come with them sometime soon.

191 Believe in Jesus

(PAGE W65) ACTS 11:19-22, 26C • JOHN 15:26—16:1

At this Mass we will hear about the spread of the Good News about Jesus Christ. For two thousand years the message has been passed on so that we ourselves received it. Now it is up to us to treasure this message and pass it on to future generations. We celebrate this Good News at this Eucharist. We pray for the grace to be worthy bearers of it to others.

Universal Prayer

The response is *"Lord, hear our prayer."*

For the worldwide Church, that members may be called to be missionaries and spread the Good News with enthusiasm, let us pray to the Lord.

For leaders of countries, that they may not block the efforts of missionaries, let us pray to the Lord.

For those who work in foreign or home missions, that they and the people they work with may enjoy the peace that comes from knowing Jesus, let us pray to the Lord.

For us, that we may have missionary hearts, let us pray to the Lord.

Special Features

- Invite a missionary to speak to the children.
- Take up a collection for the missions.
- After communion have the children light their own small candles and reflect on their call to spread the light of Christ to others. (Closely supervise this.)
- From a mission organization, obtain bookmarks that have a prayer for the missions, and distribute these after Mass.

Songs

Alleluia No. 1; All I Ask of You; He Is Lord; Jesus, Come to Us; Jesus Is Life; Jesus, Lord; Jesus, We Believe in You; My God and My All; We Walk by Faith; You Call Us to Live

Homily Ideas

Visual: A baptismal candle and another candle

Show a lighted baptismal candle and remind the children that each of them received one at their baptism. The light of the candle stands for the life of Jesus that was given to them then. Demonstrate how light can spread by lighting another candle from the flame. State that we can share the light we have with others.

· · ·

Refer to the first reading that told how the disciples brought the Good News about the Lord Jesus to people in other cities. In Antioch the disciples were first called Christians, which means "like Christ." The life we received at baptism makes us like Christ, just as the fire that touches an object sets it on fire and makes that object like itself.

· · ·

Discuss ways that the children can be true Christians, that is, like Christ. If they were like Christ, how would they pray? Talk to their parents? Treat their friends? Act in school? Respond to people in need?

· · ·

Point out that in the gospel Jesus promises that the Spirit will help us know the truth so that we can pass it on to others. Ask: How can we learn more about Jesus so that we can tell others about him? (pray, study, participate in religious activities).

· · ·

Tell the story of a great missionary such as Francis Xavier or Frances Cabrini. Francis Xavier was a Jesuit priest from Spain who longed to go to China to teach people about Jesus. He was sent to work in India and Japan, where he converted thousands of people. After ten years he finally was on his way to China, but he became ill and had to be taken off the boat. On an island so close to China that he could see it, Francis died. Mother Frances Cabrini from Italy always dreamed of being a missionary in the East like Francis Xavier. When she became a nun she even took his name. The pope, however, sent her to work with the Italian immigrants in the United States. There she and her sisters began schools, hospitals, and orphanages. She became the first American citizen to be canonized, proclaimed a saint.

• • •

Explain that missionaries are not only those who go to foreign countries. There are home missionaries who work among people in our own country. Explain that not only priests, sisters, and brothers are missionaries, but many laypeople are too. Some of them volunteer for a year or two.

• • •

Comment that the children do not have to wait until they are grown up to begin missionary work. They can talk about Jesus to their friends. They can support the missions by their prayers, money, and other gifts.

192 Preaching about Jesus

(*PAGE W67*) ACTS 16:22-34 • LUKE 9:1-6

For the fifty days of the Easter season we think about the wonderful things Jesus did to save us. At this Mass we celebrate them and are sent out into the world to let others know about them. We are to proclaim from the housetops that Jesus is Lord, that Jesus conquered death, and that God loves us very much. We pray to become good messengers.

Universal Prayer

The response is *"Lord, hear our prayer."*

That the Church may be inspired in this Easter season to proclaim the Good News more strongly, let us pray to the Lord.

That government leaders may act in ways that are in line with the teachings of Jesus, let us pray to the Lord.

That the whole world may come to believe in Jesus, let us pray to the Lord.

That we may have the courage and love for Jesus that will make us dynamic apostles, let us pray to the Lord.

Special Features

• Have several children read the first reading, taking the speaking parts.

• Add gestures to the gospel and read it as an echo pantomime with the children repeating each line and gesture.

• Highlight the proclamation of the mystery of faith by using a new melody.

• Accompany a song with trumpets.

• As a communion reflection, pray this litany:

The response is *"Lord Jesus, you are life."*

You rose from the dead. / You conquered sin and evil. / You won heaven for us. / You give us grace. / You are everything we need. / We love you.

Songs

Bring Forth the Kingdom; God Has Chosen Me; Great Is the Lord (Toolan); Here I Am; Proclaim the Good News; Send Us as Your Blessing, Lord; Take the Word of God with You; What You Hear in the Dark

Homily Ideas

Visual: A lily

Point out that the Easter lily is in the shape of a trumpet or megaphone. It reminds us of our role to be apostles. The word "apostle" means one who is sent. Jesus sends each one of us to be his messenger to others. We are to tell them the Easter news that Jesus has died and is risen.

⁕ ⁕ ⁕

Describe the zeal of Paul and Silas in being apostles and its effects. They were badly beaten and thrown into jail for speaking about Jesus. There they were chained and guarded. What did they do? They prayed aloud and sang praises to God. No one could keep them quiet. They were still delivering their message to the people around them, the other prisoners and their jailer. And what was the result? The jailer and his whole household became Christian.

⁕ ⁕ ⁕

Mention that in the gospel Jesus sent his apostles out to proclaim God's kingdom and to heal the sick. They went from village to village. Because of them, we know about Jesus.

⁕ ⁕ ⁕

Explain that Jesus uses us, too, to do his work and bring about God's kingdom. We shout out the Good News not only by our words but by the way we live. Because we believe in Jesus, we are people who pray, who celebrate Mass, who try to love others, who share, and who forgive. When others see us doing these things, they wonder why. They may realize that it's because we are Christian. They may become better Christians themselves. Someone once said that faith is caught more than it is taught.

⁕ ⁕ ⁕

Ask the children how they can be an apostle to their family and to their classmates.

⁕ ⁕ ⁕

Give an example of a person who has brought someone else to the faith. You might use a story about the children's parents or a parishioner. You might tell about the priest who became a priest because as a boy he saw his father go to Mass every day no matter what the weather.

Ordinary Time

193 Light for the World

(PAGE W73) EPHESIANS 5:8-10 • MATTHEW 5:14-16

Jesus told us to be a light for the world. Whenever we celebrate the Eucharist, we are filled more with the light of Christ's glory and have more power to be shining lights ourselves. Let us pray during this Mass to be light especially for those who are in darkness.

Universal Prayer

The response is *"Lord, hear our prayer."*

That our Holy father, bishops, priests, and deacons may reflect God's goodness, we pray to the Lord.

That our government leaders may spread the light of goodness and truth by their decisions, we pray to the Lord.

That the lives of those who suffer may be brightened by the warmth of love others show them, we pray to the Lord.

That we may have the courage and confidence to be light for people, we pray to the Lord.

That our relatives and friends who have died may soon live in the eternal light of heaven, we pray to the Lord.

Special Features

- Have an entrance procession with a child from each grade carrying a candle of different color and size. Have them set these candles on boxes covered with cloth that are arranged in the sanctuary like a mountain.

- Add gestures to the gospel and read it as an echo pantomime with the children repeating each line and gesture.

- As a communion reflection, pray Cardinal John Henry Newman's prayer "Radiating Christ":

Help me, Jesus, to spread your light everywhere I go. Fill my soul completely with your spirit and life. Then let your light shine through me so that every person I meet will feel your presence in my soul. Let others look and see no longer me but only you. Stay with me, Jesus, and I will be your light to others. The light I give to others will be coming from you; none of it will be mine. Let me praise you in the way you love best—by letting others know you, not so much by my words, but by my joyful spirit and example. I will be you shining on others through me. Amen.

Songs

Bring Forth the Kingdom; Christ Be Our Light; I Am the Light of the World; The Light of Christ; Light of the World; Sing Out His Goodness; This Little Light of Mine; Thy Word Is a Lamp; We Are the Light of the World; What You Hear in the Dark

Homily Ideas

Visuals: A flashlight and a pail or box

Ask the children how many of them have ever been afraid of the dark. Talk about the helplessness and fear that dark causes because we can't see when it's dark.

• • •

Introduce Jesus as the light of the world who came into our darkness to bring light and happiness. Explain that because we were joined to Christ at baptism, we are to be light like him. Refer to the first reading in which Paul tells us to act like people of the light. Ask what Paul says we are to do to make our light shine (be good and honest and truthful as we try to please the Lord).

• • •

Demonstrate Jesus' lesson in the gospel by putting a flashlight under a pail. Ask why the light isn't helping anyone. Tell the children that they are to be lights for other people by doing good. They are to be lights to family members at home by helping. They are to be lights to friends by helping them do what is right. They are to be lights to everyone who sees them. They are to let their love for Jesus show by praying, by participating in Mass, and by doing what they know he wants. That way they will be like a bright city on a hill. All people will see the good they do and be encouraged to do good themselves.

• • •

Talk about being light by showing how to care for others and for the world.

• • •

Mention that our spiritual batteries are recharged whenever we celebrate the sacraments. Then we can be good, steady lights, not flickering lights or lights that go out.

• • •

Tell the children the motto of the Christophers: "It's better to light one candle than to curse the darkness." Ask them what they think it means.

• • •

Give one or two examples of someone in the school or parish who is a light for others. Better yet, have a parishioner who is a light give a three-minute witness talk.

• • •

Quote Mother Teresa of Calcutta's advice, "Make all your life something beautiful for God."

Love Everyone

(*PAGE W75*) 1 CORINTHIANS 13:4–7 • MATTHEW 5:43–48

At this feast of love, the Eucharist, we gather in love to celebrate the love God has for us. We pray that we may grow in love of God and others. In communion we receive the grace to be more like Jesus in showing forth the love of the Father for everyone.

Universal Prayer

The response is *"Lord, fill us with your love."*

For the Church throughout the world, that it may show the love of Jesus for all, let us pray to the Lord.

For civil authorities, that they may have a heart for people who are in trouble, let us pray to the Lord.

For prisoners who are guilty, that they may be sorry for the evil they have done and resolve to be better, let us pray to the Lord.

For people who do not like us, that they may be blessed, let us pray to the Lord.

For ourselves, that we may see Christ in people we want to ignore, look down on, or dislike.

Special Features

- After Mass, pass out heart-shaped cookies.
- As part of the decorations, set up a heart-tree. Hang paper hearts on branches inserted in a pail of plaster of paris.
- For the communion reflection, invite everyone to stand and spread out apart from one another for the following prayer experience.

> *God asks, "How much do you love me?" You may stretch out your arms to show how much you wish to love God. (pause) Your arms are now ready to embrace others. As you embrace the people in your life, you are loving God. As you embrace those in need, you are loving God. As you embrace your enemies, you are loving God. Ask Jesus now to give you a heart like his, a heart large enough to embrace the whole world.*

Songs

The Bread That We Share; Now Let Us from This Table Rise; Service; That There May Be Bread; They'll Know We Are Christians; We Have Been Told; Where There Is Love; Whatsoever You Do

Homily Ideas

Visual: Outstretched arms

Tell the story about the person who asked Jesus, "How much do you love me?" Jesus stretched out his arms on the cross and answered, "This much." Demonstrate. Comment that God's love embraces the whole human race. We show love in return by loving others.

. . .

Refer to the gospel. Point out that Jesus told us we are to imitate our Father in heaven. We are to love even our enemies. We may hate their sinful acts, but we are still to love them as people. This means loving the person who pushes us in line, the classmate who spreads lies about us or steals from us, even the terrorist who kills innocent people. This isn't easy. It's something God does. And Jesus said we are to be perfect just as our heavenly Father is perfect.

. . .

Suggest that the children pray for their enemies. This might change their enemies and also change their attitude toward their enemies so that the relationship is healed. Sometimes a person we don't like can turn out to be one of our best friends. Tell the children to think of someone they don't particularly like. Invite them to offer this Eucharist for that person and his or her needs.

. . .

Elaborate on the gospel verse that says it's easy to be friends with those who like us. Christians are called to go out to those who are avoided by other people or who are in need. This means that the children are to be friendly with children who are considered odd: the "nerds" (or whatever term is in use for people who are different). We are even to reach out to people who don't seem to like us. People who are unlovable or mean are those most in need of love.

. . .

Point out that Jesus loved his enemies. He loved us when we had turned away from God and made ourselves God's enemies. He died on the cross for the very people who were responsible for his death. He forgave Peter after Peter denied even knowing him.

If Judas had asked his forgiveness, Jesus would have joyfully taken him back among the twelve apostles.

. . . .

Tell the story of the Green family. As they were touring Italy, someone shot into their car and killed their little boy Nicholas. Instead of directing their anger at the country, the parents donated their son's organs to Italians who were in need of them. They turned a horrible incident into a life-giving one.

Later, people in Italy who had received the new organs gathered to meet and thank the Greens.

. . . .

Reread the first reading and invite the children to insert their names wherever the word "love" is, to see if the description fits them. Use your own name as an example: Tom is kind and patient, etc. Comment that God is love. The more we love, the more we are like God.

195 This Is How You Should Pray

(PAGE W77) 1 TIMOTHY 2:1–4 • MATTHEW 6:7–13

Prayer is communicating with God. In prayer we speak to God and we listen to God. In the readings of today's Mass we hear how we are to pray. We hear Jesus give us the prayer we call the Lord's Prayer. We are gathered at this altar to pray the greatest prayer there is: the Eucharist. It is Jesus' prayer in which he offers himself to the Father. Let us make this Eucharist our prayer by echoing the words in our hearts and by joining in the prayers and songs with strong voices.

Universal Prayer

The response is *"Loving Father, hear our prayer."*

For the Church, that its leaders and people may come closer to Christ through private and public prayer, let us pray to the Lord.

For presidents, kings and queens, prime ministers, and other government officials, that they may have a heart for the poor, let us pray to the Lord.

For those who do not have enough to eat, let us pray to the Lord.

For those among us who have special needs, that these needs may be met, let us pray to the Lord.

For ourselves, that we may become persons of prayer.

Special Features

- Add to the Universal Prayer. Let individuals read specific intentions. Sing the response.
- Have the children bring intentions on slips of paper and burn them at the Universal Prayer as a sign that their petitions are rising to God.
- Highlight the Our Father by using a new melody, by holding hands, or by gathering around the altar. You might have it prayed in another language, such as sign language, with a line-by-line translation.

Songs

Children of God; Father of Peace; Gift of Finest Wheat; Glory and Praise to Our God; Our Daily Bread; Standin' in the Need of Prayer; We Belong to God's Family

Homily Ideas

Visual: Bread

Inform the students about St. Rose Philippine Duchesne, an American who was canonized. When she was in her seventies, she volunteered to work with Native Americans. Although she could not master their language, she lived among them and was an inspiration to them. Each day she would spend hours in prayer, so that the Native Americans called her "Woman Who Always Prays." There is a story that one day as Rose knelt in prayer a young boy crept up to her and sprinkled corn seed on her long skirt spread out behind her. Hours later the boy returned to find that the seed hadn't been disturbed.

• • •

Discuss what Rose was doing: lifting her mind and heart to God, being with God. Prayer is a way to grow in friendship with God. We like to be with people we love.

• • •

Point out that the first reading mentions whom we should pray for. It begins by saying we should pray for everyone. Ask if anyone remembers what we are to say to God about everyone (ask God to help and bless them; tell God thanks for each of them). Then we are to pray for kings and others in power. Ask: When do we pray for these people at Mass? (during the entire Mass, particularly at the intercessions).

• • •

Remind the children that in the gospel Jesus says that our prayers don't have to be long. God knows what we need. The point is that God does want us to pray when we or other people need help. We are happy and honored when someone asks us for help. God likes us to ask for help, too.

• • •

Explain that Jesus gave us the Our Father after the apostles noticed how often Jesus prayed and they asked him to teach them. Naturally this was a favorite early Christian prayer. One of the earliest Christian writings, the Didache (DID ah kay), says to pray it three times a day. Ask: When do we pray the Our Father? (at Mass; in the rosary). Suggest that the children pray it in their morning and night prayers.

• • •

Tell the children that in Jerusalem there is a church called the Church of Pater Noster (Our Father, in Latin). On its walls and outside walkways are large plaques that have the Our Father written in more than sixty languages.

• • •

Show bread. Point out that in the Our Father we ask for daily bread. Bread is a basic food. Ask the children to name types of breads. In the prayer, bread can mean food as well as everything else we need to survive. It can also mean the sacred bread we receive in the Eucharist. Just as earthly parents provide bread for their children, our heavenly Father provides bread for us.

• • •

Invite the children to think of a particular intention for which they would like to offer this Mass.

---

196 Store Up Riches in Heaven

(*PAGE W79*) COLOSSIANS 3:1-2 • MATTHEW 6:19-21

The Eucharist we are about to celebrate has infinite value. It is worth more than anything on Earth, for it is the sacrifice of God's only Son, Jesus Christ. Many graces are won through this sacrifice. We who offer this sacrifice with Jesus are not only doing a good deed: We are also storing up treasures in heaven for ourselves and for others.

Universal Prayer

The response is *"Lord, hear our prayer."*

That the Church may always live as if our real treasure is in heaven, let us pray to the Lord.

That government leaders may help to see that the goods of this earth are shared more equally, let us pray to the Lord.

That wealthy people may use their money wisely to help other people, let us pray to the Lord.

That we may set our hearts on storing up riches in heaven by doing good, let us pray to the Lord.

Special Features

- Begin or end Mass with a procession to a treasure chest in which the children deposit a paper coin on which they have written a good deed they intend to perform.
- Sing the refrain of the responsorial psalm using these words: "Happy Those Who Hear."
- After communion read a prayer called "Jesus, My Treasure," written by a faculty member or student.

Songs

All That I Have; Earthen Vessels; I'd Rather Have Jesus; Only in God; Seek Ye First; This Alone; Yes, I Shall Arise

Homily Ideas

Visual: A bank

Show the bank and ask the children if they have one. Ask what could happen to the money in their bank so that they wouldn't have it anymore (it could get lost; someone could steal it; they could spend it; bills could burn in a fire).

. . .

Point out that some people are always thinking about treasures like money, new clothes, cars, and other material things. Their minds and hearts are focused on them, and their lives are devoted to increasing them. Explain that Jesus taught us that there is something much more important than these things. We are to focus on heavenly treasures. Only these spiritual treasures will make us truly happy.

. . .

Describe what our treasures in heaven are: a new life after death, being with God, sharing God's life, living forever in happiness. Ask how we can obtain these treasures (by following God's laws; by loving on earth). It follows then that our lives should be centered on doing this. However, because we don't see heaven, we sometimes forget about it. Prayer will help us keep in mind what is most valuable: our everlasting life.

. . .

Tell the story of the woman who died and went to heaven. St. Peter was taking her down the street to her home in heaven. As they walked, they passed many gorgeous mansions. Finally they stopped in front of a small one-room house, and Peter said to the woman, "This one's yours." Stunned, the woman stuttered, "But…but…why isn't my house as great as the others we passed?" Peter replied, "That's all we could build with the material you sent up." Ask the children what "materials" we send ahead to heaven (prayers, acts of charity, sacrifices, good deeds).

. . .

Mention that not many saints were rich. In fact, most were poor on earth. Those who did have money did not clutch it to themselves or store it in banks. They used it to help others. For example, Katharine Drexel belonged to a wealthy family in New York. She was used to traveling, fine meals, and luxurious homes. Then God called her to become a nun. She took a vow of poverty and used the twelve million dollars she inherited to help Native Americans and black people.

. . .

Tell the children that a shroud is a sheet people used to be buried in. Ask them the meaning of the quotation, "There are no pockets in shrouds." (It is another way of saying "You can't take it with you.")

197 I Will Take Care of You

(*PAGE W81*) ISAIAH 46:4 • MATTHEW 6:25B-33

We are God's children. God made us, and we belong to God. The love God has for us is shown in what God has done for us. God even sent his only Son to save us. If God has done this incredible thing for us, won't God take care of us in other ways? Today let us celebrate God's goodness and care and give God thanks in this Eucharist.

Universal Prayer

The response is *"Loving Father, hear our prayer."*

That church members may be generous in doing God's work, we pray to the Lord.

That those who hold authority in the world may look to God for guidance, we pray to the Lord.

That people who need food, clothing, and other necessary things may receive them through others, we pray to the Lord.

That the lonely and the elderly may find joy and hope through others' care, we pray to the Lord.

That we may have hearts that trust God completely, we pray to the Lord.

Special Features

- In the sanctuary have a display of flowers and birds, perhaps a mobile.
- Allow for spontaneous intercessions.
- Read "Footprints" as a communion reflection if it is not used in the homily.
- Display a picture of the Good Shepherd and distribute holy cards of him.

Songs

Blest Be the Lord; Glory and Praise to Our God; He's Got the Whole World; Lead Me, Guide Me; The Living God; The Lord Is My True Shepherd; Praise God From Whom All Blessings Flow; Seek Ye First; Sing of the Lord's Goodness; You Are Near

Homily Ideas

Visual: A flower

Talk about the flower: how it began as a tiny seed; how it received soil, sun, and rain for life; its beauty. Explain that Jesus used flowers to teach us a lesson about God's love. He said that even King Solomon with all his wealth was not clothed as beautifully as a flower. It is God who does all these things for the flowers. Ask who takes care of the birds like *(name some in your region)*.

• • •

Read the story "Footprints" below. Point out that in the first reading God says, "I will carry you and always keep you safe."

Footprints

One night a man had a dream. He was walking along the beach with the Lord. Across the sky flashed scenes from his life. In each scene he noticed two sets of footprints in the sand: one belonging to him, and the other to the Lord. When the last scene of his life flashed before him, he looked back at the footprints in the sand. He noticed that many times along the path of his life there was only one set of footprints. He also noticed that it happened at the very lowest and saddest times in his life. This really bothered him, and he questioned the Lord about it. "Lord, you said that once I decided to follow you, you'd walk with me all the way. But I have noticed that during the most troublesome times in my life, there is only one set of footprints. I don't understand why when I needed you most, you would leave me." The Lord replied, "My precious, precious child, I love you and I would never leave you. During your times of trial and suffering, when you see only one set of footprints, it was then that I carried you." —*Source Unknown*

. . .

Reflect on the Good Shepherd in the responsorial psalm. A shepherd takes his sheep to feed in green pastures and drink cool water in safe streams. A shepherd guides his sheep along safe paths. He guards them from wolves and other dangers, even risking his own life to protect them. Compare the shepherd's care to the care the children give their pets. Then ask the children how God is a good shepherd for them.

. . .

Comment that we belong to God, and God loves us. We are more precious to God than flowers or birds. God tells us that we are not to worry about things like clothes and food. Instead, we are to be concerned about doing God's work and doing what God wants. Then God will provide these other things.

. . .

Explain the term "divine providence"—our belief that God provides good things for us. God sees that everything works for our good. The word "providence" comes from the word "provide." Remind the children that God is in charge of the world, and God is all-wise, all-powerful, and all-loving. Mention that in the song "He's Got the Whole World in His Hands" we sing about divine providence.

. . .

Comment that the things that happen to us that we consider lucky are really the result of providence.

. . .

Have the children recall something they or their parents are worried about. Invite them to shift this worry onto God's shoulders and trust that God will take care of them. Allow quiet time for them to do this.

---

198 Forgive as the Lord Has Forgiven You

(PAGE W84) COLOSSIANS 3:12–13 • MATTHEW 7:1–5

God forgives us again and again. This Mass is a celebration of how God forgives the entire human race. God forgave the original sin of the human race and forgives our personal sins as well. God asks us in turn to forgive one another. We are to be as loving to our brothers and sisters as God is to us. Let us pray for the grace of forgiveness during this Eucharist.

Universal Prayer

The response is *"Lord, hear our prayer."*

For the members of the Church, that they learn to forgive and forget, we pray to the Lord.

For world leaders, that they show mercy toward other countries and peoples, we pray to the Lord.

For people who bear grudges and seek revenge, that they learn to love, we pray to the Lord.

For victims of wars, famine, and violence, that they may soon experience peace in their lives, we pray to the Lord.

For ourselves and our families and friends, that we may put up with and encourage one another, we pray to the Lord.

Special Features

- For the sign of peace have the children say, "Peace be with you. You are good."
- At the end of Mass distribute paper logs, small sections of tree branches, or log candy as reminders not to judge others.

Songs

Forgive Our Sins; God Is Rich in Mercy; Let Us Go!; Loving and Forgiving; Prayer of St. Francis

Homily Ideas

Visuals: An eraser and a log

Show an eraser and ask what it does. Explain that God uses an eraser for our mistakes and faults. After we tell God we are sorry, God erases our wrongs and lets us start fresh. God even gave us a special sacrament that lets us start over again. Ask what it is (penance or reconciliation).

. . .

Tell the story of a woman who told her bishop that God talked to her. The bishop told the woman that the next time God talked to her she should get proof that it was really God. She was to ask what the bishop's secret sin was. The woman did this and then returned to the bishop. The bishop asked, "What did God say when you asked what my secret sin was?" The woman replied, "God said, 'I forgot.'"

. . .

Explain that all of us have some bad in us. All human beings are weak, and we sin. Even the saints sinned.

. . .

Refer to the gospel in which Jesus warns us not to judge others. He, a carpenter, asks how we can see the speck in our friend's eye, but not notice the log in our own. (Show the log.) Explain that Jesus was exaggerating to make a point: We easily see others' little faults, but are not aware of our own large faults. Give the example of a boy who thinks his sister is too bossy. He might be even bossier than she is, but he doesn't realize it.

. . .

Quote Billy Graham's words: When you find the perfect church, join it. Then it won't be perfect anymore.

. . .

Ask how we can know what our faults are (think over each day before we go to bed, making an examination of conscience; ask our parents or a good friend). Ask how we can overcome our faults (effort, prayer, the sacraments).

. . .

Comment that even though God is perfect, God puts up with us who are flawed. God loves us just as our parents do, who also put up with us. In the first reading God asks us to put up with one another. Elsewhere Jesus says, "Judge not, and you shall not be judged" (Matthew 7:1).

. . .

Tell the students that every person could wear a sign that says, "Be patient with me. God isn't finished with me yet." We are all trying to be good persons with God's grace. When someone fails, we forgive. When we fail, we hope others forgive us. Encourage the students to overlook others' faults and to make excuses for others as easily as they make them for themselves. Urge them to look for the good in others.

199 My Burden Is Light

(*PAGE W86*) PHILIPPIANS 4:8-9 • MATTHEW 11:29-30

The teachings of Jesus help us to live good, happy lives. At each Eucharist we hear these teachings in the word of God, the readings from the Bible. We also receive the grace to live by them, especially when we receive Jesus himself in communion. Let us thank God today for sharing with us the secret to living in peace and joy.

Universal Prayer

The response is *"Lord, hear our prayer."*

For our church leaders, that they may guide and inspire us in accepting the yoke of Christ, we pray to the Lord.

For people in authority, that they do not lay unnecessary burdens on others, we pray to the Lord.

For people who are sad and depressed, that Jesus and his followers may bring them happiness, we pray to the Lord.

For ourselves and those we love, that we may follow God's law of love with light hearts, we pray to the Lord.

Special Features

- Set up a large bag as part of a display. In the bag put small cards or pieces of paper that have some facet of the law of love written on them: kind words, good deeds, care for the elderly, and so on. After communion, invite each child to draw a card out of the bag and resolve to carry it for the week.
- At the end of Mass, distribute smiling face buttons as a reminder that Jesus' way of life brings about joy.

Songs

All People that on Earth Do Dwell; Come to Me; Come to Me, All Who Are Weary; Joyful, Joyful We Adore Thee; Keep in Mind; Like a Shepherd; O Jesu, Joy of Loving Hearts

Homily Ideas

Visual: A backpack containing a paper with the word "love"

Have the children think of a time they had to carry something heavy. Show the backpack and suggest that they may have many books to take to school. Remove the paper with the word "love" on it from the backpack, and ask how heavy love is (it weighs nothing).

. . .

Explain that Jesus told us that his way of life is light and easy to carry. At the time when Jesus lived, some religious leaders taught laws that made people's lives difficult. Jesus had only one main law: the law of love. He promised that if we followed that law and followed his example we would be happy.

. . .

Comment that Jesus compared his way of life to a light yoke. Ask what a yoke is (a wooden bar that joins animals at the neck, enabling them to carry a load together and share the weight). When we live for Jesus, we are not alone in carrying the burden. Jesus is our yoke partner. He helps us live in love as he did.

. . .

Elaborate on the joy of being a Christian. Talk about how Jesus' way frees us from the heavy burdens of pride, worry, unforgiveness, and hate. When we aim to be loving persons and are not selfish and self-centered, we are lighthearted and joyful. What's more, we spread happiness wherever we go.

. . .

Quote the saying, "A sad saint is a sorry saint."

. . .

Tell about St. Philip Neri, who is known for his sense of humor. His two favorite books were the New Testament and a book of jokes and riddles. Philip lived in Italy in the sixteenth century. When he was about eighteen, he went to Rome, where he studied at a university and tutored two boys. One day during prayer he had a spiritual experience that changed his life. He became a lay minister to young men in Rome. They liked Philip because he was fun to be with, and eventually he formed the men into a community of priests. Philip wore old clothes, big white shoes, and his hat cocked to one side. Once when the pope left a cardinal's hat outside Philip's door as a hint that he wanted to make him a cardinal of the Church, Philip played catch with it. Another time when people were saying that Philip was a saint, he shaved off half of his beard. Philip shows that people who are holy are happy.

. . .

Encourage the students to have a happy, positive attitude by doing what the first reading said: "Keep your minds on whatever is true, pure, right, holy, friendly, and proper."

. . .

Tell the children that Dante wrote a long poem about someone who had a tour of hell and heaven. When the person approached heaven, he didn't hear the singing of hymns, but he heard the sound of people laughing.

200 Treasures of Heaven

(PAGE W88) 1 PETER 1:3-4 • MATTHEW 13:44-46

Through baptism we became children of God. We can inherit God's kingdom of heaven. There, a wonderful world awaits us, full of treasures we can only imagine. It is possible for us to reach heaven because Christ bought it for us at the price of his own blood on the cross. At this Eucharist, we celebrate and share in Christ's sacrifice. We thank God for giving us a chance to inherit heaven.

Universal Prayer

The response is *"Lord, hear our prayer."*

That church members may desire with their whole heart to win the treasure of heaven, let us pray to the Lord.

That people in positions of power may not be blinded by greed or ambition, let us pray to the Lord.

That those people whose lives are centered only on things of this earth may wake up and think about the next life, let us pray to the Lord.

That more people may become priests, deacons, and men and women religious, let us pray to the Lord.

That we and our family members and friends may be wise enough to give up things for the sake of the kingdom of heaven, let us pray to the Lord.

Special Features

- Tape a dollar bill underneath a pew or chair, and begin the homily by having the children look for the "treasure." Let the child who finds the dollar keep it.

- Let everyone march out to the song "When the Saints Go Marching ln."

- Read the following reflection after communion:

Jesus, thank you for being with me now in a special way. In the next world I can be with you always and see you face to face. Please help me keep my heart set on heaven so that your suffering and death for me will not be in vain. Help me to love you and others even when it's hard or hurts or costs me something, so that someday I can enter heaven. For only there with you will I be truly happy.

Songs

Blest Are They; Eye Has Not Seen; I'd Rather Have Jesus; I Am the Bread of Life; I Know That My Redeemer Lives; The Love of the Lord; Seek Ye First; When the Saints Go Marching In

Homily Ideas

Visual: A lottery ticket

Show a lottery ticket and ask the children if their family has ever won a lottery. Ask if they themselves have ever won anything. Tell them to recall how they felt when they found out they were winners. (Or have them look for the dollar bill if you have put one under a seat. How does the winner feel?)

. . .

Explain that every person in the Church is a winner of a grand prize. It is worth far more than a million dollars. Ask the children if they know what it is (heaven). Tell them that God gave us heaven because God loves us very much.

. . .

Ask the children what they think heaven is like.

. . .

Refer to the gospel and explain that Jesus tried to tell us in stories called parables how marvelous God's kingdom is. He speaks of a man who discovers a treasure and is full of joy. The man sells everything he has in order to become the owner of that treasure. Another time Jesus tells about a lucky man who finds a very valuable pearl. He, too, sells everything in order to buy the pearl.

. . .

Point out that heaven is not really for sale. It was given to us as a gift from our loving Father when we were created. When we lost it through sin, Jesus won it back for us. We still have a chance to get to heaven if we live God's laws of love.

. . .

Ask the children what they would give in order to have a place in heaven. Ask if they would be willing to trade their bad habits, their sins, their time, their energy, their money. Remind them that if they wanted something bad enough, they would be willing to give up anything or do anything.

. . .

Mention that some people want to be with God in heaven so much that they do extreme things to make sure they get there. Tell the story of Francis of Assisi. He belonged to a wealthy family and was a popular young man. One day he decided to live for God alone. He gave away all he owned, even his fine clothes. He spent the rest of his life wearing the robe of a peasant and begging for what he and his companions needed. He believed that God was calling him to become holy in this way.

. . .

Explain that some people get to heaven by becoming good mothers and fathers and raising children who know and love God. Some people get to heaven by acting like Jesus where they work. Some people get to heaven by serving in the Church in a special way as a priest, deacon, sister, or brother. Some people get to heaven by being loving children in a family.

. . .

Comment that if heaven had a price tag, it would say "a heart full of love."

201 Trust in the Lord

(PAGE W90) ISAIAH 25:6–7, 9 • MATTHEW 14:22–33

God is true, and God is faithful. When God says, "I love you," we know it is the truth. Therefore, we can trust God to do what is good for us, to protect us, and to help us. We need not be afraid. This is the message of the readings today. It is a message that we celebrate with joy and thanksgiving at this Eucharist.

Universal Prayer

The response is *"Lord, have pity on us."*

That our Holy Father, the pope, may be strengthened by faith in Jesus to guide and govern us, we pray to the Lord.

That world leaders may look to God for help as they deal with matters of life and death, we pray to the Lord.

That people who are in crisis situations may look to Jesus for wisdom, courage, and comfort, we pray to the Lord.

That we may have the grace to help those who are in trouble by our words and actions, we pray to the Lord.

That we may not be needlessly worried, anxious, or fearful, we pray to the Lord.

Special Features

- Have the gospel read with the children taking the speaking parts.
- End the homily with a witness talk by someone who has been helped in a remarkable way after praying.
- Distribute cards that have Scripture's "911" number on them: "The crowds…followed him. He received them and spoke to them about the kingdom of God, and he healed those who needed to be cured" (Luke 9:11).

Songs

Be Not Afraid; Be with Me, O God; Don't Be Worried; If God Is for Us; On Eagle's Wings; Only in God (Talbot); Though the Mountains May Fall; Trust in the Lord; You Are Mine

Homily Ideas

Visual: A lucky charm, four-leaf clover, rabbit's foot, or horseshoe

Show something that people consider lucky. Explain that some people believe that certain objects bring good luck. They put their trust in things like a four-leaf clover or a rabbit's foot or the stars, which have no power at all. Point out that the rabbit that owned the foot had four of them, and it wasn't so lucky.

. . .

Explain that we trust in God, who is all-powerful. As the psalm said, we can run to God for safety. God will protect us.

. . .

Tell the story of the man who falls off a cliff and midway in his fall grabs onto a tree growing out of the side of the cliff. As he hangs there, the man calls out, "Help!" A voice answers, "This is God. Just let go. Trust me." The man thinks a bit, and then calls out, "Is there anyone else up there?" Sometimes God asks us to trust in ways that we don't understand. Then it is difficult to trust God.

. . .

Refer to the difficulty Peter had in trusting Jesus in today's gospel. Jesus told him to come to him across the water. Notice that as long as Peter trusted Jesus, he could do the impossible. He could walk on water. But when he thought of the wind and waves and when he thought of what he was doing, he became frightened. His faith in Jesus was shaken; and Peter, whose name means rock, began to sink like a rock. But he immediately called to Jesus for help and he trusted in Jesus, and so he was saved.

. . .

Explain that sometimes we feel like Peter—as though we are battered by winds and waves. We are asked to do something as challenging as walking on water. Maybe someone in our family is sick. Maybe we have a physical problem. Maybe we feel we have no friends. Maybe everything seems to go wrong. Where can we find the strength and courage to go on? In Jesus. He won't let us down. As the Angel Gabriel told Mary, "With God nothing is impossible."

. . .

Ask the children how they would feel if their friend was in trouble and didn't ask them for help. Point out that Jesus wants us to look to him for help. Just as we like to help our friends and feel good when they ask us for help, Jesus, our best friend, likes to help us. He has already helped us in fact by his death and resurrection.

. . .

Encourage the children to call on Jesus just as readily as they would call 911 in an emergency.

. . .

Have someone share how they prayed and their prayers for help were heard. Or share a time when your own prayers were answered.

202 Gifts Received from God

(PAGE W93) 1 PETER 4:10-11 • MATTHEW 25:14-29

God has given each of us many gifts, gifts of mind, body, and heart. We are to use these gifts to serve and help other people. At this Mass we celebrate God's best gift, Jesus. We thank God for Jesus and ask for the grace to imitate the way Jesus used his gifts and talents for others.

Universal Prayer

The response is *"Lord, hear our prayer."*

That the Church may be open to the Spirit alive and working within, let us pray to the Lord.

That the leaders of nations may work together to improve the life of all, let us pray to the Lord.

That those who enrich our lives with their talents and gifts may be blessed with the enthusiasm to continue, let us pray to the Lord.

That we may know what our gifts are, develop them, and then use them to serve God and others, let us pray to the Lord.

That artists, musicians, writers, and architects may be blessed, let us pray to the Lord.

Special Features

- Have the gospel read with the children taking the parts of the master and servants.
- Display a banner or give out cards that say, "What you are is God's gift to you. What you become is your gift to God."
- After communion let the children reflect on one of their gifts, thank Jesus for it, and ask him to help them use it to help others and glorify God. End with this adaptation of Cardinal John Henry Newman's prayer:

   God, you have created me to do some definite service. You have given me some work that you have not given to another. I have my mission. I am a link in a chain, a bond of connection between persons. You know what you are doing. Therefore I will trust you.

Songs

All That We Have; Every Person Is a Gift of God; For the Beauty of the Earth; Now Thank We All Our God

Homily Ideas

Visual: An object that represents a gift or talent

Show the object and explain how someone (perhaps yourself) uses it to benefit others. For example, show a musical instrument and tell how the person who plays it uses his or her musical talent to worship God and to bring joy to others.

. . .

Ask the children to name gifts they see people using to serve others. Point out that smiles, a listening ear, and a big heart are gifts.

. . .

Mention that God has given each person many gifts. Not everyone has the same gifts. We work together to bring about God's kingdom. Tell the folk tale "Stone Soup," which follows.

Three hungry soldiers came to a certain poor town. The people hid their food, for they didn't want to share the little they had. The soldiers told the villagers that they would teach them how to make stone soup. They set a large pot filled with water over a fire and put stones in it. Then the soldiers said that the soup could use some carrots. A man said, "I think I could find some." He brought out some carrots and added them to the water. "Now," said another soldier, "if only we had some potatoes." "I have a few," said a woman, and she added potatoes. Then a soldier stated that the soup needed a little meat, and someone brought meat. Ingredients were added to the soup in this way until a wonderful meal was prepared. Everyone in the village enjoyed the stone soup.

. . .

Explain that we are to develop our gifts and not waste them. The servant with the one coin didn't make it grow. He just kept it safe. We are not to be like him, but to use our gifts and not ignore them. If we have a good mind, we are to work hard in school so that later we can help others as nurses, doctors, teachers, electricians, or secretaries. If we have a talent for drawing, we are to take lessons and practice. If we can tell jokes well, we are to brighten others' lives by telling jokes.

. . .

Point out that gifts can be used for good or evil. For example, a smart man can use his intelligence to seek a cure for cancer, or he can use it to plan how to rob a bank. We must keep in mind that we were made to know, love, and serve God. All our decisions and actions should work for the good of all and for God's greater glory.

. . .

State that a certain woman lived until she was eighty, but she died when she was twenty. Ask how that could be (she stopped using her gifts as a human being). Quote this saying of St. Irenaeus: "A person fully alive is God's glory." To be fully alive means to live to our potential, to develop and use all our gifts and powers.

. . .

Give examples of people who are using their gifts, such as the president, a popular actor, a singer, a sports figure, the children's teachers, and people in your parish.

. . .

Share the quotation "What you are is God's gift to you. What you become is your gift to God."

203 The Word That I Speak

(PAGE W96) ISAIAH 55:10–11 • MARK 4:1–9

God sent us his Son, Jesus, the word made flesh, to teach us the way to life and to save us. God also speaks to us through the word of sacred Scripture. If we listen to the word of God and do what it says, we will come to know and love God. We will have a rich life full of love and we will bear much fruit. During this celebration let us listen together to God's word and pray that it will be powerful and fruitful in our lives.

Universal Prayer

The response is *"Lord, hear our prayer."*

That our church leaders may always nourish us with the word of God, we pray to the Lord.

That civil leaders may live according to God's word, we pray to the Lord.

That people who have never heard God's word may have someone bring it to them, we pray to the Lord.

That nothing may prevent God's word from growing in our hearts, we pray to the Lord.

That Scripture study and prayer groups may increase, we pray to the Lord.

Special Features

- Have an entrance procession in which the lectionary is held high and then placed on or in front of the altar. When it is time for the readings, have another procession with two lighted candles to take the lectionary to the lectern. Incense the lectionary before reading from it.
- Display banners or posters that show a dead plant and a thriving plant.
- Add gestures to the first reading and read it as an echo pantomime with the children repeating each line and the gestures.

- After communion pass around a heart-shaped box and have the children draw from it a slip of paper with a Scripture verse that they can apply to their lives.

Songs

God's Blessing Sends Us Forth; The Good News of God's Salvation; Happy Those Who Hear the Word of God; Let Us Go!; Sent Forth by God's Blessing; Song of Good News; Speak, Lord; Take the Word of God with You; Thy Word Is a Lamp

Homily Ideas

Visual: A packet of seeds

Show the packet of seeds and ask what must happen for them to become plants (they must be planted and have sun, water, and good soil). Recall that in today's gospel Jesus compares God's word to seeds. When we listen to God, we let God's word be planted in our heart. Then if we follow what God says to do, these words grow and produce much fruit.

. . .

Give an example of how something God says to do can produce good fruit, or ask the children for an example. For example, God's word in Scripture tells us to pray. If we follow this word and pray, we will become better persons. We will be happier, wiser, more courageous, more loving. We will do much good on earth for other people.

. . .

Mention that the gospel says that not all seeds grow when they are planted. Ask why not (birds eat them; the soil is not deep, so the plants can't grow roots; other bushes choke them). Explain that some people hear God's word and read God's word but it doesn't grow in their hearts. Ask why not (the people forget it; they don't follow it; they are too busy with other things). Refer to the expression "talking to a brick wall." God keeps trying to tell us how to be happy, but some people are like a brick wall. God's words don't sink in but bounce right off.

. . .

Present Mary as a model of someone who heard God's word and followed it. She prayed and listened to God. Mary gave birth to Jesus, who is the Word of God. She was full of love like Jesus. When her relative, Elizabeth, was old and pregnant, Mary hurried to help her, traveling miles on the hot, dusty roads. At the wedding at Cana when the wine ran out, Mary helped the bride and groom by asking her Son to do something. When Jesus was

dying on the cross, Mary stood there, one with him in his suffering. After the resurrection she helped the early Church. Even now she helps us when we ask for her prayers.

. . .

Point out that God's word is powerful and can change lives. Give the example of Augustine who at one time was not living a Christian life. In fact, he was quite a sinner. One day Augustine picked up a Bible and read a passage that caused him to change his life completely. He became an outstanding bishop and is now honored as a saint.

. . .

Ask the children to read a bit of the Bible every day, perhaps a verse or two each night before they go to bed.

204 I Will Help You

(PAGE W98) ISAIAH 41:14 • MARK 4:35–41

We are here to celebrate that Jesus saved us. When we were in danger of losing our eternal life, Jesus won it back for us. Over and over in life, Jesus will act as our savior. We only need to trust him and to turn to him for help. Then we will see marvelous things in our lives. Let us each offer this Mass for a special need we might have. (You might also mention a particular school or parish need.)

Universal Prayer

The response is *"Help us, O Lord!"*

That the Church may always be full of hope because it relies on God, let us pray to the Lord.

That government leaders may turn to God for guidance and help as they strive to make a better world, let us pray to the Lord.

That those who are experiencing a crisis right now may find strength and comfort in the thought of God's love for them, let us pray to the Lord.

That those who have asked us to pray for them may have their needs filled, let us pray to the Lord.

That we may never lose heart, but always be encouraged by knowing that God cares for us, let us pray to the Lord.

Special Features

- Have a group of students pantomime the gospel as it is read.
- Provide an opportunity for the children to name personal needs in spontaneous petitions.
- Give the students lifesaver candy as a reminder to turn to Jesus when they need help.

Songs

Amazing Grace; Christ Is Here; O God, Our Help in Ages Past; Save Your People; Shelter Me, O God; This Day God Gives Me; Turn to Me

Homily Ideas

Visual: Candy lifesavers or a life preserver

Share with the children this quotation: "Lord, let me remember that nothing will happen today that you and I can't handle."

. . .

Explain that in the first reading God tells the people of Israel that when others call them names or insult them, they are not to worry, for God will save them. God loves us as much as God loved Israel. God is with us and helps us even when others might think of us as little or lowly or worthless—even when we feel like Ziggy or Charlie Brown. We are always in the mind of God.

. . .

Recall the gospel in which Jesus, the all-powerful, saved his friends. They were caught in a storm, and their boat was about to capsize. Jesus saved them from drowning.

. . .

Ask for other examples of times when Jesus helped people.

. . .

Explain that Jesus is with us in the storms and difficulties of life. When we feel as if we are drowning, when we are in trouble or worried or afraid, Jesus will save us because he loves us. Jesus is our life preserver. (Show the lifesaver or candy lifesavers.) All we have to do is to put our hand in his. Even when Jesus appears to be sleeping and not answering our prayers, we can be sure of his love and care for us.

. . .

Point out that in the gospel story Jesus scolded the disciples for not having enough faith in him. If we really believe in Jesus and his love for us, then we will face our problems calmly and in peace. We know that Jesus will help us work through them. We believe that everything will work out for our good.

. . .

Mention that one of the simplest prayers is "Help!"

. . .

Tell the story of the sea captain who was caught in a terrible storm. After trying everything to save his ship, as a last resort he fell to his knees and prayed, "O God, I haven't bothered you in twenty years. Save me, and I won't bother you for another twenty." Comment that the sea captain did not have the right idea about prayer. God likes to be bothered by us every day.

. . .

Explain that Jesus has already saved us from the greatest evils—sin and eternal suffering in hell.

205 The Lord Will Help You

(PAGE W100) ISAIAH 30:19-20, 23-24, 26 or EPHESIANS 1:15-16A, 18-19A

MARK 5:21-24, 35B-36, 38-42

When we were lost in the darkness of sin and death, Jesus came into the world and brought us the light of new life. He is our rising sun. He opened our eyes to see what was good and true. He showed us the safe way through life. He warmed us with his love and care. God continues to be our saving light. At this Eucharist we celebrate God's saving actions, and we look to God to be our light this day and every day.

Universal Prayer

The response is *"Lord, hear our prayer."*

For the Holy Father, all bishops, priests, deacons, and men and women religious, that they may reflect the light of Christ for everyone, we pray to the Lord.

For those in positions of authority, that they will work with God's help to rid the world of evil, we pray to the Lord.

For those who have no hope, that they may be enlightened to realize God's love for them, we pray to the Lord.

For ourselves, that we may have the grace to always keep our eyes on Jesus, we pray to the Lord.

Special Features

- Display the Paschal candle or other candles in the sanctuary.
- Let children carry lighted candles in the entrance procession.
- Have a group of children pantomime the gospel as it is being read.
- Chant the intercessions.
- Give the children a card that says, "S.O.S." and have them put it by their light switch or lamp at home as a reminder to look to God for help.

Songs

Bless the Lord, My Soul; Center of My Life; Christ Be Our Light; Jesus, Come to Us; The Light of Christ; The Lord Is Near; Thy Word Is a Lamp; Turn to Me; Yahweh, the Faithful One

Homily Ideas

Visual: A candle or flashlight

Ask the children if they were ever afraid of the dark. Ask if they were ever lost in the dark. Explain that darkness often stands for evil because in darkness we can't see and might get hurt. (Light a candle or turn on a flashlight.) Point out that light gets rid of darkness. It conquers it. Someone said that all the darkness in the world can't put out the flame of a candle.

. . .

Recall that in the story of creation, at the beginning all was confusion and darkness. Then God created light and it was good.

. . .

Recall that after the sin of Adam and Eve the human race was in darkness and sin. God sent his Son Jesus to be light for us and save us. Jesus died and rose on Easter like the rising sun. By his death and resurrection he overcame our darkness and brought us the light of eternal life. He called himself the Light of the World.

. . .

Refer to the gospel in which Jairus' daughter was in the darkness of death. Her father knew where to get help. He went to Jesus, and Jesus brought the little girl back to life. She opened her eyes and saw the face of Jesus. She was saved from death. This miracle shows us the power of God over evil.

. . .

Mention that at Easter we use the Paschal (or Christ) candle to remind us of Jesus' presence. This candle is lit at the Easter Vigil service, and everyone's small candle is lighted from it. This demonstrates in a beautiful way how Christ's new, holy life is shared with us.

. . .

In the first reading, the blessings of God are compared to light. (Reading A: The sun will shine seven times brighter than usual. Reading B: Paul prays that light will flood the hearts of the Christians.) We can pray for this light. We can pray that God will help us in times of darkness.

. . .

Quote the saying, "Keep your eyes on the sun and you will not see the shadows." Explain that if we keep our eyes on Jesus, the risen Son, we will be full of joy. The shadows, or the troubles of life, will not disturb our inner peace. Then we will be like bright rays of light for others. Ask how we keep our eyes on Jesus (make time for prayer; read the gospels; study about Jesus; celebrate the Eucharist, the meal Jesus gave us to remember him and his saving works).

Invite the children to think about some part of their lives that is in darkness. It may be something or someone they are worried about. It may be a bad habit they have gotten into. Give them time to talk to Jesus and ask him to bring his light into their lives.

• • •

206 We Are Called God's Children

(PAGE W104) 1 JOHN 2:29B—3:1A • MARK 9:33–37

Because we are made in the image of God, we are children of God and can hope to inherit God's kingdom of heaven someday. After sin lost us the right to heaven, Jesus won it back for us. Now through baptism we are God's children once again. Today we celebrate with God's family. We praise and thank God that we are his children.

Universal Prayer

The response is *"Gracious Father, hear our prayer."*

For our Holy Father, our bishop, and all others who guide us in the Church, that they may lead us to God, we pray to the Lord.

For those who govern us, that they may act with wisdom, justice, and love as they care for God's children, we pray to the Lord.

For children everywhere, that they may come to know the love God has for them, we pray to the Lord.

For us, that we may always remember that God is our loving Father and live as God's children, we pray to the Lord.

For those who will be baptized this year, that they may always live as children of God.

Special Features

- By the baptismal font, have a sign that reads, "We are God's children."
- Before Mass give the children badges to wear that say, "I am a child of God."
- Make the Our Father special by having the children hold hands or by singing it.

Songs

Abba; Children of God; Come, My Children; Everyone Moved by the Spirit; Father, We Adore You; Glory and Praise to Our God; In Him We Live; Let Heaven Rejoice; Like a Child Rests; Sing Praise to Our Creator

Homily Ideas

Visual: A photo of a father and child (or children)

Show a photo of a father and child (or children). Comment on the relationship of the father and children: how the children come from the father, resemble the father, and are loved and cared for by him. Explain that God is our heavenly Father. When we were baptized, we became God's children. That's how much God loves us.

• • •

Comment on what a great privilege it is to be God's children. God loves us. Even adults are children in God's eyes. Jesus called his followers "little ones."

. . .

Explain how God spoils us by giving us many wonderful gifts. Ask the children to name some. Conclude that the best gift of all awaits us: a life without end with the God who loves us so much.

. . .

Point out that the first reading tells us that whoever does right is a child of God. We are to live as God's children by trying to be like our heavenly Father. We are to be good and loving. People should be able to tell that God is our Father because we resemble God, just as we resemble our earthly parents.

. . .

Comment that just as we try to obey and honor our parents on earth, we should also try to obey and honor our heavenly Father. We should do what pleases God and show love for God in return for all the love showered on us. Ask how we know what God wants (through the commandments, the Bible, what Jesus said, the Church).

. . .

Remind the children that even when we displease God through sin, God is a loving Father who forgives us.

. . .

Refer to the gospel in which Jesus tells his disciples that they are not to try to be more important and greater than others. Rather, they are to be humble and loving like little children. They are to serve others.

. . .

Point out that Jesus is the champion of children. He encourages his disciples to welcome children, not ignore them or chase them away.

. . .

Mention that whenever the children pray the Our Father, they should remember that they are really speaking to God as their Father. Jesus called God "Abba," which means "father"; and we can call God "Abba," too.

207 Jesus Blessed the Children

(PAGE W106) ISAIAH 41:10 • MARK 10:13–16

Jesus loved children. He had time for them and blessed them. He died on the cross for children, too. At Mass Jesus welcomes us, adults and children, to join with him in praising his Father. Jesus comes to us in communion and speaks to our hearts. Let us thank Jesus at this Eucharist for his love for us and ask him to bless us today, too.

Universal Prayer

The response is *"Lord, hear our prayer."*

That the Church may show the same love and con-cern for children as Jesus showed, we pray to the Lord.

That government officials may have a heart for children, especially for the children of the poor, we pray to the Lord.

That parents may not choose abortion, through which unborn children die, we pray to the Lord.

That countries in which children are forced to work long, hard hours may stop this practice, we pray to the Lord.

That all the children of the world may experience happiness and well-being, we pray to the Lord.

Special Features

- Before Mass have the children prepare paper hearts with a promise or a prayer of love for Jesus on them. Let them deposit the hearts in a basket as they enter the church, and have the hearts presented as an offering to God. The paper hearts may be burned.
- Read the following reflection after communion:

    Jesus, you are in my heart, closer than if I were sitting beside you. I know that you love me more than anyone else in the world loves me. You are my best friend. You even died for me so that I could live forever. I love you. I want to be with you forever, so please help me live in a way that shows love for you. Help me to follow your way of love for God and others. Make me kind, gentle, helpful, and prayerful. Make me just like you. Amen.

- Have the gifts brought up by children wearing ethnic dress.
- Take up a collection that will benefit needy children.
- Distribute holy cards showing Jesus with children.

Songs

Abba; Children of God; Come, My Children; Jesus Is with Us; Jesus Loves the Little Children; Jesus Loves Me; A Gift from Your Children; The Greatest Gift; Let Heaven Rejoice; Open My Eyes

Homily Ideas

Visual: A picture of a child saint, such as Dominic Savio, Tarcisius, or Maria Goretti

Tell the story of the little boy whose father had just spanked him. The boy ran crying to his mother and sobbed, "Why didn't you marry Jesus? He loved little children."

• • •

Comment that the story of Jesus and the little children is in three of the four gospels. It is an important story. Recall that the disciples didn't want the children to bother Jesus. They tried to get the parents to take their children away from him. The disciples probably thought that Jesus was too tired or too busy to spend time with children. Jesus, however, scolded the disciples and told them to let the children come to him.

• • •

Explain that Jesus probably held the children, ruffled their hair, and played with them the way people do with children. He also blessed them. The same hands that blessed the children later broke bread and then were nailed to a cross in a sacrifice given for them.

• • •

Encourage the children to come to Jesus. Ask them how they can do this (by praying, by celebrating Eucharist and receiving communion).

• • •

Point out that children are not too little to love Jesus. They can know that Jesus is their friend who loves them.

• • •

Tell the story of a child saint, for example, Dominic Savio. Dominic was one of ten children. When he was only five years old, he learned to serve Mass. At the time of his First Communion, Dominic made rules for himself. One of them was that he would rather die than commit sin. Dominic wanted to be a priest. He went to a school where a priest-friend, John Bosco, helped him to be holy—to be cheerful and wise. Dominic loved the Eucharist. He lived like Jesus and loved others. He helped other children to be good, too, by forming a club. The members helped with jobs at the school. After two years at the school, Dominic became sick. He died when he was only fifteen years old. Now he is a saint.

• • •

Ask the children how they can be a good friend to Jesus, who is such a good friend to them.

208 I Want to See Again

(*PAGE W108*) ISAIAH 42:16 • MARK 10:46-52

Jesus cures blindness. When we didn't see how to live, he came and showed us. When we were lost in the darkness of sin and death, he came to be our light. Even today when we are blinded by temptation and can't see what to do, he helps us. Just as Jesus has power over blindness of the body, he has power to heal our spiritual blindness. Let us ask at this Eucharist for the grace to see things as they really are, to see things as God sees them.

Universal Prayer

The response is *"Lord, have pity on us."*

That the holy Church of God may respond to the needs of the poor as Jesus did, we pray to the Lord.

That leaders of nations may look beyond their own countries to see and tend to the needs of the world, we pray to the Lord.

That the unemployed, the homeless, and the sick may find work, shelter, and healing, we pray to the Lord.

That people who are blind to the needs of others may receive sight, we pray to the Lord.

That when we are in need, we may remember to call out to Jesus for help, we pray to the Lord.

Special Features

- At the penitential rite mention that asking forgiveness is a way to heal spiritual blindness.
- Have a group of children pantomime the gospel.
- For the Universal Prayer, have the children raise their arms as they respond to each petition.

Songs

Open My Eyes; Open Our Hearts; Speak Lord, I'm Listening; We Walk by Faith

Homily Ideas

Visual: A pair of glasses

Show the glasses and talk about ways that vision is impaired. Some people can't see things at a distance; others can't see things close up. Some people have double vision, and some are color blind. Some people can't see at all.

• • •

Explain that there is another kind of vision: spiritual vision. Some people can see the truth about life. They know that we are made to know, love, and serve God, and they see how to do this. On the other hand, some people don't see why they are on earth and how important God is. They do not see how to live the right way. At times what is bad looks good to some people. We can be blinded by money, fame, or false teachings.

• • •

Point out that Jesus came to correct our vision and give us 20/20 vision. His grace, like glasses, helps us to see life as it really is. Jesus helps us see that God is our loving Father and that the only way to be truly happy is to love God and others. He helps us see that all people are our brothers and sisters.

• • •

Refer to the gospel in which Jesus gave Bartimaeus sight. Invite the children to imagine what it is like to be blind. Ask: What are some of the dangers of blindness? (you could hurt yourself and others; you could get lost). Comment that just as Jesus had power to heal Bartimaeus, he can heal our blindness. If we can't see what to do, we can call out to Jesus as Bartimaeus did, "Jesus, have pity on me!"

When terrible things happen and everything seems dark, we can call out, "Jesus, have pity on me!"

• • • •

Explain that we can pray to see things as Jesus sees them: to see right from wrong, to see what is best for us, to see all people as children of God. When we go to Jesus, we can throw off our blindness as quickly as Bartimaeus threw off his cloak.

• • • •

Tell the story of the religious teacher who asked his followers when the first moment of daybreak was. One disciple asked, "Is it when we can see the forest?" The teacher said, "No." Another disciple asked, "Is it when we can tell one tree from another?" The teacher said, "No. It is when we can see the face of Christ in the face of our neighbor."

• • • •

Comment that the people in the crowd who tried to silence Bartimaeus were really blind themselves. They did not see the blind beggar as someone in need of their love and help. They did not see that Jesus came to help people like Bartimaeus.

• • • •

Point out that we can learn to see Jesus not only in other people but everywhere. Read Joseph Mary Plunkett's poem "I See His Blood upon the Rose."

---

209 They Were Extremely Generous

(PAGE W110) 2 CORINTHIANS 8:1–3A, 12 • MARK 12:41–44

God's loving kindness overflows onto all the world. What marvelous things God has given us and done for us. As God's people we are to be loving like God. Our love is to be shown in generous and loving deeds. We are to give to God and to others even when it hurts. At this Eucharist we receive the strength and power to be bighearted, to be more like Jesus who shed his blood for us on the cross.

Universal Prayer

The response is *"Hear us, gracious God."*

For our Holy Father, all bishops, priests, and deacons, that they may be examples for us in showing generous love for the poor, let us pray to the Lord.

For world leaders, that they may share their country's gifts with other countries, let us pray to the Lord.

For the rich, that they may use their wealth to improve the life of the poor, let us pray to the Lord.

For the poor, that they may have enough food, clothing, and a place to stay, let us pray to the Lord.

For us, that we may not be stingy but generous with the good things that God has given us, let us pray to the Lord.

Special Features

• As a communion reflection, pray the following prayer of St. Ignatius:

> *O Lord, teach me to be generous.*
> *Teach me to serve you as you deserve;*
> *to give and not to count the cost;*
> *to fight and not to heed the wounds;*
> *to toil and not to seek for rest;*
> *to labor and not to ask for reward,*
> *save that of knowing that I am doing*
> *your holy will. Amen.*

• Take up a collection for a worthy cause. Have a child from each grade level carry up the donation during the presentation of gifts.

Songs

Each Time That You Love; Feed My Lambs; A Gift from Your Children; If You Belong to Me; Love, Love; Seek Ye First

Homily Ideas

Visual: Two pennies

Show two pennies and ask what two pennies can buy today. Explain that in the story in today's gospel a few coins like these were precious because they were everything a poor woman had. Jesus praised this woman for giving these coins to the temple treasury. She gave what little she had for God's glory. Rich people put much more money in, but they still had a lot left for themselves. The woman, whose husband had died, had nothing.

• • •

Explain that the woman is a model for us. We are to be generous with God and willing to give up everything for God's glory. What does this mean? In the first reading we heard about Christians in Macedonia who were poor, and yet who gave generously—more than they could afford—to other Christians who were in need. Ask why we should do things like this (because God has been good to us; because others are our brothers and sisters).

• • •

Offer examples of people in the parish or in the news who have given generously.

• • •

Remind the children that love is shown by giving. Ask them how God has shown tremendous love for us. Tell the children that the Bible says that Jesus emptied himself for us; in other words, he gave his all.

• • •

Explain that we can give by sharing our time, our talents, and our treasures. We can share our time by helping set the table when we'd rather be watching television. We can share our talents by reading to a younger brother or sister. We can share our treasures by giving some of our allowance to the missions. Elicit more examples of ways to show love for others.

• • •

Tell the story "Tatterrags." A boy lived in a village that had a festival each year to which everyone wore costumes. One year the boy was too poor to have a costume. His friends came to his house, and each one presented the boy with a piece of cloth from his or her own costume. The boy's mother sewed all of the pieces together to make a colorful costume. Of all the costumes at the festival, the boy's was the best, for he was clothed in the love of his friends.

• • •

Tell about St. Martin of Tours, a soldier who, when he met a poor man freezing on the road, cut his cloak in half with his sword and shared it. That night in a dream Martin saw Jesus wearing the part of the cloak he had given the beggar.

• • •

Quote these words of St. Basil: "The bread you do not use is the bread of the hungry; the garment hanging in your wardrobe is the garment of him who is naked; the shoes that you do not wear are the shoes of one who is barefoot; the money that you keep locked away is the money of the poor; the acts of charity that you do not perform are so many injustices that you commit."

• • •

Comment that Jesus is always with us. He sees our generosity the way he saw the generosity of the woman in the temple. He takes it as a sign of our love for him.

210 Kind Is the Lord

(PAGE W112) ISAIAH 30:18 • LUKE 7:1–10

God is outstanding in kindness. God showers us with gifts and plans our lives to be happy. When we call upon God for help, God hears us. Even when we turn away from God, God takes us back with loving forgiveness. God is kind to enemies. What can we do to praise and thank such a good God? We offer this Eucharist, the greatest sacrifice we can offer, the greatest prayer we can pray.

Universal Prayer

The response is *"May your kindness be upon us."*

That the Church may shine forth the kindness of God to all, let us pray to the Lord.

That those in positions of authority may be both just and kind, let us pray to the Lord.

That those who have been kind to us may be blessed, let us pray to the Lord.

That doctors, nurses, and all who care for the sick may have patience, love, and joy in their work, let us pray to the Lord.

That we may be kind and loving to all we meet, especially to our family members, let us pray to the Lord.

Special Features

- Let a group of students take parts for the gospel.
- Have the students prepare paraphrases of Psalm 136 by listing ten things they thank God for. Choose students to read their prayers with the refrain "For his love is everlasting" as part of the homily or as a communion reflection.
- After communion, invite the children to reflect on a way to be kinder to a particular person and resolve to try to do it.

Songs

Alleluia; Gentle Shepherd; How Great Thou Art; Kindness; O Bless the Lord, My Soul; Oh, How I Love Jesus; You Are Mine

Homily Ideas

Visual: A bottle of glue

Show glue and state that kindness is like glue that keeps relationships together. Friends are kind to each other. Family members are kind to each other. And God is kind to us. This kindness binds us together and heals us when something has caused a break in our relationship. Ask for examples of what it means to be kind.

• • •

Tell Aesop's fable of the lion and mouse. A lion caught a mouse who begged to be let go. The mouse promised that someday he would return the favor. The lion freed the mouse. One day the lion was trapped in a net. The mouse came and chewed the net to set the lion free.

• • •

Point out that kindness has a domino effect. When someone is kind, the person who receives the kindness passes it on.

• • •

Tell the children that there is a song that begins, "Kindness is kind of a miracle." The kindness of God to us is a great miracle. God loves us and cares for us. Elicit from the children kindnesses of God toward them.

• • •

Explain that in the Bible the word "hesed" stands for loving-kindness. This is what God shows to us over and over. We do not have to be afraid of God.

• • •

Talk about Jesus' kindness. Many of his miracles were acts of kindness, especially those in which he healed people. Refer to the gospel in which Jesus healed the army officer's servant. Point out that the officer had been kind to Jesus' people. He had built them a meeting place. He was also kind to Jesus in that he said Jesus need not come to his house. According to Jewish law, going into a Gentile's house would have made Jesus unclean, so the officer told Jesus just to say the word and his servant would be healed. Jesus responded to this kind man with kindness and granted his request.

· · ·

Encourage the children to count their blessings each night. They can look over the day and recall things that happened that showed God's kindness to them.

· · ·

Explain that the best way to thank God for kindness shown to us is to pass it on. Christians should be known for their kindness.

· · ·

Tell the children that a holy woman named Janet Stuart wrote a prayer asking for virtues. Her prayer ends with the words, "And, O Lord God, let us not forget to be kind."

---

211 I Will Save You

(PAGE W114) ISAIAH 43:1–3A, 5 • LUKE 7:11–17

The name Jesus means "God saves." Jesus is our savior who saved us from sin and death. At this Eucharist we remember and celebrate his saving acts: his suffering, death, and resurrection. As Jesus offers himself on our altar, he continues to save the world. Let us thank God wholeheartedly in song and prayer for rescuing us and sending us Jesus to be our savior.

Universal Prayer

The response is *"Hear us, saving God."*

That our church leaders may confidently rely on God and encourage us to do so, we pray to the Lord.

That government leaders may turn to God for help as they deal with problems and world situations, we pray to the Lord.

That people who are suffering or dying may look to God for strength and comfort, we pray to the Lord.

That we may grow in the virtues of faith, hope, and love, we pray to the Lord.

Special Features

- Display a picture of the Good Shepherd.
- After Mass present everyone with a card that says "S.O.S." as a reminder to call on God for help. You might have an appropriate psalm verse printed on the opposite side.
- Read "Footprints" as a communion reflection. See page 54.

Songs

All the Ends of the Earth; Be Not Afraid; Blessed Be the Lord, My Rock; Blest Be the Lord; He Is the Lord; The Lord Is My Hope; Path of Life; Tell Out, My Soul; Save Us, O Lord; Sing to the Mountains

Homily Ideas

Visual: A card that says "S.O.S."

Tell the children that someone called the Bible a book drenched in love. The stories in the Bible show God saving people out of love for them. Ask the children for some examples (Adam and Eve, the Israelites in Egypt, the three young men in the fiery furnace, Esther, David, healing stories about Jesus, Jesus' death and resurrection).

· · · ·

Call attention to the first reading from Isaiah, in which God promised the Israelites to be with them and keep them from drowning when they crossed deep rivers. God promised that when they walked through fire, they wouldn't be burned by the flames. Comment that God tells us the same thing today: "Don't be afraid. I am with you."

· · · ·

State that God is with us at all times. God is not only Most High but Most Near. Tell about the little fish in the ocean who asked a big fish, "Where is the ocean?" God is like that ocean. Tell about the little boy whose mother asked him to get the broom from the dark closet. Because the boy was afraid and because he believed that God is everywhere, he called into the closet, "OK, God, hand me the broom."

· · · ·

Ask the children to name frightening times they have experienced when God was with them. Offer examples yourself from recent happenings.

· · · ·

Point out that the story in the gospel shows Jesus saving two people. Because the widow's only son died, there was no one left to support her. Jesus saved the boy from death and saved the woman from a life of poverty. Comment that the gospel says that Jesus felt sorry for the woman and told her not to cry. Jesus is God. He shows us that God is full of compassion. God has a heart for us. God cares for us and helps us when we are in trouble.

· · · ·

Explain that this gospel story foreshadowed what happened to Jesus. When Mary was a widow, Jesus, her only son, would die, too. Where the son of the widow of Nain was brought back to life, Mary's son would rise with a new, everlasting life. Through his death and rising, Jesus will someday raise us up to new life.

· · · ·

Share a story from your own experience when God helped and comforted someone who was going through a crisis.

· · · ·

Show the S.O.S. card and encourage the children to look to God when they face hard times. When they call on God, God will hear them and come to their rescue. Remind them that Jesus called himself the Good Shepherd. He is a shepherd who keeps his sheep safe. Just as a good shepherd helps his sheep who are lost or hungry or in danger from wild animals, Jesus helps us. Just as a good shepherd risks his life to protect his sheep, Jesus laid down his life to save us.

· · · ·

Read to the children more verses from Isaiah that assure them of God's love for them:

> "I have grasped you by the hand" (42:6).
>
> "You are precious in my eyes and glorious… I love you" (43:4).
>
> "Can a mother forget her infant?…Even if she forget, I will never forget you" (49:15).
>
> "See, upon the palms of my hands I have written your name" (49:16).
>
> "Though the mountains leave their place and the hills be shaken, my love shall never leave you" (54:10).

212 God Is Love

(*PAGE W116*) 1 JOHN 4:7-10 • LUKE 7:36-50

God's love for us is seen in God's forgiveness. Not only has God forgiven our entire human race and sent his Son to win eternal life for us, but God forgives each one of us. Whenever we are sorry for our sins, God welcomes us back as generously and lovingly as parents forgive their children. At this Mass we recall the great sacrifice of forgiveness, Jesus' death on the cross. We ask forgiveness and pray for the grace to love with our whole heart, the way God loves us.

Universal Prayer

The response is *"Lord, hear our prayer."*

That church members may be filled with a great love for God, we pray to the Lord.

That government leaders may show love and forgiveness in their decisions, we pray to the Lord.

That sinners may realize how much God loves them, we pray to the Lord.

That we may treat others with mercy and love, we pray to the Lord.

That we may make time for God in our lives, we pray to the Lord.

Special Features

- As a communion reflection, have a student pray this prayer of St. Ignatius (or play a recording of the song version):

  Take, Lord, and receive all my liberty, my memory, my understanding, and my entire will. Whatever I have and possess you have given all to me. To you, Lord, I now return it. All is yours. Dispose of it according to your will. Give me only your love and your grace. I will be rich enough; that is enough for me.

- Make the penitential rite special. For example, sprinkle the congregation with holy water.
- Have the gospel read with children taking parts.
- Give each person a yellow ribbon as a reminder of God's forgiving love.

Songs

Bread for the World Broken; Bread, Blessed and Broken; God Is Love; The Good News of God's Salvation; I Have Loved You; Jesus, Lord; Jesus, You Love Us; Love That's Freely Given; Lover of Us All; Only a Shadow; Sing Out, Earth and Skies; Taste and See (Hurd); There's a Wideness in God's Mercy; We Have Been Told; We Remember

Homily Ideas

Visual: A container of perfume

Tell the children that John the Evangelist wrote a beautiful description of God in the Bible. He said that God is love. Love is the most outstanding quality of our good God. We see it over and over. Point out that we don't have to be beautiful, rich, or intelligent to be loved by God. No matter what we're like, God loves us and surrounds us with tender care. God loves us the way parents love a baby who can't even return their love yet.

. . .

Explain to the children that God loves us through others, for example, through their mothers and fathers who stay up caring for them when they are sick during the night.

. . .

Ask the children to name some signs of God's love for them. If they don't mention God's forgiveness, do so.

. . .

Invite the children to recall a time when they hurt someone and then were forgiven. Have them recall the relief and joy they felt when they knew they were loved again.

. . .

Show the perfume and point out that in the gospel we see Jesus with a woman who has been forgiven. She responded with a love that is like perfume. As she poured the perfume on Jesus, its pleasant fragrance filled the room and reached everyone in it. Jesus was happy to receive this sign of her love. He explained to Simon, who was a religious leader, that he (Simon) had not shown even basic signs of courtesy and affection that a host ordinarily showed guests in those days. In comparison, the sinful woman who was forgiven showed Jesus tremendous love.

. . .

Explain that God longs to forgive us as the father in this story forgave his son. The boy was angry and restless and ran away from home. While he worked as a migrant worker in the vineyards, he came to realize that he had made a mistake. He longed to return home and be friends with his father again. So the boy wrote his father and told him he would be passing the family farm on a certain day. He asked the father to tie a yellow ribbon on a tree in their orchard if he was willing to take him back. The boy got a ride home with a truck driver. When they came to the boy's house, the boy was afraid to look. He asked the truck driver to tell him if there was a yellow ribbon on a tree. The truck driver replied, "Son, every tree in the orchard has a yellow ribbon!"

. . .

Comment that the children have been forgiven by God. Encourage them to live in a way that shows they have been forgiven and are full of love. Suggest that they show love for God by the perfume of prayer, the perfume of good works, and the perfume of sacrifice. They could praise and thank God in the morning and evening and wholeheartedly at each Mass. They could follow God's laws and be kind and loving to others. They could do hard things and offer them to God. Then, as the responsorial psalm says, they "will sing for joy."

---

213 Sent to Preach the Kingdom of God

(PAGE W119) JEREMIAH 1:4–8 • LUKE 9:1–6

At every Eucharist we hear the Good News about Jesus and celebrate it. We also receive grace to go out into the world and proclaim it to others. Each of us has this mission. We are to preach Christ by our words and actions. In this way others will be drawn to him and come to know and love him. Let us listen carefully today as Jesus tells us in Scripture and in our hearts to be his apostles.

Universal Prayer

The response is *"Lord, hear our prayer."*

For those who lead us in spreading the Good News, that they may always have enthusiasm, energy, and love for their mission, we pray to the Lord.

For people in authority, that they may live by the values of Jesus, we pray to the Lord.

For missionaries everywhere and the people they serve, that faith may grow in their hearts, we pray to the Lord.

For our families, friends, and ourselves, that we may answer Christ's call to spread the news of his love to others, we pray to the Lord.

Special Features

- Display a globe, map, or a banner that pictures the world.
- Take up a special collection for the missions.
- At the end of Mass have the assembly process out as a sign of going out to spread the Good News to the world.

Songs

Go; God Has Chosen Me; Great Is the Lord; Here I Am, Lord; Mighty Lord; Proclaim the Good News; Send Us as Your Blessing, Lord; What You Hear in the Dark; Wherever I Am, God Is; Yahweh, the Faithful One; You Are Near

Homily Ideas

Visual: A battery

Tell the children that God wants the whole world to know the Good News of how much God loves us. Both readings are about God choosing and sending people to speak to nations. The first reading talks about Jeremiah the prophet, and the gospel is about the twelve apostles. God also has chosen and sent us.

• • •

Comment that in the first reading Jeremiah argues that he is too young for the job. God ignores this and promises to be with him. Point out to the children that none of them is too young to carry the Good News to others either. At their baptism they received the mission to spread the gospel. They are to share with others the truths that God loves us and that Jesus has saved us.

• • •

Explain that carrying out this mission shouldn't be hard. Ask the children what they usually do when they hear some good news (tell others). Jesus is the best news of all. We should be so excited about him that we want to run and tell others all about him. Comment that in this world that is so full of bad news, it is wonderful to have some good news.

• • •

Refer to the responsorial psalm in which they repeated, "Proclaim God's marvelous deeds to all the nations." Ask the children to name some of God's marvelous deeds for them.

• • •

Tell the story of someone who has carried the Good News to other nations. This may be someone you know, someone written up in a mission magazine, or a saint like Mother Cabrini, Francis Xavier, or Isaac Jogues.

• • •

Ask the children how they can spread the Good News (talk to others about Jesus, invite others to Mass or other religious services, live as Jesus taught). Emphasize that actions speak louder than words. Children can teach the message of God's love by showing they believe it through deeds of love.

• • •

Show a battery and explain that it takes a lot of energy to spread the Good News. Sometimes we get tired or too busy about other things. We can be recharged during Mass. Jesus offers us graces at the Eucharist to carry on the work of apostles. Point out that at the end of Mass the presider sends everyone out to love and serve the Lord. We are to take Christ's message to the world: to our family, relatives, neighbors, and friends.

214 Who Is My Neighbor?

(PAGE W112) 1 JOHN 3:11, 18 • LUKE 10:25-37

In today's Mass we focus on the greatest law of all: the commandment to love. Love is what Christianity is all about. Jesus taught us to love God, others, and even our enemies. He showed us the meaning of love by the way he treated the people he met. But most of all he showed us the meaning of love when he offered himself for us on the cross. This great act of Jesus' love is represented here today. We join in his sacrifice of love and offer him and ourselves to the Father.

Universal Prayer

The response is *"Lord, hear our prayer."*

That the Church may always teach the way of love, we pray to the Lord.

That world leaders may realize that all people are brothers and sisters, we pray to the Lord.

That those who are most in need of someone's love may find it, we pray to the Lord.

That those who are hurting from alcohol or drugs may be helped, we pray to the Lord.

That we may have the grace to love God and others wholeheartedly, we pray to the Lord.

Special Features

- Invite the children to hold hands during the Our Father.
- For the sign of peace, invite the children to greet one another with, "The peace of Christ be with you, brother (sister)."

Songs

Bread for the World; Feed My Lambs; God of the Hungry; Neighbors; A New Commandment; Send Us Forth; Service; Song of the Body of Christ; We Are Many Parts; Whatsoever You Do

Homily Ideas

Visual: A card with "XOXOXO" on it

Show the card and ask the children what these marks mean on a letter or card (kisses and hugs). Explain that we tell people we love them by our words and with kisses and hugs; but, as the first reading points out, we really show love by helping others.

⋅ ⋅ ⋅

Tell the children that Jesus was the greatest lover in the world, and he commands his followers to imitate him. Ask the children how Jesus showed love for people (he healed them, fed them, taught them, and died for them).

⋅ ⋅ ⋅

Ask the children how they can show love for the people in their lives: their parents, brothers and sisters, classmates, and neighbors.

⋅ ⋅ ⋅

Comment that Jesus explained how we were to love by telling the story of the Good Samaritan. A man was beaten and robbed. He needed someone to love him enough to help him. Two people passed him right by. One man stopped to help and bound up his wounds, took him to an inn, and cared for him during the night. The next day he even paid the innkeeper to care for the man and promised to repay him if it cost more. This man was a Samaritan, someone who was an enemy of the man who was beaten. Yet, the Samaritan treated the man in need as if he were a brother.

⋅ ⋅ ⋅

Ask the children to name some people who are in need of their help. Guide them to give practical suggestions, such as a child who is shunned by other children, a person who has a disability, a parent who is overworked, a neighbor who is sad or lonely.

⋅ ⋅ ⋅

Mention that St. John of the Cross said that at the end of the world we will be judged on love. Someone else said that when God measures a person's greatness, God puts a tape measure around the person's heart, not his or her head. Love is the most important thing we can do as human beings.

* * *

Point out that it isn't always easy to really love someone. It takes courage, strength, and sacrifice.

* * *

Tell O. Henry's story the "Gift of the Magi." Della and Jim were a young married couple. They were rich in love for each other, but didn't have much money. Della's prize possession was her beautiful, long hair. Jim's prize possession was his watch. At Christmas Della cut and sold her hair to buy a chain for Jim's watch, only to find out that he had sold his watch to buy lovely combs for her hair.

* * *

Refer to the Boys Town picture that shows a boy carrying a younger boy on his back. The caption is "He's not heavy. He's my brother." Encourage the children to care about every person as their brother or sister. In reality that is what we are, for we are all children of God.

---

215 Ask and You Will Receive

(*PAGE W124*) JAMES 5:16C–18 • LUKE 11:5–10

When we are in trouble or need help, we are not alone. Jesus revealed that God invites us to come with our needs. God welcomes our prayers, for the all-powerful and all-wise God is all-loving, too. Just as a good parent or a good friend cares about us, God is ready to do what is best for us. At this Eucharist we turn to God in praise and thanksgiving for past favors, and we place our current needs before God. Because of God's goodness and love, we trust that our prayers will be answered.

Universal Prayer

The response is *"Lord, hear our prayer."*

That all of us in the Church may be prayerful people, let us pray to the Lord.

That world leaders may turn to God in prayer for help with their serious concerns, let us pray to the Lord.

That people who are in trouble and have not prayed about it may be inspired to pray, let us pray to the Lord.

That we may have the habit of turning to God first in time of need, let us pray to the Lord.

Special Features

- Before Mass have the children write prayer requests on slips of paper. During the prayers of the faithful, include the intention: "That the requests we have written on paper be answered, let us pray to the Lord." Later burn or bury the papers.
- Before the Our Father point out that in this prayer we ask for "our daily bread," which means everything we need to live. Like the friend in the parable, we ask for bread.

Songs

All My Days; Answer When I Call; Be with Us, Lord; Christ Is Here; The Cry of the Poor; Dwelling Place; Lord, Be with Us; O Lord, Hear My Prayer; Remember Your Love

Homily Ideas

Visual: A small piece of paper

Show a small piece of paper and tell the children that in Jerusalem the foundation of the Western Wall of the Temple still stands. For centuries Jews have been placing slips of paper with prayer requests in between its giant stones. Periodically these papers are removed and buried.

· · ·

Explain that we ask God for things because we believe that God has power to help us and wants to help us. In the first reading we saw that God's prophet, Elijah, could control rain through his prayers. Even though we are not famous prophets, our prayers can have wonderful results, too. Jesus promised that this is true. He encouraged his followers to pray to God with trust.

· · ·

Tell the children that a poet wrote, "More things are wrought by prayer than this world dreams of." Ask what they think the line means.

· · ·

Ask the children who they would go to for help if they had a broken bone (doctor); if they had trouble with understanding a math problem (teacher); if they were lonely and wanted someone to play with (a friend). We go to people who can help us. It makes sense then that we should go to God for help because God has more power than anyone on earth to help us.

· · ·

Ask the children how they feel when someone asks them for help (glad to help, honored). State that God likes to be asked for help, too.

· · ·

Point out that in the gospel parable Jesus is telling us never to give up praying. Just as a neighbor gets up to answer his friend's knock on the door—because the friend won't go away—God will answer us if we keep asking.

· · ·

Comment that we must make an effort to pray. Jesus says we must ask, search, and knock. If we don't ever pray, how can God answer our prayers?

· · ·

Tell the story about St. Monica who prayed for years that her son, Augustine, would change his evil ways and turn to Christ. A bishop named Anselm promised her that her tears would not be in vain. Eventually one day something Augustine read in the Bible led him to have a change of heart. He went on to become a bishop himself and is now honored as a saint.

· · ·

Quote the advice "Pray as if everything depended on God, and work as if everything depended on you."

· · ·

Caution the children that sometimes God answers our prayers with no. Ask why this might be (because God has a better idea in mind; God knows that what we ask won't be good for us). Give the example of a mother who says no to a child when the child asks for something harmful.

· · ·

Conclude that it is good to be beggars, to beg God for help. We will not be disappointed.

216 Become Stronger in Your Faith

(PAGE W126) COLOSSIANS 2:6–7 • LUKE 13:6–9

At baptism we received divine life. Just as our natural life grows and develops, our spiritual life should grow. Our faith should become stronger. At every Eucharist, we are fed with the words of the Bible and with heavenly food and drink. This makes our spiritual life grow. If we are open to God's grace, we leave Mass a little holier and more ready to live like Jesus did.

Universal Prayer

The response is *"Lord, hear our prayer."*

For our Holy Father, all bishops, priests, deacons, and religious, that they may be strong in their lives of faith, we pray to the Lord.

For those in authority, that they may grow in faith in God and follow God's laws, we pray to the Lord.

For people who are losing their faith or who have lost it, that they may have the grace to believe, we pray to the Lord.

For those we love, that through faith they may grow to become all they are meant to be, we pray to the Lord.

Special Features

- Add gestures to the first reading or the gospel, and read it as an echo pantomime with the children repeating each line and the gestures.
- Conclude the homily with this simple act of faith:

    O my God, I firmly believe that you are one God in three divine Persons, Father, Son, and Holy Spirit; I believe that your divine Son became man and died for our sins, and that he will come to judge the living and the dead. I believe these and all the truths which the holy

Catholic Church teaches, because you have revealed them who can neither deceive nor be deceived.

- After the homily have the children renew their baptismal promises, and then sprinkle the children with holy water.
- Pray the Apostles' Creed.

Songs

Heal Me, O God; I Believe in the Sun; Jesus, Lord; Jesus, We Believe in You; We Walk by Faith; Without Seeing You

Homily Ideas

Visual: An apple, orange, or other fruit

Tell the children that the first reading and the gospel talk about trees as if they were fruit trees. Ask what trees need to grow (good soil, sun, water). Comment that if a tree grows well, it produces good fruit. Show a piece of fruit.

· · ·

Ask the children if anyone remembers where the first reading says we are to plant our roots (in Christ). From Christ and divine grace we can draw life and the strength to grow. Ask how we can come into contact with Christ (in prayer, in the Eucharist and other sacraments, in Scripture). The more we are in touch with Christ and the more deeply we are rooted in Christ, the greater our faith will be. Ask the children to reflect in their hearts on how much time they spend with Christ each day.

· · ·

Explain that like trees, we are expected to bear fruit. Ask the children what kind of fruit, or good results, a life rooted in Christ would show (peace, joy, goodness, love, patience, gentleness, self-control). State that these are good, desirable qualities.

. . . .

Point out that some people never grow in faith. They are like midgets in the faith. People who separate themselves from Christ shrivel up like a dying tree. They are not happy and their lives do not do much good.

. . . .

Tell the children that one way to grow in faith is to practice it. If they believe in God, they should pray. If they believe that Jesus' teachings are true, they should live by them. If they believe that Mary is the Mother of God, they should pray to her. If they believe that they have God living in them since baptism, they should respect themselves and others. If they believe that Jesus saved them, they should be happy and celebrate it.

. . . .

Ask the children what signs in their homes and in their lives show that they have faith.

. . . .

Admit that it is difficult to have faith sometimes because we don't see God. We don't see Jesus. We don't see heaven. Recall that Jesus told Thomas, "Blessed are they who have not seen and yet have believed." Tell them that we can pray the prayer of a father who hoped that Jesus would cure his son: "Lord, I believe. Help my unbelief." Explain that faith is a gift.

. . . .

Comment that the Church prays a creed at Mass in which we state everything that we believe. Encourage the children to pray the Apostles' Creed or a simple act of faith.

---

217 Show Faith by Actions

(PAGE W128) JAMES 2:14–18 • LUKE 14:12–14

We have come here to celebrate our faith, to celebrate that God loves us and has saved us. We also come here to grow in faith. Here at the Eucharist we find the reasons to live by faith and receive the grace to do it. As we pray as God's people, let us make up our minds to be faith-filled people. Let us be believers who are not afraid to let our faith show.

Universal Prayer

The response is *"Lord, hear our prayer."*

That the Church's work for the rights of the poor may be successful, we pray to the Lord.
That government officials may make laws that improve the conditions of the poor and needy, we pray to the Lord.
That movies, television, radio, publications, and computers promote good and not evil, we pray to the Lord.
That the poor, the homeless, and the disabled may be helped by other people, we pray to the Lord.
That we may have a heart for the poor and take action on their behalf, we pray to the Lord.

Special Features

- Invite someone who works for the poor to explain his or her work as part of the homily.
- Have a special collection for the poor and take up some of the food or clothing during the presentation of gifts.

Songs

Beatitude People; God's Blessing Sends Us Forth; Here I Am, Lord; Let Your Light Shine; Jesu, Jesu, Fill Us with Your Love; Sent Forth by God's Blessing; What Shall I Give?

Homily Ideas

Visual: A report card

Show a report card and ask the children if God were to give them a grade in Christianity, what would they get? Ask how God would determine their grade. The grade would not be just for knowing the facts about the faith. It would tell how well they are living the faith, in other words, how much they are deepening their relationship with God and how well they are keeping God's commandments.

• • •

Ask the children what the first reading and gospel say we should be doing if we have faith (helping those in need, especially the poor). Tell the children that one Peanuts cartoon shows children on a wet and stormy night gathered around a shivering dog. They say to him, "Be of good cheer." Ask what the dog really needs instead of good wishes (a warm, dry blanket).

• • •

Point out that the gospel tells us to do things for those who can't repay us. We are to help them out of sheer love. We are to show selfless love.

• • •

Present the story of St. Katharine Drexel from Philadelphia. Her father was a wealthy international banker. The Drexels had a chapel in their house and prayed for a half hour each night. Her mother opened their home to the poor three days a week.

Katharine became concerned about the Native Americans in the west. At the suggestion of the pope, she began a religious community dedicated to spreading the gospel among Native Americans and blacks. She spent her inheritance of twelve million dollars on this work. Because of her, the Church and the country became more aware of the needs of the poor.

• • •

Explain that some people feel bad about the sufferings of other people but don't lift a finger to help them. As Christians we are bound to love others by doing kind deeds. Ask what the children can do to help the poor and needy although they are only children (give from their allowance; help with a food or clothing drive; pray for them; do errands for someone with a disability; send cards to the sick).

• • •

Tell the story of Trevor Ferrell. When he was eleven years old, Trevor saw a program on television about homeless people who were sleeping on the streets of Philadelphia. Trevor begged his parents to take him there that night so he could give someone a blanket and one of his pillows. Every night after that the Ferrells went downtown, taking clothing and blankets that Trevor had gathered. Friends began to help. The movement grew, and now there is a building called Trevor's Place where homeless people find shelter.

• • •

Tell the children about a local organization that helps the needy.

• • •

Express the wish that the children may merit an A+ in Christianity someday because of the love they show toward the poor.

218 The Good Shepherd

(PAGE W130) ISAIAH 40:10–11 or EZEKIEL 34:11–15 • LUKE 15:1–7

In Jesus' parable, the good shepherd who finds and brings back his lost sheep calls for a celebration. We are gathered here to celebrate because Jesus, our good shepherd, has saved all of us. He gave his life so that we could someday enjoy life everlasting in heaven. As we think together today about the kindness God shows us, may our hearts be filled with joy and gratitude that we belong to God.

Universal Prayer

The response is *"Lord, hear our prayer."*

That all the shepherds of the Church may show Christ's love and care for people, we pray to the Lord.

That those who rule over people may realize that their job is one of service, we pray to the Lord.

That sinners who have left the flock may return to God, we pray to the Lord.

That we may always follow our good shepherd, we pray to the Lord.

Special Features

- Have an entrance procession in which everyone follows a statue of Jesus or a crucifix into the church.
- Add gestures to the first reading (A) and read it as an echo pantomime, with the children repeating each line and gestures.
- When the gifts are brought up, have children bring up lambs they have made to represent themselves.
- After communion have a reflection period during which a song about Jesus, the good shepherd, is played and slides are shown.

Songs

Gentle Shepherd; God Is So Good; Jesus, Shepherd; Like a Shepherd; The Lord Is My True Shepherd; My Shepherd, Lord; Oh, How I Love Jesus

Homily Ideas

Visual: Sheep from a nativity set

Tell the children that the earliest paintings that Christians did on the catacomb walls showed Jesus as the good shepherd. We actually got the idea of calling God a shepherd from Scripture. In the first reading, the prophet talks about God as a shepherd who cares for his sheep. (Reading A: Isaiah says God carries his lambs near his heart. Reading B: Ezekiel says God rescues the sheep that have wandered away.)

* * *

Recall that in the gospel when Jesus is accused of being friends with sinners, he asks if a shepherd who loses a sheep wouldn't go after it. State that later Jesus called himself the good shepherd who lays down his life for his sheep.

* * *

Show the sheep and explain that we are like God's sheep. We belong to God and God calls us by name. Sometimes, like sheep, we are rather stupid. We do things that hurt us. We wander away from the path we should follow by not keeping God's laws. Tell the children that sometimes lost sheep lie down and can't get up again. Gases build up in them and stop the circulation. Wolves and other wild animals can easily attack them. A good shepherd looks for such sheep. When he finds one, he holds it up and rubs its limbs to restore the circulation. When we are like a lost sheep, God searches for us to bring us back to where we can be safe and happy.

* * *

Explain that a shepherd feeds his flock, cares for it, and protects it. He even sleeps across the entrance of the cave where the sheep are so that he forms a gate to protect them. God gives us food for our table and also the sacred bread and wine at Mass to make us strong. God cares for us by providing people who love us. God protects us by keeping us from harm. We belong to God, and God loves us as a shepherd loves his flock.

• • •

Tell the children that a poet named Francis Thompson, who was not living a life pleasing to God, suddenly changed his ways. He described what had happened to him in a poem called "The Hound of Heaven." In the poem he speaks of God as a hound that constantly, patiently searched for him until he found him. This is the way God looks for us if we sin. God wants us back.

• • •

Invite the children to share times in their lives when they experienced the love and care of God as their good shepherd.

219 Give Thanks to God

(PAGE W133) 1 THESSALONIANS 5:16–18 • LUKE 17:11–19

One of the basic kinds of prayer is the prayer of thanksgiving. When we realize all the wonderful things God has done for us, our hearts are filled with gratitude. We respond by expressing our thanks. The greatest prayer of thanks is the Eucharist. Even the word "Eucharist" means thanksgiving. Mindful of what God has done for our human race and for us personally, we join together in offering our prayers and the sacrifice of Jesus in thanksgiving.

Special Features

- Display a banner or cartons covered with pictures of things for which we thank God.
- Make a giant thank-you card to present to God at Mass. Let each child write on it something for which he or she is particularly grateful.
- Highlight the thanksgiving after communion by having one or more students read a personal prayer of thanks to Jesus.

Universal Prayer

The response is *"Lord, hear our prayer."*

That the Church may always teach us to give thanks, we pray to the Lord.

That people who serve in government offices may always remember that God is the source of their power and gifts, we pray to the Lord.

That people who are not thanked begin to be appreciated, we pray to the Lord.

That we may always have grateful hearts, we pray to the Lord.

Songs

All Our Joy; All Praise and Glad Thanksgiving; Alleluia; At the Table of Jesus; God Is So Good; In Memory of Jesus; Jesus, Thank You; Mountains and Hills; Sing to the Mountains; Song of Thanksgiving; We Are Grateful; We Thank You; We Thank You, Father

Homily Ideas

Visual: A thank-you card

Tell the children that a post office worker once said that before Christmas the post office receives many letters to Santa at the North Pole, but after Christmas he has never found a thank-you note to Santa.

. . . .

Show a thank-you card. Ask the children if their parents have them write thank-you cards for birthday and Christmas gifts. Point out that we are expected to thank people who have given us gifts and tell them how much we like the gifts and how we will use them. It is natural to express gratitude.

. . . .

Point out that everything we have is a gift from God. We owe God thanks more than anyone else. God has given us life, our bodies, our friends, good things to eat, the world and everything in it. Best of all, God has given us Jesus to teach us how to live and to win eternal life for us. That is why the first reading says, "Whatever happens, keep thanking God because of Jesus Christ."

. . . .

Explain that the word "thank" comes from the word "think." We thank someone when we think about what they have done for us. In the gospel Jesus healed ten lepers, but only one of them thought to thank him. This cure was a marvelous, kind deed. Lepers had a terrible disease that was painful and very contagious. They were kept away from other people and treated like outcasts.

They could not work or enjoy their families and friends. After Jesus cured the lepers, they were able to return to normal life. In their excitement, nine of them forgot to thank Jesus. But one man did, and he was a Samaritan, an enemy of the Jews. Ask the children how they think Jesus felt.

. . . .

Point out that Jesus has healed us, too. By his death and resurrection he has healed us from sin and death. We now can live forever in heaven with God.

. . . .

Ask the children to suggest ways they can thank God (prayer, celebrating Thanksgiving Day, the Eucharist). Tell them that the Eucharist is the most perfect way to thank God and the way most pleasing to God.

. . . .

Tell the children that someone once said that thanksgiving is "thanksliving." Ask them what they think that means. Clarify the point by stating that we show appreciation for a gift by the way we use it. We show gratitude for life by using it the right way: taking care of ourselves and what God has given us, using it the way God meant it to be used.

. . . .

Comment that a grateful heart is a joyful heart. Encourage the children to express thanks today not only to God, but to others who show love to them.

. . . .

Mention that thanksgiving is the best petition.

---

220 Pray Always

(*PAGE W135*) EPHESIANS 6:18B–19A, 20B • LUKE 18:1–8A

God loves us the way parents love their children. Because our mothers and fathers love us, they like to be with us, to talk with us, and to give us things we need. God is no different. God wants us to come and ask for things. This is what we hear in the read- *ings of today's Mass. So let us put our needs, our concerns, our worries, and our troubles before God. Let us trust that God will hear and answer our prayers.*

Universal Prayer

The response is *"Lord, hear our prayer."*

That all church members may be people of prayer, let us pray to the Lord.

That those in authority may have the courage and wisdom to lead and care for others, let us pray to the Lord.

That those who most need our prayers may be helped, let us pray to the Lord.

That through prayer we may realize how great God is, let us pray to the Lord.

That we may have the grace to pray always, let us pray to the Lord.

Special Features

- Present each person with a small prayer book or prayer card, perhaps a homemade one.
- During the prayers of the faithful, burn incense to represent your petitions rising to heaven.
- Set up a petition tree and invite the children to write and attach (with twist ties) special requests to be prayed for during the Mass.

Songs

Answer When I Call; The Cry of the Poor; The Giving King; I Lift Up My Soul; See Us, Lord, about Your Altar

Homily Ideas

Visual: A prayer book

Tell the children that in Burma the people have the custom of playing tug of war to bring on a change of weather. One side stands for rain and the other a dry spell. Holding a rope, they pull each other until one side is pulled over the center line. If the rain side wins, they believe rain will come. If the other side wins, they expect the end of rain or a delay in rain.

• • • •

Explain that as Christians we do not believe in games, stars, or superstitions to direct our lives. We believe that a loving God watches over us and plans our lives. Show a prayer book and state that we can pray about things. God has promised to hear our petitions. In the gospel Jesus tells a story that teaches us to "bother" God with our needs and keep bothering God until we receive an answer.

• • • •

Point out that in the first reading Paul tells the early Christians to pray always. He asks them to pray for him. Comment that we can pray for ourselves and for other people. Ask the children to name some personal needs they can pray for. (Their answers should include spiritual needs such as the grace to be holy, the grace to pray, and a stronger faith, hope, and love.) Ask them to name needs others have that they might pray for.

• • • •

Give an example of a time when you or the parish experienced an answer to prayer. For example, one pastor did not have enough money to pay a large bill. He prayed to the Sacred Heart, and shortly after, he received a check from a donor for the exact amount he needed.

• • • •

Ask the children how they can pray always. Suggest the practice of offering short prayers during the day, such as "Jesus, I love you."

• • • •

Share the quotation "A life hemmed in by prayer is less likely to unravel." Encourage children to pray morning and night prayers. When they wake up, they can offer their day to God and ask for help in meeting the day's challenges. At night they can express sorrow to God for any way they have failed to show love that day. They can thank God for good things that happened, and they can ask God to bless those they love.

• • • •

Invite the children to think of something they are worried about. Give them time to talk to God about it and ask God for help.

221 God Loves Us

(PAGE W137) HOSEA 11:3–4 • JOHN 3:16–17

We are here to celebrate God's great love for us. God has loved us by creating us and giving us life. God has loved us by giving us Jesus, who became a human being like us to save us from sin and death. God has loved us by giving us the Eucharist, a special way Christ is with us. Let us show God love in return by worshiping him today with our whole heart and soul.

Universal Prayer

The response is *"Loving God, hear our prayer."*

That church leaders may realize and teach everyone how much God loves us, let us pray to the Lord.

That government leaders may realize God's love for them and for each one of the people they serve, let us pray to the Lord.

That people may show great love for God by becoming priests, deacons, or religious brothers and sisters, let us pray to the Lord.

That we may witness to God's love by living in peace with everyone, let us pray to the Lord.

Special Features

• During the entrance procession or the presentation of gifts, have children carry up flowers and put them in a vase or vases as a sign of their love for God.

• As a communion reflection, have a student recite a prayer based on the gospel.

• Give each child a small cross to place on his or her pillow or to carry in his or her pocket.

• Distribute buttons that say, "Smile, God loves you!"

Songs

Before the Sun Burned Bright; By Name I Have Called You; Give Thanks to the Lord; His Banner Over Us Is Love; I Have Loved You; If God Is for Us; Isaiah 49; Oh, How I Love Jesus; Psalm 89; Yahweh, the Faithful One; You Are Near

Homily Ideas

Visual: A flower

Show the flower and comment that to show love for others, we sometimes send flowers. Ask the children: Who gave us all the flowers on earth? Tell them that God gave us more than flowers to show love. God has shown us love by many deeds.

. . .

Recall the first reading, which speaks about God's love for the chosen people. God's love for them was like a parent's love for a child. God took them by the hand and taught them to walk. God healed them, freed them from slavery, and fed them. God loved them tenderly.

. . .

Explain that God loves us in the same way. God's love has surrounded us from the first moments of our existence in our mother's womb. God has watched over us and cared for us with great love. Invite the children to recall a time when they felt God's love for them, and have them silently reflect on it.

. . .

Tell the children to look at their hands. Comment that their fingerprints are unlike anyone else's. God made them special and loves them in a special way. Even when it seems no one else loves them, God does.

. . .

Tell the story of the little girl who was afraid to go to sleep in the dark. Her mother came and told her not to worry because God was with her. The girl replied, "I know, but I want someone with skin." Comment that although God doesn't have skin and is not visible to us, God is with us. God treats us as beloved sons and daughters.

. . .

Refer to the gospel, which says that God loved us so much he gave his only Son so that we could have eternal life. Ask the children if they think their parents would give them up to save the life of someone who doesn't belong to their family. Stress that God really must have loved us to do this amazing thing: to send his Son to save us.

. . .

Remind the children that God wants them to respond with love. When we like someone, we want that person to like us back. God loved us first, and really wants us to love in return. Ask the children if it is hard to love God.

. . .

Explain that the cross is a sign of God's love. Seeing it should remind us of God's love and also stir us to love God. Invite the children to look at the crucifix with wonder and awe at how much God loves them.

. . .

Tell the children that in heaven we will be with God. Someone once said that heaven is a hug that never ends.

222 We Are the People of God

(PAGE W139) JEREMIAH 31:33 or 1 PETER 2:9-10 • JOHN 13:34-35

God tells us who we are. We are somebody because we belong to God. We are somebody special because we are members of God's people. We are royal people because we belong to the king of heaven and earth. We gather as God's holy people today to celebrate who we are. We praise and thank God for calling us to be a holy people and for forming us into disciples who shine with love.

That people who do not think they are worth much may grow in love for themselves, we pray to the Lord.

That widows, orphans, and single parents may find love and support, we pray to the Lord.

That we may follow Jesus' command to love and bear with one another's faults, we pray to the Lord.

Universal Prayer

The response is *"Make us into your holy people."*

That the Church throughout the world may love like Christ, we pray to the Lord.

That the leaders of nations may recognize that all people belong to God, we pray to the Lord.

Special Features

- Pass out VIP buttons.
- Begin Mass by having the children form a circle around the entire church. Invite them to see themselves as God's people.
- Display banners or mobiles with words that show love in action: concern, care, honesty, truthfulness, responsibility, helpfulness, kindness, gentleness.

Songs

Church of God; Come, Worship the Lord; Gather Your People; Lead Us On, O Lord; Now as We Gather; Sing Alleluia Sing; Song of the Body of Christ; We Are the Church; We Are the Family; A Wondrous Work of Art

Homily Ideas

Visual: An ID card

Ask, "Who are you?" and let some children answer. Tell them that they could also answer "a child of God," "one of God's holy people," "a sheep in God's flock," "a disciple of Jesus."

. . .

Show an ID card and tell the children that an identification card lets everyone know who we are. Point out that the gospel says that their "lives" should let people know that they are Christians, people who follow Jesus. Ask how they can do this (by showing love). Jesus told us we must love one another, just as he has loved us.

. . .

Refer to the first reading and explain that the people of Israel became God's people by making an agreement with God. They promised, "We will do everything that God says." God became their God, and the Israelites became God's people. Ask the children how they think the Israelites felt at being God's chosen people.

. . .

Ask when we became a member of God's people (at baptism). Ask what God wants us to do (follow the commandments, live like Jesus).

. . .

Tell the children that because they belong to God's people, they are royal people. They are like princes and princesses. Real royal people love and serve. Ask the children how they can live like a royal person at home, in school, and in their neighborhood.

. . .

Quote the saying "What you do speaks so loud I can't hear what you are saying." Ask what the quotation means. Elaborate that our lives should show what we believe. We should teach others the way of Jesus by our lives. That way people will be drawn to him.

. . .

Tell the children that Abraham Lincoln once asked, "If you called a dog's tail a leg, how many legs would it have?" Ask the children what they would have answered. Tell them that the answer would still be four because just calling a tail a leg doesn't make it a leg. Some people call what God's law says is wrong right. They say it's all right to take things from stores. They say it's all right to have sex before marriage. They say it's all right to kill unborn babies. Calling wrong things right doesn't make them right. As God's people we follow what Jesus and his Church tell us even when many people act differently.

. . .

State that there are no "nobodies" in the Church. Each person is a VIP, a very important person. Each person is loved by God and has been saved by God. Tell the children that when they look in the mirror they can say, "Thank you, God, for making me special" and smile.

223 The Spirit Has Given Us Life

(PAGE W141) GALATIANS 5:22-23, 25-26 • JOHN 14:15-17

God has sent us the gift of the Spirit to lead us to life everlasting. The Spirit guides us along the path of life and helps us do what is right, what is loving. This Spirit of Jesus within us makes us more and more like Jesus. Let us pray during this celebration to be open to the Spirit, to listen to the Spirit, and follow what the Spirit prompts us to do.

Universal Prayer

The response is *"Lord, hear our prayer."*

For members of the Church, that they may be filled with the gifts of the Holy Spirit, let us pray to the Lord.

For government officials, that they may follow the lead of the Holy Spirit and not give in to evil, let us pray to the Lord.

For people who do not accept the Holy Spirit, that their eyes and hearts may be opened, let us pray to the Lord.

For our families, friends, and ourselves, that we may always be guided by the Holy Spirit, let us pray to the Lord.

Special Features

- Hang paper dove mobiles in the church with a gift or fruit of the Spirit written on each dove.
- Begin with everyone in an entrance procession in the dark, following a flashlight or candle to symbolize the light of the Holy Spirit.
- As a communion reflection, pray this prayer of St. Augustine and distribute copies:

  Breathe into me, Holy Spirit, that my mind may turn to what is holy. Move me, Holy Spirit, that I may do what is holy. Stir me, Holy Spirit, that I may love what is holy. Strengthen me, Holy Spirit, that I may preserve what is holy. Protect me, Holy Spirit, that I may never lose what is holy.

Songs

Come, Holy Ghost; Everyone Moved by the Spirit; Holy Is the Spirit of the Lord; Holy Spirit; Send Us Your Spirit; Spirit of God, Come to Us; Spirit of Love; Spirit of Our God; Spirit, Come

Homily Ideas

Visual: A compass or a map

State that we are on a journey. Ask the children where all of us are ultimately headed (heaven). Ask what we use on a trip to keep going in the right direction. Show a compass or map. Tell the children that God the Father has sent us a living guide to reach heaven, the Holy Spirit.

• • •

Explain that the Holy Spirit came to the whole Church on Pentecost after Jesus died and rose and returned to heaven. But the Spirit came to live in the children when they were baptized. Since then the Spirit has been hard at work in them to make them good, loving children so that they will reach heaven someday.

• • •

Point out that the first reading tells us that the Spirit makes us loving, happy, peaceful, patient, kind, good, faithful, gentle, and self-controlled. Acknowledge that the children are not always this way. Sometimes they feel like hurting someone on purpose, not listening to their parents, damaging something, or not doing their homework or other duties. Suggest that at such times, they can call upon the Spirit within them for help.

• • •

Mention that when the Holy Spirit overshadowed the Blessed Virgin Mary, she became the Mother of God. She brought forth Christ to the world. The Holy Spirit can help make us like Christ, too, so that we can bring his love and goodness to the world.

. . .

Ask the children to recall and tell about times when they saw people who showed one of those qualities listed in the first reading. Comment that those people were following the Spirit's guidance.

. . .

State that the Spirit is always with the children, ready to be of assistance. The Spirit teaches them about Jesus and about what is good and true. The Spirit is a real friend to them.

. . .

Comment that the Holy Spirit is the third person of the Blessed Trinity. The Holy Spirit is God and has the same powers and the same love for us as God the Father and God the Son have. Ask the children to name prayers that mention the Holy Spirit.

. . .

Explain that a dove sometimes is used to stand for the Spirit because in the gospel when Jesus was baptized, the Spirit was present in the form of a dove.

224 Peace I Leave with You

(PAGE W143) ISAIAH 11:1B, 5–9 or COLOSSIANS 3:15–16 • JOHN 14:27

Jesus is the prince of peace. By his cross he made peace between God and the human race. His mercy and forgiveness give us peace after we have sinned. His love and grace bring peace to our hearts when we are troubled, worried, or fearful. At this Eucharist we celebrate the saving acts of Jesus that brought peace and the promise of an everlasting peace and joy in heaven.

Universal Prayer

The response is *"Lord, save your people."*

That the Church may teach the world the secret to true and lasting peace, we pray to the Lord.

That world leaders may work for justice and respect for people's rights that lead to peace, we pray to the Lord.

That people who cause violence and pain may have a change of heart, we pray to the Lord.

That people who are not at peace may find it in Christ, we pray to the Lord.

That there be an end to wars and violence, we pray to the Lord.

Special Features

- Sing the Lamb of God, calling attention to the last petition in which we pray, "Grant us peace."
- Exhort the children to really mean the sign of peace when they exchange it.
- As a communion reflection, have someone pray the World Peace Prayer below. You might sing or play Marty Haugen's musical setting for it (GIA).

> *Lead me from death to life,*
> *from falsehood to truth.*
> *Lead me from despair to hope,*
> *from fear to trust.*
> *Lead me from hate to love,*
> *from war to peace.*
> *Let peace fill our hearts, our world,*
> *our universe.*

Songs

Let There Be Peace on Earth; Peace Is Flowing like a River; Peace Prayer; Peace Time; Peace

Homily Ideas

Visual: A peace symbol

Show a peace symbol and ask the children what it stands for. Tell them that everyone longs for peace. Invite them to imagine an ocean that is peaceful, a sky that is peaceful, a landscape that is peaceful. Ask them what is meant by peace. Ask the children for signs that we do not have peace.

. . .

Explain that the savior the Israelites waited for was to be someone who would bring peace to the world. A prophet talked about this peaceful period as a time when wolves and lambs would lie down together and when young children could put their hands in the nests of poisonous snakes and not be hurt.

. . .

Have the children imagine what the world would be like if there were peace like this. No one would have to lock their homes or hide their valuables. No one would worry about being shot or attacked. There would be no more gangs or wars.

. . .

Point out that God meant for us to live in peace. Peace was destroyed when sin came into the world.

God still plans for us to live together in peace. Jesus came to bring it to us and showed us how to bring it about.

. . .

Remind the children that in the gospel Jesus said to his disciples, "I give you peace. So don't be worried or afraid." Ask the children if they have a peaceful place they go to when they are upset, or if they know a peaceful person they can talk to when they have a problem. Comment that Jesus, too, gives them peace. They can go to him when they are disturbed, and he will comfort them. Remind them that during a terrific storm at sea, Jesus said, "Peace, be still," and the wind and waves died down.

. . .

Tell the children that they can carry on the work of Christ and be peacemakers, too. Ask them to suggest ways to do this, especially in their families. Give examples of people in the news who have acted as peacemakers.

. . .

Mention that one of the beatitudes is "Blessed are the peacemakers; they will be called children of God." Ask the children if they would rather be known as a peacemaker or a peacebreaker.

. . .

Encourage the children to celebrate the sacrament of reconciliation to experience the peace that Jesus gives to sinners.

---

225 One with Jesus

(PAGE W145) 1 CORINTHIANS 12:12–13 • JOHN 15:1–5

We are the body of Christ. We became joined to Christ at baptism. As long as we remain united with him, we have a full life of peace and joy. Through this eucharistic celebration we strengthen our union with Christ and with one another. Together as one we now offer Jesus and ourselves to the Father in the perfect sacrifice of praise.

Universal Prayer

The response is *"Lord, hear our prayer."*

For all church members, that they may grow ever closer to Christ, we pray to the Lord.

For those who are in positions of authority, that their lives may bear good fruit, we pray to the Lord.

For those who do not yet know Jesus, that they may come to believe in him, we pray to the Lord.

For the people in our parish, that we may show our union with Christ and one another by our love, we pray to the Lord.

For sinners, that they may realize they need Christ and repent, we pray to the Lord.

Special Features

- As a communion reflection have students read personal meditations on how they can be Christ in the world.
- Display a large outline of Christ with student photos or self-portraits inside of it.

Songs

Gather Us Together; Jesu, Jesu, Fill Us with Your Love; One Bread, One Body; One Lord; Take My Hands; We Are Many Parts; We Are Your Hands; A Wondrous Work of Art

Homily Ideas

Visual: An ivy or other plant

Show the ivy and ask the children what would happen to one of the leaves if you broke it off. Tell them that Jesus spoke of himself as a vine. We are all branches growing out from him. If we separate ourselves from him, we are like a separated leaf or branch. We will have no life and will produce no good fruit.

· · ·

Explain to the children that when we are united with Christ, his life flows through us. We share in his power, his energy, his love. We are able to do much good. Ask the children to tell kinds of "fruit" or good works we will bear, as long as we have Christ's life of grace in us.

· · ·

Mention that it was at baptism that we first became joined to Christ and to the other believers.

· · ·

Recall that the first reading said we all were different parts of the body of Christ. Invite the children to think of the part of Christ's body they would like to be and why.

· · ·

Explain that we each have different gifts and do different things. We live in different countries all over the world. Tell the children that one artist drew a face of Christ that was made up of many people including famous Christians.

· · ·

Ask the children to share ways they can stay united with Christ (prayer, celebration of the Eucharist).

· · ·

Name some outstanding Catholics, and comment that it is wonderful to be one with them in the body of Christ.

· · ·

Point out that at communion we all receive Jesus himself. He gave us this gift so that he could be our food and, like any food, become part of us. We are united with him and one another most closely during these moments. That is why communion has the word "union" in it. That is why we sing and join our voices together at this time.

· · ·

Tell the story of the statue of Christ which was shattered in the bombings during a world war. The hands were missing. Someone hung a sign on the statue that read, "I have no hands but yours." Ask the children how they can be hands for Jesus (hug a lonely person), eyes (see where help is needed), ears (listen to someone who needs to talk), feet (run to pick up something that is fallen), and heart (care for a person who is hurting). Encourage the children to be Christ to others.

• • •

Comment that the more the children are united to Christ, the more like him they will be. People will look at them and see Jesus. Ask: When people look at you, do they see Jesus?

---

226 May Your Joy Be Complete

(PAGE W147) ROMANS 5:10B-11 • JOHN 15:9-11

Jesus has given us the gift of joy. Because he has conquered sin and death for us, we can again be happy. We can again have the hope of living forever. When our days on earth are marked by pain and suffering, we are cheered and comforted by Jesus' promise of eternal happiness at the end. We rejoice in Jesus our savior. We celebrate what is truly Good News.

Universal Prayer

The response is *"Lord, hear our prayer."*

That our church leaders may guide us to joy and hope, we pray to the Lord.

That world leaders may have their life of cares and responsibilities lightened by a spirit of joy, we pray to the Lord.

That people who are unhappy may have their spirits lifted, we pray to the Lord.

That we may be people of joy who make others happy, we pray to the Lord.

Special Features

• Since dancing is a sign of joy, have children dance as part of the entrance procession, communion reflection, or recessional. They might carry and wave streamers.

• Distribute smiling face buttons or badges with the word "Joy."

Songs

City of God; For You Are My God; I've Got the Joy, Joy, Joy; Let Heaven Rejoice; New Life; Rejoice in the Lord Always; Sing a New Song

Homily Ideas

Visuals: A recipe or cookbook and a sheet of paper with the word "Joy" on it

Ask the children if they ever get the mopes or the grumpies. Ask if they ever have bad things happen that make them sad. Show a recipe or a cookbook and ask, "Wouldn't it be nice if we had a recipe for happiness?" Tell them that we do. Jesus told us the ingredients for happiness. All we have to do is follow his recipe.

• • •

Ask the children what Jesus told us to do (love God, love others). Ask the children how they feel when they do something kind for someone. Ask how they feel when they hurt another person. Conclude that the more loving we are, the happier we'll be.

• • •

Explain that Jesus himself makes us happy. When Jesus came to earth he taught and proved to us that God loves us. This thought alone is reason to be happy. Then Jesus died and rose again. He promised that we, too, could rise with new life and live forever. This promise also makes us happy. Jesus gave us the secret to be happy on earth. In the gospel we heard him say that to be completely happy, all we have to do is obey him.

• • • •

Tell the children that when we do what Jesus says and are close to him, we have a deep inner joy. No one or nothing that happens can take this deep joy from us.

• • • •

Present the example of St. Julie Billiart. As a child she taught others about the good God. One day someone shot at her father. Julie, who witnessed the attack, was so shocked that she became an invalid and confined to bed. Sometimes she was paralyzed to a degree that she could barely talk. Yet, Julie gathered children around her bed and prepared them for First Communion. She became known as the smiling saint.

Because it was the time of the French Revolution and the Church was being persecuted, some people tried to capture and kill Julie, but she escaped by being hidden under straw in a farm wagon. She began a religious community of sisters. She was cured of her illness, but she continued to have serious problems. Bishops and even members of her own community turned against her. Through every crisis Julie kept her faith in the good God. She continued to smile.

• • • •

Point out that joy is a sign of a Christian. When someone loves us, we are happy. If the children are Christians who truly believe that God loves them, they should be happy and laughing. Joy is a fruit of the Holy Spirit. When we live as the Spirit of Jesus guides us to live, then we have joy.

• • • •

Mention that a psalm verse states, "My joy lies in being close to God" (Psalm 73:28). When we know and love Jesus, we have joy. Show the word "joy" on a card and tell the children it is made from putting nothing (O) between Jesus (J) and you (Y).

227 You Are My Friends

(*PAGE W149*) 1 JOHN 3:1, 23 • JOHN 15:12–15

Jesus showed he was our greatest friend by dying for us. He asks that to be good friends of his we love one another. At this love feast of the Eucharist we remember the love of our friend Jesus. As we share the sacred bread and wine that is himself, we ask for the grace to be good friends to one another, to love one another as he loves us.

Universal Prayer
The response is *"Lord, hear our prayer."*

For the Church, that we may lead others to know Christ through our love, let us pray to the Lord.
For leaders of nations, that they may work for a world where all people are friends, let us pray to the Lord.
For people who are lonely and have no friends, that someone may show them love, let us pray to the Lord.
For our friends, that we may be good friends to them, let us pray to the Lord.

Special Features
- Hang hoops as decorations to stand for friendship rings.
- As a communion reflection pray a poem or prayer entitled "Jesus, My Friend" composed by a faculty or staff member or a student.

Songs

Jesus Is with Us; A Joyful Sound; My God and My All; No Greater Love; Sing to the Lord a Joyful Song; We Have Been Told; You Are Always with Me; You Are Mine; You Are My Friends

Homily Ideas

Visual: A ring

Show a ring and state that marriage partners exchange rings as a sign of their love and that some people exchange friendship rings as a sign of their devotion to each other. Ask why the ring is a good sign for love. (It is a circle that has no beginning or end. The love the partners pledge is meant to be forever.)

• • •

Ask the children to think of their good friends. Invite them to reflect on why they like their friends. Ask them if they know who their best friend is (Jesus). Ask them why he is their best friend. (He loves them more than anyone does. He died for them. He will always help them.)

• • •

Comment that sometimes two friends became "blood" sisters or brothers by nicking themselves and mixing their blood as a sign of being loyal to one another. Explain that Jesus did more than that with us. He shed his blood on the cross as a sign of his love for us. Even now he offers himself at every Mass for us and gives us his body and blood as food and drink in holy communion.

• • •

Point out that in the gospel Jesus told his apostles they were not servants but friends. He spoke to them not as someone who was above them but as a friend. He let them know everything the Father told him. Comment that Jesus regards us as his friends, too. Ask the children how they can treat Jesus like a friend (spend time with him; talk to him; do what he wishes; try to please him).

• • •

Explain that the best way to make our friend Jesus happy is to love one another. Both the first reading and the gospel of the Mass point this out. Jesus showed love by dying for us. We don't usually die for other people, but there are other ways to show love that may be difficult. Give suggestions: Maybe you don't like to do homework, but you know that your parents and your teacher want you to do it, so you do it. Maybe you see someone that no one else in the class likes, and you are kind to that person. Maybe your neighbor is elderly and sick, and you run errands for him or her. Let the children suggest other ways to show love.

• • •

Comment that when we obey Jesus we are happy because Jesus does not tell us to do what is senseless or harmful. His commands are such that by following them we become loving and happy. Jesus does exactly what any good friend does. He helps us to become better persons, the persons we ought to be.

Last Weeks in Ordinary Time

228 Entering the Kingdom of Heaven

(PAGE W151) JAMES 2:14–17 • MATTHEW 7:21, 24–27

In today's readings we will hear about the key for entering the kingdom of heaven. Although Jesus has won for us the right to live forever in heaven, we must live in such a way that we are worthy of heaven. We must live by faith, doing what Jesus taught. In the Eucharist, we praise and thank God with all those who are already in God's kingdom. We ask for the grace to someday be counted among them.

Universal Prayer

The response is *"Lord, hear our prayer."*

For the Church, that it may take to heart the words of Jesus, we pray to the Lord.

For those in public office, that they may act with justice and honesty, we pray to the Lord.

For those whose lives are based on false values, that they may realize their foolishness, we pray to the Lord.

For our families, friends, and ourselves, that we may be inspired to do good deeds and have the strength to do them, we pray to the Lord.

Special Features

- Decorate the church with large paper rocks that each have a saying of Christ written on them.
- Add gestures to the gospel and read it as an echo pantomime with the children repeating each line and gesture.
- As a communion reflection, have the children pray the following litany:
  Response: Hear me, Jesus, my rock.
  May my life be founded on your words. / May my life be founded on your truth. / May my life be founded on your holiness. / May my life be founded on your wisdom. / May my life be founded on your goodness. / May my life be founded on your mercy. / May my life be founded on your love.
- Distribute rocks to the participants.

Songs

Blest Are They; God Has Chosen Me; Here I Am, Lord; The House Built on the Rock; In the Day of the Lord; Let Us Go!; On the Journey to the Kingdom; Out of Darkness; Song of the Body of Christ; Take the Word of God with You

Homily Ideas
Visual: A Bible

Tell the story of the little leaguer who had rounded third base and was coming in for a run. As he neared home plate, his coach waved him back to third. Afterwards the boy asked, "Why did you do that?" The coach said, "Because you didn't touch third base." "But the umpire didn't see," argued the boy. "No, but I did," the coach responded. Comment that the coach was living by the principle of honesty and doing what was right. The coach was like the man in the gospel who built his house on rock, and he was trying to teach young boys to live this way.

. . .

Ask the children to give examples of times their parents or others who loved them taught them to do the right thing. You might begin by telling how someone taught you to live as Jesus said.

. . .

Comment that Jesus taught us to be people of faith who live a law of love. He told the story of the two men who built houses to show us that it is wise to live by his teachings. If we don't follow them, our whole world will collapse around us.

. . .

Point out that the first reading tells us not just to say we have faith; we must live our faith. We must act on what we believe and do what Jesus says. Ask the children how they know what they are supposed to do (read the Bible, pray, listen to people who love them). Show the Bible. Ask the children to tell some of the things Jesus said to do (follow the ten commandments, love, share, be kind, pray). Mention that the ten commandments are called commandments, not suggestions. We are supposed to follow them.

. . .

Quote the saying "The road to hell is paved with good intentions," and ask what it means.

. . .

Encourage the children to read the Bible, pay attention in religion class, and pray to the Holy Spirit in order to really know and live their faith.

. . .

Comment that we should be on fire with love for Jesus and the desire to live and love as he did.

. . .

Tell about someone in your parish or in the news who is living out the faith. For example, a house burned down to the ground, and a group of teenagers stood in front of the house and collected money from people who came by to look at it. They raised $600 for the family who had lived in the house.

229 The Banquet of the Kingdom
(*PAGE W153*) ISAIAH 25:6, 9 • MATTHEW 8:5–11

The banquet we are about to celebrate is a foretaste of the banquet we will enjoy in heaven forever. We are joined in love here in an act of total adoration of God. All of the angels, Mary, the saints, and our loved ones in heaven are present. They are united with us as we sing and pray, offering Jesus and ourselves to God.

Universal Prayer
The response is *"Lord, hear our prayer."*

That the Church may be generous in meeting the needs of the poor, let us pray to the Lord.
That civil leaders may work for the good of all people, let us pray to the Lord.

That those who are taken up with the things of this world may begin to think of the afterlife, let us pray to the Lord.

That we may respond to Jesus' invitation with faith and love, let us pray to the Lord.

That those who do not have enough to eat, especially hungry children, may soon receive food, let us pray to the Lord.

Special Features

- Call the children around the altar for the Eucharistic Prayer.
- Pass out cards to the children that say, "You are invited to come to the banquet of the Lord. RSVP."

Songs

As Grains of Wheat; I Am the Bread of Life; In My Father's House; If You Belong to Me; Gift of Finest Wheat; Sing and Rejoice; When We Eat This Bread

Homily Ideas

Visual: An invitation

Show an invitation. Tell the children that they were invited to a wonderful banquet and that they obviously accepted the invitation. They are gathered at the table of the Lord to feast together with all his friends. They will share in the sacred bread that is his body and the sacred wine that is his blood.

. . .

Explain that they have another invitation. This one has an RSVP. Ask what that means (a response is requested). This invitation is the invitation to the unending banquet in the kingdom of God. This banquet is described in the first reading: "The Lord will prepare for all nations a feast of the finest foods. Choice wines and the best meat will be served." Comment that one man wrote a play called *Green Pastures* in which he imagined that heaven was like a giant fish fry.

. . .

Point out that in the gospel Jesus says that many people will come from all over to enjoy this heavenly feast. We give our RSVP when we act like the non-Jewish officer in the gospel and show we have faith in Jesus.

. . .

Ask the children how the officer showed faith (by asking Jesus to heal his servant at a distance; by his words alone). Ask the children how they can show faith in Jesus (by praying, learning more about him, doing what he says). Ask the children if they can tell in one four-letter word what Jesus teaches us to do (love). Comment that love will gain us entrance into the great feast of heaven.

. . .

Tell the story of a man's vision of hell and heaven. In hell he saw people around tables laden with food. However, the people were gloomy. No one was eating because the only way they could eat was with three-foot-long chopsticks. Then the man saw a vision of heaven. As in hell there were tables laden with food to be eaten with three-foot-long chopsticks. But in heaven the people were laughing, talking, and having a grand time. They were using the sticks to feed one another!

. . .

Explain that our life on earth prepares us for our life in heaven. Ask the children how we can practice "feeding" people on earth (provide food for the physically hungry; give attention to those thirsting for love; do good to those who hunger for kindness; help teach those who hunger for knowledge; work for the rights of those who are hungry for justice).

. . .

Comment that whenever we partake of the Eucharist, we receive nourishment and strength to feed other people, to be bread for them, to show them love in action. Tell the children that Mother Teresa of Calcutta, who worked for the poorest of the poor, used to tell the Sisters in her community, "Let the people eat you up." Ask the children what she meant by that.

230 The Lord Is Coming Soon

(PAGE W155) PHILIPPIANS 4:4–7 • LUKE 12:35–40

We believe that someday Jesus Christ will come again to judge the living and the dead. We look forward to that day when his glory will be shown to all the nations. We live in preparation for the next world and celebrate at each Eucharist the saving deeds of Christ that made our entry into the kingdom of heaven possible.

Universal Prayer

The response is *"Lord, hear our prayer."*

The members of the Church are servants of God. That we may always do the things that please God, let us pray to the Lord.

Leaders have the task of making the world a better place. That they may carry out this task with faith and love, let us pray to the Lord.

Many people will die today and enter into eternal life. That they may be prepared to meet God, let us pray to the Lord.

We want to keep our lamps burning. That we may show love for God and others, let us pray to the Lord.

Sinners always have a chance to receive God's forgiveness. That they may be sorry and make up their minds to sin no more, let us pray to the Lord.

Special Features

- For the entrance procession, have students carefully carry lighted candles and arrange them in a display in the sanctuary.
- Highlight the penitential rite by introducing it as a way to be prepared to meet God.
- Give each participant a card that says, "Always be prepared!"

Songs

Eye Has Not Seen; The Lord Is with You; O, How I Long to See; Stay Awake; We Long for You, O Lord

Homily Ideas

Visual: A calendar

Show the calendar and tell the children that no one knows the day or the time when the world will end. Neither does anyone know exactly how or when his or her own life will come to an end. Explain that Jesus told us to be ready at all times. He gave the example of servants who wait for the master to return from a wedding feast. They keep their lamps burning and are alert so that as soon as he comes they can open the door for him. Jesus said that if these servants carry out their duty well, the master will serve them!

• • •

Ask the children how they are to get ready for Jesus' coming, how they should prepare to meet him face to face without any shame (live the way he told us).

• • •

Ask the children what they would do if they knew a thief was coming to their house at seven o'clock that night. Then remind them that in the gospel Jesus said he himself will surprise us. We don't know if he is coming this night, tomorrow, or ten years from now. We have to be ready at all times for him to come.

• • •

Tell the children that when St. Ignatius was asked what he would do if he knew that his life would end in an hour, he replied that he would continue to do just what he had been doing.

• • •

Suggest that the children make it a practice to pray an Act of Contrition often. Explain that in this prayer they tell Jesus they are sorry for all the ways they have committed sin by failing to love.

• • •

Recommend that each night before the children go to bed they play back the day as if there were a television screen in their mind and look for two things: good things that happened to them, for which they will thank God, and ways they failed to show God's love, for which they will express sorrow and ask forgiveness.

. . .

Tell the children that some stories and movies are about people who have died and are given a chance to come back to earth to live their lives over again. Comment that this does not really happen. We get only one chance to live a good life, and we'd better do it right. Emphasize, however, that God is totally forgiving, and even when we fail, we can be assured of a fresh start.

. . .

Point out to the children that we are not to be afraid of the end of the world and the end of our lives. The first reading tells us to be glad and not to worry about anything. Jesus' coming again will be a time of great joy. Ask the children why we should look forward to Jesus' coming. (We will see him. All suffering will be ended. Jesus will bring God's kingdom of peace and joy.) Invite the children to reflect on what they will say to Jesus when they first see him.

. . .

Comment that Jesus talks of being ready in terms of keeping our lamps burning. We might compare that to the fire of love in our hearts. We are to keep love for God and others burning in our hearts at all time. This isn't easy, but it is our task. It is what God made us for.

---

231 The Kingdom of God Is Among You

(PAGE W157) EPHESIANS 3:16B–17, 20–21 • LUKE 17:20–21

In the Our Father we pray, "Thy kingdom come." Jesus told us that God's kingdom is already among us. Every time we make peace, God's kingdom is here. Every time justice is shown, God's kingdom is here. Every time someone does an act of love, God's kingdom is here. As people of God's kingdom we come together to praise and thank God. We pray that through us God's kingdom will be shown to all the world more and more.

Universal Prayer

The response is *"Lord, may your kingdom come."*

For the Church, that we may grow in faith, we pray to the Lord.

For leaders, that they may work for the spread of peace and justice throughout the world, we pray to the Lord.

For those who devote their lives to the spreading of God's kingdom, that they may have the strength to go on, we pray to the Lord.

For people we know who appear to be outside of God's kingdom, that they may know its peace and joy, we pray to the Lord.

Special Features

- Set up a display of building blocks labeled with qualities that contribute to God's kingdom, such as peace, goodness, justice, mercy, generosity, humility, patience, gentleness.

- Before this Mass, have a class design a flag for the kingdom of God. Have a student carry the flag in the entrance procession.

- Add gestures to the first reading and read it as an echo pantomime with the children repeating each line and gestures.

- Invite someone to give a witness talk as part of the homily, telling about how he or she sees the kingdom in his or her life.

Songs

Beatitudes; Blest Are We; Bring Forth the Kingdom; Christ Be Our Light; Christ Is Here; Christ Is Our Light; City of God; Dwelling Place; Where Two or Three Are Gathered

Homily Ideas

Visual: A key

Show a key and explain that sometimes a mayor honors a person by presenting him or her with the key to the city. That means that the honored person is welcome to the city and is free to feel at home in it. He or she has power and authority there.

* * *

Explain that by his death and rising Jesus has given us the key to the city of God. We are free to live as children of God's kingdom. Jesus is at work within us to bring about the kingdom more each day.

* * *

Tell the children that the kingdom of God is not so much a place as a certain way of being. God's kingdom is among us when we are at peace with one another and justice is done. God's kingdom is among us when love and care are shown. God's kingdom is among us when people are good to one another.

* * *

Comment that God's kingdom is on earth when Christ reigns in our hearts. Refer to the first reading, in which Paul prays that Christ will live in the hearts of Christians because of their faith. He tells them to stand firm in the faith. He means that they are not to give it up but to make it grow stronger by practicing it. Paul tells the Christians to be deeply rooted in Christ's love. Ask the children what that means (to believe that Christ loves them, to show Christ's love to others).

* * *

Direct the children to join their thumbs and then their forefingers. Ask them what their fingers form (a heart). Point out how this heart is wide open. Air can pass through it. People can see through it. Explain that our hearts should be open like this: open to God. People should be able to see that God is in our hearts.

* * *

Tell the children that when we have Christ in our hearts, his power can do far more than we dare ask or imagine. Relate a story about a person who seemed to be weak, yet because of faith did marvelous things. You might tell about St. Bernadette who was physically weak and had asthma. She was the one chosen to see the Blessed Mother at Lourdes and start the famous shrine there. Tell about Solanus Casey, a Franciscan priest who was not allowed to give homilies at Mass or hear confessions because it was thought that he wasn't smart enough. Through him God worked many miracles of healing. Tell about Pope John XXIII who was so old when he was elected pope that no one thought he would do much, and yet he called for the Church council that began a great renewal of the Catholic Church.

* * *

Point out that the people who hold the key to God's kingdom are the beatitude people: the poor in spirit, the sorrowing, the meek, those who hunger and thirst for what is right, the merciful, the pure of heart, and those who are persecuted for the sake of what is right.

* * *

Mention that Jesus said that to enter God's kingdom we must be like children. Ask what he meant by that (that we have the simplicity, love, trust, and innocence of children).

* * *

Ask the children what they might do to help bring about the kingdom of God in their homes, their neighborhood, the world.

PROPER *of* SAINTS

Numbers followed by "A" or "B" denote celebrations found in the New Roman Missal but not in the *Lectionary for Masses with Children.*

JANUARY

234 JANUARY 1
Octave of Christmas,
Mary, Mother of God (SOLEMNITY)

235 JANUARY 2
Basil the Great and Gregory Nazianzen,
Bishops, Doctors of the Church (MEMORIAL)

Basil and Gregory were bishops who lived in the fourth century. They were good friends who studied together in Athens, Greece. When Basil formed a group of monks, Gregory joined him, and for about five years they lived in the same monastery. Basil preached against a heresy called Arianism, which denied that Jesus was God. He also wrote rules for monks that are still followed today. Gregory was an outstanding preacher. For a time he was bishop of Constantinople, a city where the Church was sadly divided because of Arianism. Both Basil and Gregory worked for peace and unity in the Church.

Themes: Friendship in the faith, monks, divinity of Christ

235A JANUARY 3
Most Holy Name of Jesus (MEMORIAL)

Soon after his birth, Jesus received his name officially. Through an angel God directed Mary and Joseph to name his Son Jesus. This name is fitting for the savior of the world because it means "God saves." The name of Jesus is powerful. He told us that whatever we ask the Father in his name will be given to us. The name of Jesus is holy because it stands for him, the Son of God. The Bible says that the name Jesus is "the name that is above every name" (Philippians 2:9). That is why we are careful how we use it. We say it with love and respect. Saying the name Jesus is one of the simplest ways to pray.

236 JANUARY 4
Elizabeth Ann Seton,
Married Woman, Religious Founder (MEMORIAL)

Elizabeth Ann Seton is the first American-born person to be canonized a saint. Born in New York

City in 1774, she belonged to a wealthy Episcopalian family and even attended George Washington's inauguration. Even as a young girl she cared for poor people in her neighborhood. When she was nineteen, she married William Seton. The couple had five children. When her husband's business went bankrupt and he became sick, they traveled to Italy, where after a few weeks William died. In Italy Elizabeth stayed with a Catholic family. When she returned to America, she and her children became Catholics. In Baltimore in 1808 Elizabeth Ann began the first American parish school. The next year in Emmitsburg, Maryland, she began the first religious community in America, the Sisters of Charity.

Themes: Vocations, serving the needy

237 JANUARY 5
John Neumann,
Bishop, Religious, Missionary (MEMORIAL)

John Neumann, a humble, hardworking saint, was born in Bohemia in 1811. He had a strong desire to work as a missionary in the United States. Before he was twenty-four years old, he had mastered six languages and had completed studies for the priesthood. Because his bishop thought there were enough priests in his country, John was not ordained. He sailed for America and arrived with one suit of clothes and one dollar. Three weeks later he was ordained in New York. At first John did missionary work with German-speaking people, traveling miles on horseback. He joined the Redemptorists and then became bishop of Philadelphia. There he had to deal with an anti-Catholic group and people who did not accept him personally. He encouraged Catholic schools and began the practice of Forty Hours (eucharistic devotion) in the United States.

Themes: The priesthood, the Eucharist

238 JANUARY 6
André Bessette, *Religious*

André Bessette was born in Montreal, Canada. His parents died young, and he was adopted when he was twelve. André could barely read or write; and when he tried to be a shoemaker, baker, and blacksmith he was unsuccessful. He joined the Congregation of the Holy Cross and was asked to leave because of his bad health.

A wise bishop persuaded the community to let André stay. Brother André was the doorkeeper at the College of Notre Dame for forty years. A man of deep prayer, he had the gift of healing. Throngs of people visited him daily for a cure or spiritual direction. Each year he received 80,000 letters. André gave St. Joseph the credit for his healing miracles.

When his community tried in vain to purchase nearby land, André buried a medal of St. Joseph on the property. The owners suddenly changed their minds. Andre raised money bit by bit to have a church built in honor of St. Joseph. At the church, people he cured left behind their crutches and canes. It took fifty years to build St. Joseph's Oratory, which stands because of Brother André's devotion to St. Joseph.

Themes: St. Joseph, ministry of healing, sacrament of the anointing of the sick

239 JANUARY 7
Raymond of Penyafort, *Presbyter, Religious*

Raymond lived almost a hundred years, from about 1175 to 1275. He was born near Barcelona, Spain, where he became a priest and professor of philosophy and canon law. At the age of forty-seven he joined the Dominicans, who had him write a four-volume work about the sacrament of penance. Then the pope called him to Rome to be his confessor and to make a collection of canon law. When the pope told Raymond that he was going to make him an archbishop, Raymond begged him not to. The pope granted his request. Raymond was allowed to return to Spain, where he became head of his order. The last thirty-five years of his life were spent carrying out his dream: evangelizing the Jews and Muslims in Spain. St. Raymond is the patron of lawyers.

Themes: The sacrament of reconciliation, evangelizing

240 JANUARY 13
Hilary, *Bishop, Doctor of the Church*

Hilary was born in Poitiers, France, in the beginning of the fourth century. He married and had a daughter. An educated man, Hilary became a Christian from reading Scripture, especially the opening of John's gospel. The people of Poitiers chose him to be their bishop. At that time the Emperor Constantius followed the Arian heresy, which held that Jesus was not God. When Hilary refused to go along with this heresy and attacked it with vigor, he was exiled to Phrygia. There for three years he preached, wrote, suffered, and offered to debate the Arian bishops. The Arians in Phrygia asked the emperor to send Hilary home, which he did. The emperor called Hilary "disturber of the peace." Hilary is one of the first Latin hymn writers. He used these hymns, too, to fight Arianism.

Themes: Scripture, Jesus, standing up for what is right and true

241 JANUARY 17
Anthony, *Abbot* (MEMORIAL)

Anthony was born in Egypt around the year 250. When he was twenty and his parents died, Anthony gave away his property and possessions to the poor and went to the desert. There he lived alone and learned from a hermit the life of prayer and penance. People attracted by his holiness came to see him and learn from him. At the age of fifty-four Anthony founded a type of monastery for hermits and wrote a rule for them. During the persecution of Christians, Anthony wanted to be a martyr, so he left the desert for a time to take care of those in prison. Later he again left the desert to preach against Arianism, a heresy that denied the divinity of Jesus. It is said that Anthony died in a cave when he was more than a hundred years old. He is called the Father of Eastern Monasticism.

Themes: Penance, prayer, solitude, holiness

242 JANUARY 20
Fabian, *Pope, Martyr*

Fabian was a farmer who was present the day people were preparing to elect a new pope in the third century. A church historian named Eusebius wrote that a dove flew in and rested on Fabian's head. The people took this as a sign that Fabian should be pope, and so this layman promptly was made a bishop. Fabian was pope for fourteen years until Emperor Decius ruled that Christians should suffer the death penalty. Pope Fabian was among the first to die for the faith in this persecution. His courage was inspiring to all.

Themes: Living the faith, martyrs, the pope

243 also JANUARY 20
Sebastian, *Martyr*

Sebastian was martyred during the last Roman persecution, which started in the year 300. The traditional story of this saint is that he was a Christian army officer who comforted the martyrs in prison. His fellow soldiers shot him with arrows, and when this failed to kill him, he was clubbed to death. His tomb is in the catacombs on the Appian Way in Rome. He is one of the Fourteen Holy Helpers.

Themes: Loyalty to Christ, martyrs, compassion

244 JANUARY 21
Agnes, *Virgin, Martyr* (MEMORIAL)

Agnes lived in Rome near the end of the third century when Christians were being persecuted. When she was about thirteen years old, she was martyred for her belief in Christ. A traditional story tells us that Agnes was beautiful and many men wanted to marry her, but she declared, "Christ is my bridegroom. He is the first to choose me. I shall be his alone." One of her disappointed suitors was so angry that he reported to the governor that Agnes was a Christian. The governor threatened her with torture and had her taken to a house of prostitution where she was not harmed. St. Ambrose wrote that Agnes went to the place of execution more cheerfully than others go to their wedding. Because the name Agnes means lamb, St. Agnes is often depicted with that animal of gentleness and innocence. On this day at the basilica of St. Agnes in Rome, lambs are blessed. Their wool is used to make palliums, stoles that go over the shoulders and have a piece hanging in the front and back. Palliums are worn by the pope and metropolitan archbishops.

Themes: Consecrated lives, love of Christ, innocence

245 JANUARY 22
Vincent, *Deacon, Martyr*

St. Vincent, the first martyr of Spain, died in the persecution of Diocletian in the year 304. He was ordained a deacon by Bishop Valerius of the Church of Saragossa. This bishop was imprisoned for holding Christian services. Caught visiting the bishop by the governor, Vincent, too, was imprisoned. They were given no food and experienced extreme sufferings and torture. It is said that Vincent survived being roasted on a gridiron and then was thrown in a dungeon filled with broken pottery. There he converted the jailer. Moved to a regular prison, Vincent was comforted by his friends until he died.

Themes: Suffering for the faith, serving as a deacon

246 JANUARY 24
Francis de Sales, *Bishop, Religious Founder, Doctor of the Church* (MEMORIAL)

St. Francis was born in France in 1547 into a family of nobility. He studied to be a lawyer but then became a priest. He worked tirelessly to teach the Catholic faith in the years after the Protestant Reformation. As the bishop of Geneva, the seat of Calvinism, he was ideal. He was a friend to Catholics and Protestants. He guided people in the spiritual life and strengthened their faith by his writings. His book *Introduction to the Devout Life* is still read today. He guided St. Jane de Chantal in founding the Visitation religious order. Although he once had a quick temper, Francis eventually became known as "the gentleman saint." He is the patron of writers and editors.

Themes: Holiness, learning about the faith, controlling anger

247 JANUARY 25
The Conversion of Paul, *Apostle* (FEAST)

Paul, once one of the Church's greatest enemies, became one of its greatest apostles. Today we celebrate the day the risen Christ called Paul to spread the Good News. We also celebrate the many ways Paul contributed to the early Church. We pray at this Eucharist that we may have the grace to

follow Christ with the devotion and love that Paul had for him.

Universal Prayer

The response is *"Lord, hear our prayer."*

That the Church may continue to welcome all people into it, let us pray to the Lord.

That world leaders may work to ensure freedom of religion, let us pray to the Lord.

That missionaries may have the strength and courage they need to endure sufferings for Christ, let us pray to the Lord.

That unbelievers today open their hearts to the Good News of salvation, let us pray to the Lord.

That we may bring people closer to Christ by our good example, let us pray to the Lord.

Special Features

- Display a map or overhead transparency showing where Paul's travels took him.
- Have children take parts for the first reading about Paul's conversion.

Songs

Center of My Life; Here I Am, Lord; Jesus the Lord; Only This I Want; Paul's Prayer; Whatsoever You Do

Homily Ideas

Visuals: A glass of water and food coloring

Add a drop of food coloring to the water. Remark that the colorless water has now changed to a color. This change is nothing compared to the change that occurred in the man called Saul, who is now called St. Paul. Ask the children to recall what Saul did to Christians before he met Christ (arrested them, had them killed).

. . .

Explain that an apostle is someone who has seen the risen Lord and is sent to tell others the Good News about him. As Saul was on his way to hunt for Christians, Jesus spoke to him. Jesus told Saul that in harming his people he was being cruel to Jesus himself. A bright light blinded Saul, so Jesus sent him to a city where Ananias would come and cure him. When Saul could see again, Ananias told him he was chosen to tell others about Jesus. He told Saul to be baptized. Now Saul could see the world again, and he could also see the truth about Jesus. He changed his name to Paul, and he became a zealous preacher.

. . .

Tell the children some of Paul's accomplishments: he spread the Good News and began churches throughout the known world, he made three missionary journeys, he wrote letters that are part of the Bible, he helped the Church realize that not only Jewish people but everyone could belong to it.

. . .

Tell about some of Paul's hardships as an apostle. He was whipped five times, beaten with rods three times, stoned by people, shipwrecked three times. His journeys put him in many dangerous situations. He had nights without sleep, he suffered hunger and thirst, and he was often out in the cold and other bad weather.

. . .

Point out that the reason Paul was willing to do all these things and suffer all these things was that he had a great love for Christ. Read aloud some things Paul wrote in his letters about Jesus:

What will separate us from the love of Christ?…I am convinced that neither death, nor life, nor angels, nor principalities, nor present things, nor future things, nor powers, nor height, nor depth, nor any other creature will be able to separate us from the love of God in Christ Jesus our Lord (Romans 8:35–39).

For to me life is Christ, and death is gain (Philippians 1:21).

I even consider everything as a loss because of the supreme good of knowing Christ Jesus my Lord (Philippians 3:8).

Whatever you do, in word or in deed, do everything in the name of the Lord Jesus, giving thanks to God the Father through him (Colossians 3:17).

. . .

Ask the children how they can spread the Good News like Paul (by learning about it, by talking to others about it, by inviting others to religious activities, by living it).

248 JANUARY 26
Timothy and Titus, *Bishops* (MEMORIAL)

Timothy and Titus were disciples and assistants of the apostle Paul. Timothy was converted by Paul and became his close companion. Timothy became the young bishop of Ephesus, and Titus the bishop of Crete. They did much to guide the growth of the early Church. In the Bible there are two letters to Timothy and one to Titus. These are called pastoral epistles because they contain advice for pastors in dealing with their communities.

Special Features

- As an introduction to the homily, children can be prepared to take the roles of Timothy and Titus and be interviewed. Use the previous paragraph and the suggested first readings for information.
- No matter which reading is selected, in the homily point out the strong, personal relationship Paul had with these two early bishops. He regarded them as his children and expressed prayers for them. This is the kind of unity and love that should characterize the members of the Church today.

Themes: Church leadership, epistles in the Bible

249 JANUARY 27
Angela Merici, *Virgin, Religious Founder*

St. Angela founded the Ursulines, the oldest teaching order in the Church. Born in northern Italy in 1470, she became a Third Order Franciscan. At that time many girls were uneducated. While she was in Brescia, Angela began to teach girls about the faith. She knew the importance of Christian families, and she firmly believed in this motto: "Convert the woman and one converts the family." At the age of fifty-seven, Angela formed a group of women named the Company of St. Ursula. These religious women had special permission to live in their own homes as they taught and did other works of mercy. They met once a month for prayer. Forty years later the Sisters were asked to live in convents and wear habits.

Themes: Sisters, faith in families, women in the Church

250 JANUARY 28
Thomas Aquinas, *Presbyter, Religious, Doctor of the Church* (MEMORIAL)

Thomas Aquinas is the patron of Catholic schools. He was born in Italy around the year 1225. He was brilliant, but because he was large and very quiet, his classmates called him "the dumb ox." Thomas wanted to be a Dominican against the wishes of his wealthy family. They even imprisoned him for a year in the family castle, but this didn't change his mind. Thomas studied under St. Albert the Great and became a teacher himself. He wrote much about God and prayed much. One day while celebrating Mass Thomas had a religious experience that led him to say that all his writing was just straw in view of the mystery of God. He never wrote again. His most famous work is the *Summa Theologica*, which contains his thought on all the Christian mysteries. Invited to the Council of Lyons by the pope, he died on the way there at the age of forty-nine. St. Thomas is known as "the angelic doctor" because of his purity and knowledge.

Themes: Learning more about the faith, prayer

251 JANUARY 31
John Bosco, *Presbyter, Religious Founder* (MEMORIAL)

John Bosco was born in Italy in 1815, the youngest son of a peasant family. At that time hundreds of orphaned boys and poor boys lived and worked in cities. They fought, used bad language, stole, and hurt others. As a priest, John Bosco's ministry was to teach them the faith and the way of Christ. For these boys he formed Sunday expeditions that began with Mass. In 1850, he opened his first home for forty boys with his mother as housekeeper. In his homes he trained the boys in a trade, gave them a religious education, and provided a healthy social life for them. John Bosco founded the Salesians, a religious congregation that works with poor boys. He also wrote much about the faith. John Bosco, the apostle of youth, used his gifts and attractive personality to serve the Church. He is also called "Don" Bosco. "Don" means Father.

Themes: Using talents for God, the importance of Mass

FEBRUARY

252 FEBRUARY 2
The Presentation of the Lord (FEAST)

Today we celebrate Christ the light of the world. Forty days after his birth, Jesus was brought to the Temple by Mary and Joseph to be consecrated to God. There Simeon recognized Jesus as the savior who would be a light to all nations. Jesus is the one who brought us out of the darkness of sin and death. He saved us and gave us truth and eternal life. For this we praise and thank God today in this Eucharist.

Universal Prayer
The response is *"Lord, hear our prayer."*

For the Church, that it may be a light for all people, let us pray to the Lord.

For countries that are struggling against the evil of wars and crime, that they may soon experience the light and peace of Christ, let us pray to the Lord.

For mothers who are expecting babies, that they may have safe births, let us pray to the Lord.

For the elderly, that they may grow ever stronger in their faith, let us pray to the Lord.

For ourselves, that we may be like shining lights to our families, friends, and other people we meet.

Special Features
- Hold the blessing of candles.
- Have a candlelight (or unlighted candle) procession after the blessing.
- Give each child a blessed candle to take home.

Songs

Canticle of Zachary; Christ Is the World's True Light; I Am the Light; I Want to Walk as a Child of the Light; Joy to the World; The Light of Christ; The Lord Is My Light; This Little Light of Mine; We Are the Light of the World

Homily Ideas

Visual: A candle

Show the candle and light it. Ask the children how candles are used (to give light so we can see, in worship to praise God, to celebrate birthdays).

Tell the children that today is the feast of the Presentation when Jesus was presented and consecrated to God the Father in the Temple. Another name for the feast is Candlemas. Candles are blessed on this day.

• • •

Explain that the connection between candles and the Presentation is found in a prayer that the children heard in the gospel. When Jesus was taken to the Temple, an old man named Simeon had been sent there by God. Simeon had been promised by God that he would not die until he had seen the savior. When he saw Mary and Joseph's baby, Simeon knew that Jesus was the messiah that everyone had been waiting and longing for. He praised God in a beautiful song. In the song he called Jesus a light to the Gentiles. Jesus enabled the whole world to see the truth about God and our lives.

• • •

Point out or ask for other customs that remind us that Jesus is our light. (We keep a sanctuary light burning in church near the tabernacle. At our baptism we receive a candle as a sign that we share Jesus' life. At the Easter Vigil a large Easter candle is lighted and carried in procession as a symbol of the light of Christ. At Christmas and Easter people place candles in bags or bottles of sand and set them in their yards. When someone receives the anointing of the sick at home, a candle is lighted.)

Encourage the children to keep a blessed candle in their homes.

• • •

Comment that the Presentation is the fourth Joyful Mystery of the rosary. We remember this mystery in our personal prayer this way. Also every evening the Church prays the song of Simeon in the Divine Office, the official prayer of the Church.

• • •

Explain that Jewish law required a woman who had a son to make an offering to God in the Temple. She could sacrifice a lamb, or if she could not afford it, a pigeon or turtledove. Mary and Joseph gave the offering of the poor. The couple also came to offer their son to God. This custom came from the time in Egypt when the firstborn sons of the Jewish people were not killed in the tenth plague. The Jewish people continued to thank and praise God for their sons.

• • •

Remind the children that they are to show forth the light of Christ in their own corners of the world: their homes, their neighborhoods, and their schools.

253 FEBRUARY 3

Blase, *Bishop, Martyr*

St. Blase was the bishop of Sebaste, a town that is now in Turkey. He was martyred during a persecution in the early fourth century. Many legends are told of him. The most famous is that one day a woman came to him with her son who was choking on a fish bone. When Blase prayed over him, the boy was cured. For this reason, Blase is the patron of those who have throat diseases. It is said that in prison, he was condemned to darkness, but someone smuggled him some candles. On the feast of St. Blase the Church blesses throats using two candles bound together in the form of an X.

Themes: Sacramentals, praying to saints

254 also FEBRUARY 3
Ansgar, *Bishop, Missionary*

St. Ansgar is called the "apostle to the North" because he worked to evangelize the Scandinavian countries. He was born in France about the year 801. Ansgar joined the Benedictines and became a missionary in Denmark for three years. Although he was a wonderful preacher and teacher, he had little success. He became a bishop in Hamburg where he became known for his preaching, love for the poor, and prayer. After thirteen years, however, Hamburg was invaded and destroyed, and the people gave up their faith. Ansgar then became a missionary to Sweden and Denmark. After his death Sweden, too, turned away from the faith.

Themes: Perseverance, evangelizing

255 FEBRUARY 5
Agatha, *Virgin, Martyr*

St. Agatha was martyred in Sicily in Italy during the persecution of Decius in the middle of the third century. According to stories told of her, she was born of noble parents and was so kind and lovely that the governor of Sicily proposed to her. When she rejected his proposal, he sent her to a house of prostitution, but she was not harmed. Then he sent her to prison for being a Christian. There she was tortured and died. A year after her death, when the city survived the volcano on Mt. Etna, people said it was through Agatha's prayers. Agatha became such a popular saint that her name was included in a Eucharistic Prayer. It is the oldest Eucharistic Prayer and is still used today. In Italy St. Agatha's feast day is celebrated with fireworks. The name Agatha means "good" in Greek.

Themes: Witnessing to the faith, purity

256 FEBRUARY 6
Paul Miki, *Religious, Missionary, Martyr*, and His Companions, *Martyrs* (MEMORIAL)

Paul was born in Japan in the middle of the sixteenth century. When he was a Jesuit brother preparing to be the first Japanese priest, a new leader came into power who banished missionaries and began to persecute Christians. More than 3,000 people were martyred. Paul was arrested and condemned to crucifixion with twenty-five others, including boys as young as ten and thirteen. The prisoners were tortured and then marched 300 miles through snow and ice to the mountain in Nagasaki where they would be killed. Along the way they sang psalms, prayed, and preached to people, telling them their martyrdom was a cause for rejoicing. From his cross St. Paul said, "I hope my blood will fall on my fellow men as fruitful rain."

Themes: Suffering for Christ, missionaries

257 FEBRUARY 8
Jerome Emiliani, *Presbyter, Religious Founder*

When Jerome was a twenty-five-year-old soldier in Venice, he was captured in battle and imprisoned. While in prison he thought about his life. He decided to change his sinful ways and dedicated himself to Mary. After escaping from prison, Jerome cared for the sick and poor and studied for the priesthood.

As a priest he devoted himself to caring for orphans, training them to make a living and teaching them about the faith. Jerome and two other priests founded a congregation originally called Servants for the Poor, known later as the Clerks Regular of Samascha. Jerome died of the plague, which he caught from his patients. His last words were "Jesus" and "Mary."

Themes: Works of mercy, conversion of heart

257A also FEBRUARY 8
Josephine Bakhita, *Virgin*

When this saint was a young girl in the Sudan, slave traders captured her. They called her Bakhita, which means "lucky." As a slave, she was sold several times. Some owners treated her cruelly. Finally she was given to a kind Italian family. When the parents went to Africa, they sent Bakhita and their daughter to stay at a Canossian convent in Venice. There Bakhita's love for God grew. When the parents returned, to their dismay Bakhita asked to stay with the Sisters. A court ruled that she was free. At baptism Bakhita received the name Josephine. She joined the Canossian Daughters of Charity and worked as a cook, seamstress, and doorkeeper. She had a missionary heart. Everyone loved this friendly, gentle Sister. They called her Mother Moretta, "our black mother," and regarded her as a saint. She died in 1947.

Themes: Hope, trust in God, patience in suffering

258 FEBRUARY 10
Scholastica, *Virgin, Religious* (MEMORIAL)

Scholastica lived in Italy in the sixth century. She was the twin sister of St. Benedict, who founded the Benedictines. Vowing herself to God, Scholastica followed her brother to his monastery at Monte Cassino and helped him found a community of religious women. St. Gregory the Great said of her, "She could do more because she loved more." A story about her is that once when Benedict visited her, they talked late into the night. Scholastica begged him to stay still later, but he refused, saying that his rule required the monks to be in the monastery at night. At that, Scholastica put her head down on the table and cried and prayed. A terrible storm came up, and Benedict exclaimed, "What have you done?" Scholastica said that since he would not grant her favor she had turned to God, who had an-

swered. The two talked and prayed together until morning. Three days later Scholastica died.

Themes: Holiness, the law of love

259 FEBRUARY 11
Our Lady of Lourdes

On February 11, 1858, Mary appeared to fourteen-year-old Bernadette Soubirous in Lourdes, France. Bernadette was collecting firewood with her sister and a friend. Because she was sickly, she lagged behind. In a grotto she saw a beautiful lady dressed in white with a blue sash. The lady had a rosary and prayed it with her. Eighteen more times the lady appeared to Bernadette. She told her to do penance and to pray for sinners. She identified herself as the Immaculate Conception and told Bernadette to instruct the priest to have a chapel built on the site and to hold processions there. One day Mary had Bernadette dig in the soil. A spring gushed forth that produced healing waters. People make pilgrimages to Lourdes today and are healed spiritually and physically.

Themes: Mary, the rosary, healing, penance

260 FEBRUARY 14
Cyril, *Religious, Missionary*, and
Methodius, *Bishop, Missionary* (MEMORIAL)

Cyril and Methodius were two brothers born in Greece in the ninth century. They are known as the "apostles of the Slavs." They served as a spiritual bridge between Eastern and Western traditions. Cyril was a brilliant philosopher who became a priest. Methodius was a governor who became a monk. The brothers were sent as missionaries to Russia and then to Moravia in Eastern Europe. They developed an alphabet in order to translate the gospels into the Slavic language, and at Mass they preached in Slavic. German bishops who did not trust the brothers had them called to Rome to defend their actions. This led to the decision to make the brothers bishops! Cyril, however, died before he could be consecrated a bishop. Methodius was made a bishop and returned to Moravia, but he continued to be accused until his death. At one time a German Synod of bishops deposed him and imprisoned him for two years until the pope ordered him freed.

Themes: Missionary work, long-suffering, courage

261 FEBRUARY 17
Seven Founders of the Order of Servites, *Religious*

In the middle of the thirteenth century seven wealthy businessmen in Italy were dismayed by the evils in society. They decided to follow Christ completely and left the city to lead lives of prayer and penance in the mountains. Calling themselves the Servants of Mary, or Servites, they gradually moved from being monks living apart from the world to being men actively helping the poor and needy. Six of the seven became priests. Alexis Falconieri, who was more than a century old, was the last of the seven to die.

Themes: Ways to fight evil, Mary as model, life priorities

262 FEBRUARY 21
Peter Damian, *Bishop, Doctor of the Church*

St. Peter Damian was born in Ravenna, Italy, in 1007. He became a teacher and then was ordained a priest. Later he entered a Benedictine monastery where the monks lived in twos in small hermitages in which they prayed, fasted, and performed penances. When he was elected abbot, Peter reformed the order. Then he was made bishop and cardinal and was called on to serve the Church by settling disputes, fighting abuses, and going on diplomatic missions. He worked to reform the leaders of the empire as well as the clergy. Through his writings he encouraged people to reform their lives and practice discipline.

Themes: Reforming our lives, prayer

263 FEBRUARY 22
The Chair of the Apostle Peter (FEAST)

The pope and bishops act as our shepherds, teaching us and helping us to become holy. In a special way the pope is a sign of Christ's love and presence with us on earth. Today we thank and praise God for giving the Church leaders down through the centuries. We pray for our pope and for the Church of which he is the head.

Universal Prayer
The response is *"Lord, hear our prayer."*

For Pope (N), that the Holy Spirit may fill him with wisdom and courage to carry out his task of governing and caring for the Church, we pray to the Lord.

For all bishops, that they may be united in their teachings and their love for Christ, one another, and the Church, we pray to the Lord.

For all priests, deacons, and other church leaders who carry on the work of Christ, that they may be blessed, we pray to the Lord.

For us, that we may be open to the guidance of the pope and bishops and follow their leadership, we pray to the Lord.

Special Features
- Have a display of pictures and articles about the present pope and/or your local bishop.
- Read the gospel with students taking parts.

Songs

Center of My Life; The Church's One Foundation; Do You Really Love Me?; Faith of Our Fathers; Like a Shepherd; The Lord Is My True Shepherd; Lord, to Whom Shall We Go?; My Shepherd, Lord; Song of the Body of Christ

Homily Ideas

Visual: A picture of the pope or the Vatican

Show the picture of the pope or the Vatican. Explain that today's feast is a celebration of the leadership God gives us in the Church. Christ called certain followers to be bishops who would guide us in his name. The pope is the bishop of Rome who is recognized as having primacy or a specialness as the chief leader of the Church.

. . .

Tell the children that this feast is called the Chair of Peter. The chair from which a bishop presides at Mass is a symbol of his authority. The chair of Peter refers to St. Peter, the prince of the apostles, and the more than 260 popes who followed him.

. . .

Explain that Scripture and tradition show that St. Peter held a position as head of the apostles. He often spoke for the others and was the first to preach after Pentecost. The gospel of this Mass tells how Jesus singled out Peter to be head of the Church. When Jesus asked the apostles who they thought he was, Simon declared, "You are the messiah, the Son of the living God." Jesus changed Simon's name to Peter, which means rock, and stated that he would found his Church on this rock. Jesus said he gave Peter the keys of the kingdom; in other words, Peter had authority in the Church.

. . .

Mention that at the Last Supper Jesus told Peter that he had prayed for him and that Peter must strengthen his brothers.

. . .

Recall that after the resurrection Jesus asked Peter three times if he loved him. Each time that Peter answered yes, Jesus told him, "Feed my lambs" or "Feed my sheep." Explain that the pope is called the servant of the servants of God. He cares for all of us like a good shepherd in place of Christ, who is the chief shepherd.

. . .

Tell the children that from Rome the pope teaches, guides, and shepherds the flock of the Church. He also speaks out on world issues and gives advice to world leaders. He travels to different countries and has the respect of people all over the world, even those who are not Catholic.

. . .

State that Peter wrote two letters that are in the Bible. These instruct the other church leaders how to act. Today the pope and bishops write letters to everyone. Suggest that as the children grow older, they try to learn what the pope and bishops are teaching by reading these letters.

. . .

Comment that Peter was not perfect. He denied Christ and was not brave enough to be there when Jesus was crucified. Other popes have had their faults, too, because they are human beings. We trust the Holy Spirit, though, to guide the Church through these leaders.

. . .

Encourage the children to pray for our pope and bishops. Their job is not easy. They are to be examples to the world.

264 FEBRUARY 23
Polycarp, *Bishop, Martyr* (MEMORIAL)

Polycarp was a disciple of the apostle John. Because he knew and was taught by an apostle, Polycarp is called an Apostolic Father. He was the much-beloved bishop of Smyrna in Asia Minor and a friend of St. Ignatius of Antioch. During a persecution around the year 155, he was captured and pressed to give up his faith in Christ. He declared, "For eighty-six years I have served Jesus Christ and he has never abandoned me. How could I curse my blessed king and savior?" In the stadium of Smyrna, Polycarp was burned at the stake. An eye-witness account states that when the flames didn't harm him, he was killed by the sword.

Themes: Faithfulness, the handing on of faith

MARCH

265 MARCH 3
Katharine Drexel,
Virgin, Religious Founder

Katharine Drexel was born into a wealthy family from Philadelphia in 1858. For three years she nursed her stepmother, who had cancer. The experience led Katharine to think about becoming a nun. A trip to the West made her concerned about the Native Americans. In a visit with the pope, she asked him to send missionaries to Wyoming. He suggested that she become one. She joined the Sisters of Mercy for two years and then made her vows as the first Sister of the Blessed Sacrament, an order she founded to share the gospel and the Eucharist among Native Americans and blacks. Mother Drexel spent the rest of her life and her inheritance on her work, establishing fifty missions for Native Americans in sixteen states, Catholic schools for blacks, mission centers, rural schools, and Xavier University in New Orleans for blacks. After suffering a heart attack, St. Katharine spent the last nineteen years of her life praying in a room overlooking the convent chapel sanctuary. She died at the age of ninety-six and is now the patron of racial justice and philanthropists.

Themes: Taking action, fighting racism, sacrificing for Christ

266 MARCH 4
Casimir

Casimir was the son of the king of Poland. He was so outstanding that when he was fourteen years old, nobles in Hungary wanted him as their king. His father sent him with an army to take over Hungary, but when Casimir heard the pope had asked his father not to do it, he returned home. For this, Casimir was banished to a castle for three months where he studied and prayed. He made up his mind to govern only by peaceful means and never to marry. When Casimir's father was in Lithuania, Casimir ruled for a short time. In 1484, when he was only twenty-six, St. Casimir died of a lung disease. This prince was known as "brother and defender of the poor" and had a great devotion to Mary and the Eucharist.

Themes: Fulfilling responsibilities, obedience to God, love for the poor

267 MARCH 7
Perpetua and Felicity, *Martyrs* (MEMORIAL)

Perpetua and Felicity were martyred in a persecution in 203 in Carthage, North Africa, because they were preparing to be baptized. Perpetua was a twenty-two-year-old noblewoman who had a young son.

Felicity was her slave who was expecting a child. The two women and four other catechumens were sentenced to be martyred as entertainment on a national holiday. Their teacher joined them so that he, too, might die for Christ. Perpetua kept a diary as she awaited her execution. Her father, a pagan, begged her to sacrifice to the pagan god to be free, but she refused. Felicity had a baby girl in prison. All six prisoners were baptized there. In the end they suffered death by wild beasts and the sword. In addition to Perpetua's diary we have the writing of someone who witnessed the death of these early martyrs.

Themes: Faith, suffering for the faith, baptism

268 MARCH 8
John of God, *Religious Founder*

John was born in Portugal in 1495. He became a soldier in Spain and led a wild life. At age forty he left the army, decided to change his way of life, and opened a religious bookstore. One day he heard a sermon of St. John of Avila that caused him to sorrow for his sins so much that he ran outside and acted like a madman. As a result he was put in a mental institution. There John of Avila came and advised him to care for the sick and poor. John opened a hospital where the poorest sick people found help. He died shortly after saving a drowning man. After John's death, his helpers formed a religious community now called the Order of Hospitallers of Saint John of God.

Themes: Helping the poor, conversion, repentance

269 MARCH 9
Frances of Rome,
Married Woman, Religious Founder

Frances was from a wealthy family and married when she was only thirteen. She and her sister-in-law cared for the sick and the poor even when other family members looked down on them for it. Frances also took care of her children and the castle. When floods and famine came to Rome, Frances changed her house into a hospital and distributed food and clothing. During an invasion, her husband was kidnapped and three of her children died. Frances founded the Benedictine Oblates of St. Mary who served the poor. After her husband died, she joined them. It is said that for twenty-three years Frances could see her guardian angel.

Themes: Love of the poor, devotion to duty

270 MARCH 17
Patrick, *Bishop, Missionary*

St. Patrick was born in Britain around 385. He was kidnapped when he was a young man and sold in Ireland where he had to tend sheep. He escaped, became a priest, and decided to return to Ireland to evangelize. The pope ordained him a bishop and sent him to northern and western Ireland, where the gospel had never been preached. St. Patrick is known as the apostle of Ireland. He dealt with the pagan clans, preached tirelessly, converted many people, and organized the Church. He is known for using a shamrock to teach about the Trinity.

Themes: The Trinity, sharing our faith with others

Special Features
- As a communion reflection, pray the prayer "Breastplate of St. Patrick."
- Sing the song versions of prayers attributed to St. Patrick, such as This Day God Gives Me or Christ Be Beside Me, or sing songs in honor of the Trinity, such as All Hail, Adored Trinity; All Praise and Glad Thanksgiving; God Father, Praise and Glory; and The Living God.

- Use shamrocks as decorations.
- Have the children wear green.

271 MARCH 18
Cyril of Jerusalem, *Bishop, Doctor of the Church*

Cyril was born to Christian parents in Jerusalem in the year 315. He became bishop of Jerusalem at a time when the heresy of Arianism was popular. This heresy denied that Jesus was divine. Cyril wrote well to explain church teachings, but three times he was sent into exile by other bishops who favored the Arians. St. Gregory of Nyssa who was sent to help him with his diocese gave up when faced with its problems. Cyril is known for his sermons preparing those to be baptized.

Themes: Divinity of Jesus, teaching the faith

272 MARCH 19
Joseph, *Husband of the Virgin Mary* (SOLEMNITY)

At this Eucharist we honor St. Joseph, the husband of the Virgin Mary. Joseph was called to be the legal father of Jesus and protector of the Holy Family. He was the right man for this job. Now we look to him as the protector of the Church. We pray that we have the courage to follow God's plans for our lives as well as Joseph did.

Universal Prayer
The response is *"Lord, hear our prayer."*

For the Church, that through the prayers and protection of St. Joseph, we may spread the kingdom of God on earth, we pray to the Lord.

For world leaders, that they may be just, we pray to the Lord.

For parents everywhere, that they may carry out their responsibilities, we pray to the Lord.

For us, that we may be obedient to God and to the people God puts in charge of us, we pray to the Lord.

Special Features
- Set up a display of a statue of St. Joseph, flowers, and candles.
- Begin the homily by having someone tell about a time St. Joseph answered a prayer, such as a prayer for selling a house.
- Distribute cards with a prayer to St. Joseph.

Songs
Holy Patron, Thee Saluting; Joseph of Nazareth; Look Down to Us, Saint Joseph; St. Joseph, Great Protector

Homily Ideas
Visual: A statue or picture of St. Joseph

Refer to a statue or picture of St. Joseph and tell the children that we know little about the man who was called to be the legal father of God's Son, Jesus. We know he was a carpenter in Nazareth of Galilee. He was a Jewish man and a descendant of King David. The Bible calls Joseph a just man. He always tried to do what was right.

. . .

Ask the children how they would feel if they had to be responsible for raising God's Son. Tell them that Joseph had a role of honor to play in the world, but it was a difficult role. Explain to the children that when Joseph was engaged to Mary, he learned that she was going to have a baby. Knowing that it wasn't his baby, Joseph was shocked and hurt. According to Jewish law he could have had Mary punished severely, but he decided just to separate from her quietly. Then in a dream an angel told Joseph that Mary's child was through God's power and that this child would be the savior.

. . .

Mention that according to the Bible, Joseph obeyed the law when the emperor ordered people to go to their hometown for a census. He took Mary with him even though her baby was due. In Bethlehem he was frustrated when he couldn't find a better place than a barn to spend the night. After Jesus was born, Joseph was told that King Herod was seeking to kill the child. Joseph fled to Egypt with Mary and Jesus. He had to make a home for them and get a job in this foreign land until it was safe to return to Nazareth. Later Joseph suffered again when twelve-year-old Jesus was missing for three days in Jerusalem. Point out that often Joseph didn't understand what God was doing with his life, but he always tried to obey God.

● ● ●

Explain that Joseph was privileged to protect and provide for Jesus. He taught Jesus Jewish ways and how to be a carpenter. Jesus was known as the carpenter's son. Point out to the children that Jesus obeyed Joseph just as they obey their fathers. Joseph was also privileged to be married to the most wonderful woman, Mary.

● ● ●

Tell the children that sometime before Jesus left home, Joseph must have died. Jesus and Mary were probably with him when he died. For this reason the Church prays to Joseph as the patron of a happy death.

● ● ●

Mention that Joseph is also patron of the whole Church, Christ's body. Encourage the children to pray to him.

273 MARCH 23
Toribio of Mogrovejo, *Bishop*

Toribio was born into a wealthy Spanish family about the year 1538. He became a professor of law. Then the pope appointed this brilliant layman bishop of Lima, Peru. Toribio resisted this until he realized that God needed him there to help bring the gospel, peace, and justice. In Lima he visited people in his diocese, traveling thousands of miles in unmapped regions. He called councils and synods to deal with problems, to reform religion, and to care for the people, especially the poor Indians who had been neglected by the priests and oppressed by the Spanish conquerors. Toribio was not afraid to speak out against injustices. When he died, he left all his belongings to his servants and the poor.

Themes: Justice, care for the poor, spreading the faith

274 MARCH 25
The Annunciation of the Lord (SOLEMNITY)

At this Eucharist we celebrate the day God first made known the plan to save the world. God sent the Angel Gabriel to Mary with the astounding news that she would be the mother of God's Son. Because Mary agreed to God's plan, Jesus was able to live as a human being. By dying and rising he was able to redeem us from sin and win for us eternal life. We remember today the tremendous love God has for us. We give thanks and praise for this love.

Universal Prayer
The response is *"Lord, hear our prayer."*

For the Church, that the members may continue to make Christ present in the world, we pray to the Lord.

For leaders of nations, that they may govern according to God's plan, we pray to the Lord.

For women who are expecting babies, that they may give birth safely and with joy, we pray to the Lord.

For us who are gathered here, that like Mary we may always be open to God's will for us, we pray to the Lord.

Special Features

- Decorate the church with blue, white, and gold.
- For the gospel, have children take the parts of Mary and Gabriel.
- Pray the following prayer after communion:

  O God, you who are almighty became a helpless baby. You who are pure spirit took on a human form. You who made the universe and its billions of stars became a few feet high. You who cannot be described ate, walked, talked, and slept. You who are awesome felt cold, hunger, thirst, pain, and death. I thank you for your great love that made you become like me in order to save. I thank you for coming to me now in the even lowlier forms of bread and wine. Your humility makes me realize how truly great you are.

Songs

Be It Done unto Me; Blest of the Lord; The God Whom Earth and Sea and Sky; Hail Mary: Gentle Woman; I Say "Yes," Lord; I Sing a Maid; Mary Full of Grace; Mary's Joy; My Soul Rejoices; O Holy Mary; O Mary, of All Women; Sing of Mary; Song of Jesus Christ

Homily Ideas

Visual: A pair of shoes

Show a pair of shoes. State that there is a saying that to understand someone you have to walk a mile in that person's shoes. Ask the children what this means. (You have to experience what is going on in that person's life.) Comment that God decided to walk in our shoes for a while by becoming a human being.

· · ·

Explain that God became human so that we could know what God is like. Watching and listening to Jesus, who is God, we learned about God. Ask the children what God is like, judging from Jesus'

words and actions (kind, loving, brave, merciful). God became human in order to teach us how to live. Jesus gave us guidelines for a good life and showed us what it really meant to love. He taught his followers and made them teachers, too. God also became human to repair the damage of sin. By dying on the cross and rising, Jesus made up for our sins and gave us the chance to live forever.

· · ·

Tell the children that God became human with the help of a young Jewish girl named Mary. God sent the Angel Gabriel as a messenger to Mary and told her that she would have a son named Jesus. Her son would be the Son of God and a king. Because Mary was only engaged to Joseph and not yet married, she asked how this would happen. Gabriel told her that it would happen through the power of the Holy Spirit. He told her that her elderly relative Elizabeth was also going to have a son even though she was never able to have one before.

· · ·

Point out that Mary's immediate response to Gabriel was to call herself God's servant. She said, "Let it happen as you have said." Recall that Gabriel told Mary that God was pleased with her. Mary always tried to do what God wanted. Because she had always been so open to God, Mary easily met the challenge of accepting this hard thing God was asking of her.

· · ·

Explain that as soon as Mary said yes to God, Jesus came to be within her. His flesh and blood were taken from her. She became God's mother.

· · ·

Ask the children why being the Mother of God was not easy. (It was mysterious and puzzling. Joseph would not understand and neither would other people. And Mary had to suffer when Jesus suffered and died.)

· · ·

Tell the children that Mary was so holy that God chose her above all other women who ever lived. She is not only the mother of Christ, but our mother, too. We should try to be like her. If we listen to God and try to be loving as Mary was, then in a way Christ will be born in us and we, too, can bring him forth to the world.

. . .

Show the shoes again and explain that Mary's son told us how to live and showed us how. Now we, Mary's other children, are to follow in his footsteps. Being in step with Jesus sometimes means being out of step with the rest of the world.

. . .

Encourage the children to pray to Mary. Remind them that the Hail Mary repeats Gabriel's greeting, "Hail, Mary, full of grace, the Lord is with you." Each time we pray it, we remind ourselves and Mary of the moment when God became one of us. The Angelus, a prayer in which we pray three Hail Marys, is also in honor of the mystery of the incarnation.

APRIL

275 APRIL 2
Francis of Paola, *Hermit, Religious Founder*

St. Francis was born in southern Italy in 1416. When he was fifteen, he became a hermit and lived in a cave overlooking the sea. Others joined him and they became an order of hermits called Franciscan Minim Friars. Minim means "little ones." The hermits did penance and made a vow always to fast as in Lent. The pope had Francis go to Rome and then France to teach others about holiness. Francis helped bring about peace between France and Britain and between France and Spain. He combined the contemplative life—a quiet, prayerful one—with an active one.

Themes: Fasting, peacemaking

276 APRIL 4
Isidore of Seville, *Bishop, Doctor of the Church*

Isidore was born in Seville, Spain, about the year 560. After his father died, he was raised by his brother. As a boy he disliked studying. One day he noticed how ropes had worn grooves in a stone well. He realized that he could succeed in studying if he kept at it. As a result, he became a very learned man. Isidore followed his brother as bishop of Seville. He worked hard to build up the Church, holding councils to solve problems and establishing seminaries. He wrote much, including an encyclopedia containing all the knowledge available at the time. During the last months of his life, his house was filled with the poor all day.

Themes: Helping the poor, knowledge, persistence

277 APRIL 5
Vincent Ferrer, *Presbyter, Religious, Missionary*

Vincent was born in 1350 in Spain and entered the Dominican order when he was eighteen. This was a terrible time, because there were constant wars between France and England, three men claimed to be pope, and the Eastern and Western churches had split. St. Vincent became a traveling preacher and taught the faith and encouraged reform throughout France, Switzerland, and North Italy. Large crowds assembled outside to hear this "mouthpiece of God" who lived what he preached.

Themes: Holding to the faith, encouraging others in the faith

278 APRIL 7
John Baptist de la Salle,
Presbyter, Religious Founder (MEMORIAL)

In 1651, John was born into a powerful, wealthy family at Rheims in France. After being ordained, this handsome, intelligent man was expected to have a high office in the Church. However, John became interested in schools for poor children. He trained teachers to be religious educators and gave away his fortune in order to identify with the poor. Eventually he founded the Brothers of Christian Schools (Christian Brothers). He also founded schools for delinquent wealthy boys. Teachers at other schools who were envious of John's schools tried to ruin his work by lawsuits. John suffered great trials in silence and died on Good Friday.

Themes: Value of religious education, a heart for the poor, suffering

279 APRIL 11
Stanislaus, *Bishop, Martyr* (MEMORIAL)

Stanislaus was born in Poland around 1030. When the diocese of Crakow needed a bishop, they begged the pope to appoint Stanislaus, a priest known for his generosity to the poor. As bishop, Stanislaus was a good shepherd, working for religious education and forming the clergy. Boleslaw, the king of Poland, invaded Russia, cheated the poor, kid-

napped a nobleman's wife, and allowed violence. Stanislaus courageously spoke out against these wrongs. The angry king accused him of crimes and continued in his corrupt ways until Stanislaus declared that he was excommunicated, or cut off from the Church. While Stanislaus was celebrating Mass, the furious Boleslaw killed him with his sword. Later the king repented.

Themes: Speaking up for what is right, serving the poor

280 APRIL 13
Martin I, *Pope, Martyr*

Martin is the last of the martyr popes. He was born in Italy and became a priest of Rome. He was elected pope in 649 and called a council to condemn a heresy. The emperor in Constantinople, who had forbidden any more discussion of the heresy, accused Martin of plotting against him. He had Martin arrested and brought to Constantinople. On the journey Martin was given little to eat and was not allowed to wash for forty-seven days. In Constantinople he was accused in an unjust trial, insulted by the people, humiliated, and condemned to death. The Church elected a new pope. In the end, Martin was exiled to Crimea. There he died abandoned by all, including his friends and relatives.

Themes: False accusations, standing for the truth

281 APRIL 21
Anselm, *Bishop, Religious, Doctor of the Church*

St. Anselm was born in Italy in 1033. His father tried to squelch Anselm's desire to be a priest by introducing him to court life. Despite this, Anselm joined the Benedictines in France. He became a great teacher and preacher and eventually the archbishop of Canterbury. He was famous for his virtue. For a time when the rulers insisted on appointing bishops, Anselm fought for the freedom of the Church and was exiled twice. Finally, the pope worked out a compromise. Anselm is known for his writings in theology.

Themes: Being virtuous, standing up for rights

282 APRIL 23
George, *Martyr*

In the fourth century in Palestine, George was venerated as a soldier who was martyred about 303 for defending the faith and encouraging other Christians. During the Crusades he was chosen as the patron saint of England. A famous legend about him tells of a dragon that terrorized people and demanded human beings for food. The day the king's daughter was chosen by lot to be served, George killed the dragon. He refused any reward but made the king promise to build churches and show compassion to the poor.

Themes: Courage, selflessness

282A also APRIL 23
Adalbert, *Bishop, Martyr*

Adalbert was born into a noble family in Bohemia about 956. As bishop of Prague, he chose a life of poverty and charity. He resigned and lived as a hermit in a monastery for four years. The pope sent him back to be bishop of Prague, where he stayed until enemies forced him out. Adalbert went to Hungary as a missionary, where he probably baptized the king and his son. He went on to Poland as a missionary. Then the pope sent him to Prussia, where the people were pagans. The Prussians resented Adalbert's efforts to convert them and eventually killed him and his companions. Boleslas I,

Prince of Poland, is said to have ransomed his body for its weight in gold.

Themes: Missionary work, charity

283 APRIL 24
Fidelis of Sigmaringen,
Presbyter, Religious, Martyr

Born in Sigmaringen in Germany in 1578 and baptized Mark Roy, Fidelis became known as the poor man's lawyer. He got a doctorate in philosophy and law and at first tutored young boys from noble families. Then he became a lawyer and took only cases for the poor and oppressed. Later he distributed his wealth to the poor and became a Capuchin. His charity and prayerfulness were well known. Sent to preach to the Swiss people who had revolted against the Catholic Church, Fidelis was killed in a church by a group of angry peasants.

Themes: Generosity, prayerfulness

284 APRIL 25
Mark, *Evangelist* (FEAST)

Mark, one of the first Christians, worked with St. Paul and St. Peter. We think it was Mark who wrote the earliest gospel. Although Mark was not one of the twelve apostles, he followed Christ with his whole heart and helped shape our Christian faith. It is believed that Mark became a bishop in Alexandria, Egypt, where he was martyred. Let us pray at this Eucharist to be as devoted to Christ as Mark was.

Universal Prayer
The response is *"Lord, hear our prayer."*

For church leaders, that they may be good examples to the people they serve, let us pray to the Lord.

For civic leaders, that they may be selfless and just, let us pray to the Lord.

For people who have a ministry related to Scripture, that their work may bring others closer to God, let us pray to the Lord.

For ourselves, that we may have a deeper love and knowledge of God through praying and studying the gospel, let us pray to the Lord.

Special Features

- Display a banner with the symbol of a winged lion for St. Mark.
- Distribute booklets of the Gospel of St. Mark.

Songs

Proclaim the Good News; Take the Word of God with You; Thy Word Is a Lamp; We Hear God's Word

Homily Ideas

Visual: A gospel book

Show the gospel book and explain that the Bible contains four gospels, or accounts of the life and teachings of Jesus. The shortest and what may be the oldest gospel is thought to have been written by St. Mark. Mark was a good friend of St. Peter. In the first reading, Peter said Mark was like a son to him. Because of this, much of the material in Mark's gospel probably came from Peter.

· · ·

Tell the children that the Gospel of Mark is direct, simple, and fast-moving. It shows Christ as the Son of God who suffers to save us. It teaches that we, too, must accept the cross, or hard things, in our lives.

· · ·

Comment that the symbol for St. Mark is a winged lion because his gospel opens with John the Baptist calling people to repent like a roaring lion.

· · ·

Point out that the gospel reading of the day is taken from Mark's gospel. In the passage is Jesus' command to the disciples to go out to spread the Good News. Mark did as Jesus said. He not only worked as a missionary to spread the faith and as a bishop, but he wrote down the Good News so that even today, two thousand years later, the message has reached us.

· · ·

Encourage the children to read Mark's gospel. Suggest that they read a few lines each day. Older children might read the whole gospel in one day.

· · ·

Tell the children that the first Christians were just as human as we are. On one missionary journey, Mark was with his cousin Barnabas and Paul. Mark decided to return to Jerusalem. This caused an argument between Paul and Barnabas. Later, however, the three men must have made up, for when Paul was in prison he wrote to Timothy to ask for Mark's help.

· · ·

Have someone talk about what Scripture means to him or her.

· · ·

Ask the children what they could do at their age to spread the Good News to others.

285 APRIL 28
Peter Chanel,
Presbyter, Religious, Missionary, Martyr

Peter Chanel was born to a peasant family in France in 1803. His parish priest helped him enter the seminary. After being a parish priest for three years, Peter joined the new congregation, the Society of Mary (Marists). For five years he taught in a seminary. Then his dream of being a missionary came true, and he was sent to the islands in the South Pacific. The work there was difficult and discouraging. Cannibalism still existed, and the language was hard to learn. There were few natives interested in the Catholic faith. When the chief's son asked to be baptized, the chief had his warriors club Peter to death. Two years later the whole island of Fortuna was Catholic.

Themes: Missionary work, the RCIA

285A also APRIL 28
Louis Mary de Montfort, *Priest*

Louis Mary was born in France in 1673. He studied theology and lived and worked with the poor. He became a priest and a Third Order Dominican. Compelled to preach, he travelled widely, giving parish missions. Louis also wrote numerous hymns. His devotion to Our Lady led to his writing books on her such as the classics *True Devotion to Mary* and *The Secret of the Rosary*. Louis founded The Company of Mary, a community of missionary priests and brothers. He also founded Daughters of Wisdom, a community that taught and ministered to the sick. Louis died in 1716. His focus on going to Jesus through Mary has influenced the Church for centuries.

Themes: Serving the poor, Mary, proclaiming the Good News

286 APRIL 29
Catherine of Siena,
Virgin, Doctor of the Church (MEMORIAL)

Catherine was born in Siena, Italy, in 1347, the youngest of twenty-three children. As a child, she was drawn to the spiritual life and had visions. At sixteen she joined the Third Order of St. Dominic and lived in silence and solitude in her home. After three years, Jesus ordered her to serve her neighbors, and she began to do works of mercy. She became the spiritual guide to a large group of followers and traveled through Italy urging people to repent. Catherine dictated many letters to popes, rulers, leaders of armies, men, and women and wrote two books. She is best known for persuading the pope, who was residing in Avignon in France, to return to Rome. A mystic, Catherine had the stigmata, the wounds of Christ, miraculously on her body although others could not see them. She also experienced a spiritual marriage with Christ. In 1970, Catherine and St. Teresa of Avila were the first women to receive the title doctor of the Church. This title honors teachers who write and preach to guide others to holiness. Catherine died when she was thirty-three years old.

Themes: Spiritual life, prayer

287 APRIL 30
Pius V, *Pope, Religious*

Pope Pius V was born in 1504 to a poor Italian family. He became a Dominican and then a bishop and a cardinal. When he was elected pope, the Council of Trent had ended three years before, and his task was to carry out its decisions. A man of great holiness and self-discipline, Pope Pius V reformed the Church and renewed the liturgy. He had a catechism published and revised the books used for liturgy. He had seminaries and CCD classes established. In 1571 the Christians overcame the Muslim Turks in the Battle of Lepanto. The victory was attributed to Mary, and Pius V encouraged praying the rosary. After six years as pope, he died of a painful disease.

Themes: Holiness, self-denial, Mary's intercession

MAY

288 MAY 1
Joseph the Worker

The Church has made today a day to think about work by celebrating a feast in honor of St. Joseph. Joseph, the legal father of Jesus, was a carpenter who made things out of wood and stone. No doubt he taught Jesus this line of work. As Christians we respect all workers and ask God to bless them. We gather here to carry out our most noble work, the work of worshiping God in the Eucharist.

Universal Prayer
The response is *"Lord, hear our prayer."*

That the Church may safeguard everyone's right to work and to receive just payment, we pray to the Lord.

That government and business leaders may act with concern for the rights of workers, we pray to the Lord.

That those who are unemployed may find a job, we pray to the Lord.

That there may be fairness in workplaces, we pray to the Lord.

That we may work hard and cheerfully at the tasks we are called to do, we pray to the Lord.

Special Features
- As part of the homily or as a communion reflection, show slides of people doing various types of work.
- Display a banner or poster about St. Joseph the Worker.
- Give the children a copy of the Morning Offering in which we offer God our works.
- Before or after Mass hold a blessing of tools or other equipment for work. Rites for this are found in the *Book of Blessings.*

Songs
Holy Patron, Thee Saluting; Joseph of Nazareth; Look Down to Us, Saint Joseph; St. Joseph, Great Protector

Homily Ideas
Visual: A hammer

Show a hammer and comment that everyone has work to do. Even God worked for six days creating the universe. Work is good. Ask the children why work is good (it contributes to the common good, improves the world, keeps us busy, and provides money for needs).

. . .

Explain that St. Joseph worked as a carpenter to support Mary and Jesus. He was not a wealthy man who did not need to work. Like other types of manual labor, carpentry is hard work, especially on hot days. A carpenter has to be strong, smart, and exact. Ask why Joseph probably liked being a carpenter. (It is satisfying to make things out of wood and stone. What he made was useful to others in the town. He was able to afford food and clothing for his family.)

. . .

Mention that Jesus worked too. He probably helped Joseph in the carpenter shop and then took over the business when Joseph died. People referred to Jesus as the son of the carpenter. Jesus also worked as a teacher and a healer. He walked from town to town in all kinds of weather doing the work of preaching and teaching that God gave him.

. . .

Ask the children to name other occupations, such as the jobs their parents do. Then ask them what their own job is (to be a student). Ask them what is hard about being a student.

. . .

Tell the children that all work is good and all workers deserve to be respected. Ask them who is more important, a lawyer or a mail carrier? a doctor or a sanitation engineer? Conclude that jobs are different but all are important.

. . .

Explain that work not only serves other people but serves God. We can offer what we do as a gift to God. One way to do this is by praying the Morning Offering. Another way is to mentally place all our works with the hosts at Mass and to offer them to God. Encourage the children to always do their best work so that they have a good gift to offer God.

. . .

Present a person the children know as a model of a good worker.

. . .

Quote sayings about work: "Idleness is the devil's workshop" or "The one who doesn't work, shouldn't eat."

289 MAY 2
Athanasius,
Bishop, Doctor of the Church (MEMORIAL)

Athanasius was born in Alexandria in Egypt in 295. He spent four years in the desert where he met St. Anthony the Hermit. Then he became a priest. At this time the heresy of Arianism arose, which held that Jesus was not God. Athanasius became bishop of Alexandria, and for forty-five years he battled Arianism. Five times he was accused of crimes and exiled. In the face of these hardships and humiliations, he courageously wrote much in defense of the truths of the faith. Throughout the conflicts, Athanasius treated his enemies with meekness and charity.

Themes: Jesus' divinity, our faith, response to enemies

290 MAY 3
Philip and James, *Apostles* (FEAST)

Philip was the apostle who brought his friend Nathanael to Jesus and then brought some Greek Gentiles to Jesus. James, the son of Alpheus, is called James the Less. This might be because he was shorter or younger than the other apostle James. James is thought to have been the first bishop of Jerusalem. Both Philip and James were martyred.

Themes: Evangelizing, suffering for Christ

291 MAY 12
Nereus and Achilleus, *Martyrs*

Nereus and Achilleus were among the first martyrs to be venerated as saints. Possibly they died in the second century. It is thought that they were Roman soldiers who, after they were baptized, left the Roman army. They were captured and put to death. A basilica stands over their tombs in Rome. One of the early popes, St. Damasus, wrote the epitaph for their tombstone. The epitaph says that faith caused Nereus and Achilleus to "throw away their shields, their armor, and their bloodstained javelins." It continues, "Confessing the faith of Christ, they rejoice to bear testimony to its triumph. Learn now from the words of Damasus what great things the glory of Christ can accomplish."

Themes: Peace, faith

292 also MAY 12
Pancras, *Martyr*

Pancras was no more than fourteen years old when he was martyred in Rome, probably in the early fourth century. It is said that he was orphaned as a young child. His uncle took him to Rome, where they both became Christians. A church stands over the tomb of St. Pancras in Rome. St. Augustine of Canterbury, a missionary to England, named the first church there after him.

Themes: What children can do for Christ, valuing the faith

292A MAY 13
Our Lady of Fatima

On this day in Fatima, Portugal, in 1917, Our Lady appeared to three shepherd children who were herding sheep. They were Lucia dos Santos and her cousins Jacinta and Francesco Marto. This was the first of six monthly visits. Mary encouraged the children to do penance, sacrifice for sinners, and pray the rosary every day. She said that practicing these things would bring about peace. Mary promised that a miracle would occur at her last visit. A huge crowd assembled to watch then and saw the sun do extraordinary things. After Pope John Paul II was shot on May 13, he gave Mary of Fatima the credit for saving his life.

Themes: Mary, the rosary, penance

293 MAY 14
Matthias, *Apostle* (FEAST)

Matthias was the man chosen to replace Judas as one of the twelve apostles. In the Acts of the Apostles we learn how this happened. A large group of disciples were gathered. Peter told them how Judas died. He explained that another man was to take his place. This should be someone who followed Jesus from his baptism to his ascension. Two good men were proposed: Joseph the Just and Matthias. The apostles prayed to God, who knows

all hearts, and then cast lots. The lots indicated that Matthias was the correct choice. So Matthias became a member of the group who witnessed to the world the Good News about Jesus.

Special Feature
- Have children take parts for the first reading which tells about St. Matthias being chosen to replace the apostle Judas.

294 MAY 15
Isidore the Farmer, *Married Man*

St. Isidore was a farmer in Spain who lived from 1070 to 1130. All his life he worked the land for the same rich landowner. His wife, Maria, is also honored as a saint. Their only child died as a young boy. Every morning Isidore went to church. As he worked hard in the fields, he prayed. He and Maria provided food for the poor, sometimes miraculously. St. Isidore is honored in Spain and in rural parts of the United States. He is the patron of the National Catholic Rural Life Conference.

Themes: Respect for manual labor, caring for the earth, feeding the hungry

295 MAY 18
John I, *Pope, Martyr*

Pope John I was born in Italy. He became pope in 523 when the Arian heresy, which held that Jesus was not God, was still causing trouble. Justin, the Eastern emperor in Constantinople, was persecuting the Arians there. Theodoric, the Western emperor who was an Arian, sent Pope John to Constantinople to persuade Justin to stop his persecutions. John was warmly received and was successful in his mission, but Theodoric distrusted John's relationship with Justin. When Pope John returned, Theodoric had him imprisoned. John died in prison, probably of starvation. He is honored as a martyr.

Themes: The pope, the divinity of Christ, unjust suffering

296 MAY 20
Bernardine of Siena,
Presbyter, Religious, Missionary

Bernardine was born in Italy in 1380 to a noble family. Because his parents died when he was young, he was raised by his aunt. Bernardine became a Franciscan and was ordained. In 1419 Bernardine began traveling through Italy by foot or by donkey, preaching the loving mercy of God. He was a remarkable preacher. He used IHS as a symbol of his message. These are letters from the Greek word for Jesus. Bernardine spread devotion to the holy name of Jesus. He also wrote works on theology. When Bernardine became head of his order, it grew from thirty to four thousand members. He preached and traveled even when he was dying.

Themes: The name of Jesus, salvation

296A MAY 21
Christopher Magallanes, *Priest, Martyr,*
and His Companions, *Martyrs*

Christopher was born in Mexico in 1869. He was the son of farmers. As a parish priest, Christopher helped found schools and a carpentry shop and plan a dam. He began a mission among the native people and established a seminary in his parish. Although Fr. Christopher preached against armed rebellion, he was falsely accused of supporting the Cristero Rebellion. He was arrested on the way to celebrate Mass and was executed without a trial.

On this day we remember him and all others who were martyred during the Mexican Cristero War.

Themes: Courage, faithfulness, evangelization

296B MAY 22
Rita of Cascia, *Religious*

Rita had several roles in life. She was born in Italy in 1381. Although she wished to enter the convent, through an arranged marriage she became the wife of a mean and immoral man. Her patience and kindness changed him. After eighteen years of marriage, Rita became a widow when her husband was murdered. Her two sons wanted revenge, but Rita prayed and soon they too had a change of heart. Rita became an Augustinian Sister. One day she prayed to share Christ's suffering. A thorn from a statue of the crucified Christ fell on her forehead and created a miraculous wound that did not heal. Rita is the patron of impossible cases.

Themes: Perseverance, prayer

297 MAY 25
Bede the Venerable,
Presbyter, Religious, Doctor of the Church

St. Bede, the patron of historians, lived in England from 672 to 735. He was a Benedictine monk who was ordained at the age of twenty-nine. He spent his life in the monastery teaching and writing. His book *Ecclesiastical History of the English People* earned him the title "the Father of English History." During his lifetime people called him venerable out of respect for his work. Thirty of the forty-five books Bede wrote are about Scripture. He died singing the Glory Be.

Themes: The importance of studying, Scripture

298 also MAY 25
Gregory VII, *Pope, Religious*

Gregory was born in the early part of the eleventh century. When Gregory was a young Benedictine monk named Hildebrand, the pope, who had been his teacher, called him to Rome to be his advisor. Hildebrand also advised the next five popes, helping to reform the Church. Elected pope himself in 1073, Gregory fought against the practice of the king or emperor appointing bishops and other church ministers. His chief opponent was the German emperor, Henry IV, whom he once excommunicated, or declared cut off from the Church. With the support of other rulers, Gregory had Henry ask for forgiveness. In the end, however, Henry forced Gregory to go into exile from Rome to Salerno, where the pope died.

Themes: Serving the Church, the pope

299 also MAY 25
Mary Magdalene de' Pazzi, *Virgin, Religious*

Catherine de' Pazzi was born in Italy in 1566. Although her family was quite wealthy, she surprised people by entering the Carmelites when she was sixteen. Her religious name was Mary Magdalene. As a nun, she led a life of prayer and penance. She had the special gift of ecstasy or union with God. She renewed her order and wrote to bishops and the pope to encourage them to reform the Church. For three years before her death she suffered much. She not only had a severe illness but could find no comfort in prayer. Life looked terrible to her, and she experienced temptations. Throughout this difficult time, she remained cheerful and kind to all.

Themes: Prayer, offering up sufferings

300 MAY 26
Philip Neri, *Presbyter* (MEMORIAL)

St. Philip Neri is remembered for his sense of humor as well as his holiness. He was born in Florence in 1515. He went to Rome where he attended a university and tutored two boys. While praying in the catacombs, he had a mystical experience that changed his life. He began to minister to the young men of Rome. For thirteen years he encouraged them to pray and do good works. They enjoyed being with him doing works of mercy. Eventually he formed these men into a community called the Oratorians whose motto is "Love alone." Philip gave spiritual advice to others, including many saints, popes, cardinals, and bishops. He was humble and simple. When people said he was a saint, he shaved off half his beard. He wore old clothes, big white shoes, and a hat cocked to the side.

Themes: Joy, good works, using your gifts for Christ

301 MAY 27
Augustine of Canterbury,
Bishop, Religious, Missionary

In 596, Pope Gregory the Great sent thirty Roman monks under the leadership of Augustine to England as missionaries. Hearing of the dangerous English Channel and fierce tribes in England, the monks persuaded Augustine to return to Rome and ask if they could give up the journey. The pope encouraged them to go and continued to give advice to Augustine through letters. Augustine was met and helped by Ethelbert, the ruler of Kent who was married to a Christian from Paris. In time Ethelbert and others in England were baptized. Augustine became the first Archbishop of Canterbury.

Themes: Courage, witness to the faith, evangelizing

302 MAY 31
The Visit of the Virgin Mary to Elizabeth
(FEAST)

At the Annunciation the Angel Gabriel told Mary that her relative Elizabeth was pregnant. After Mary agreed to be the mother of Jesus, she went in a hurry to visit and help Elizabeth. Today we recall and celebrate the time Mary, carrying Christ within her, brought him to Elizabeth. At this Eucharist Christ will come to us, too. May we take him with us to others.

Universal Prayer

The response is *"Lord, hear our prayer."*

That the Church may look to Mary as a model of Christian love, we pray to the Lord.

That world leaders may respond to those in need with concern and care, we pray to the Lord.

That women who are pregnant may give birth to their babies safely, we pray to the Lord.

That we may bring Christ to the world by loving acts, as Mary did, we pray to the Lord.

Special Features

- As part of the homily have a few students prepared to demonstrate how they can help others.
- Have a group of students do interpretive dance to a song about Mary at the presentation of gifts or after communion.
- Distribute small towels or packs of moisturized paper towels as a reminder to serve others.
- Pray the Magnificat after communion.

Songs

The Good News of God's Salvation; Holy Is His Name; Immaculate Mary; Mary's Joy; Mary's Song; My Soul Rejoices; Service; Sing of Mary; The Visit

Homily Ideas
Visual: A towel

Show a towel, and state that a towel has been a symbol of service ever since Jesus washed the feet of his disciples at the Last Supper. His mother Mary probably taught him to be kind as she teaches us. Right after she learned she was going to be God's mother, Mary went out on an errand of mercy. She could have stayed at home, taking care of herself and the baby within her. Instead, she made the long, hot, dusty journey to another town to help her relative Elizabeth. She had no car but had to walk or ride a donkey.

. . . .

Explain that Elizabeth had never had children and now she was too old. God, however, did the impossible and let her become pregnant. Her son would be John the Baptist, the one who would prepare people to accept Jesus as the savior.

. . . .

Ask the children what kind of things Mary might have done to help Elizabeth and her husband, Zechariah (cooked, cleaned, talked to them, gotten water from the well for them). Mention that she stayed with them three months and then made the long journey home again.

. . . .

Point out that Mary is the perfect Christian. She shows the love and all the virtues that Scripture tells us to practice. As a result God loves her very much.

. . . .

Recall that in the gospel the Holy Spirit let Elizabeth know that Mary was the Mother of God. Elizabeth called Mary and her child blessed. We repeat Elizabeth's words each time we pray the Hail Mary: "Blessed are you, and blessed is the fruit of your womb."

. . . .

Tell the children that Mary's response to Elizabeth's greeting was a beautiful song of praise to God. In this song Mary thanked God for doing such great things for her, and she foretold that everyone would call her blessed. She also proclaimed that God helps the chosen people, humble people, and the poor. Comment that the Church prays this song of Mary, called the Magnificat, each day in Evening Prayer.

. . .

Ask the children to suggest practical ways they could imitate their mother Mary's selfless love, or have groups of children demonstrate such ways.

303 SATURDAY FOLLOWING THE SECOND SUNDAY AFTER PENTECOST
The Immaculate Heart of Mary

At the beginning of the Second World War, Pope Pius XII consecrated the world to the Immaculate Heart of Mary. Mary's heart is a sorrowful heart. As Simeon foretold, it was pierced by a sword of grief. (Pious tradition says seven swords for the seven sorrows of Mary; see September 15). Her heart is a mother's heart. It is filled with love for Jesus and all her children. Mary's heart is an immaculate heart. The Angel Gabriel called her "full of grace" because Mary was pure and sinless. Her heart and her life were fixed on God and God's will. In the story of the finding of Jesus in the Temple, Scripture remarks that Mary pondered all these things in her heart. Today we ponder the mysteries related to Mary, the Mother of God.

Themes: Devotion to Mary, sinlessness, sorrows of Mary

JUNE

304 JUNE 1
Justin, *Martyr* (MEMORIAL)

Justin was born in Samaria around the year 100 and studied different philosophies in various cities. At the age of thirty, after reading the books of the Old Testament prophets, he became a Christian. In Rome he began a school of Christian philosophy that had public debates. He also wrote books defending and explaining Christian beliefs and practices. About the year 165, during the persecution carried out under the Emperor Marcus Aurelius, Justin was arrested for being a Christian. Because this committed layman refused to deny his faith in Jesus, he was beheaded.

Themes: Loyalty to Christ, learning about the faith

305 JUNE 2
Marcellinus and Peter, *Martyrs*

These two saints lived about the year 300. We know about them from Pope Damasus, who learned about them from their executioner. Peter was a Christian exorcist who was in prison for his faith. (An exorcist has power to drive out evil spirits.) While in prison, Peter converted the jailer and his family. He asked Marcellinus, a priest who probably lived in Rome, to baptize the family. The governor learned of the baptisms and ordered Peter and Marcellinus to offer incense to false gods. When they refused, he had them tortured and killed. Some years later the Emperor Constantine had a basilica built over their tombs. An inscription of Pope Damasus said that the two men showed an inspiring peace in the face of death.

Themes: The value of faith, courage in doing what is right, evangelization

306 JUNE 3
Charles Lwanga, *Catechist, Martyr,* and His Companions, *Martyrs* (MEMORIAL)

Charles Lwanga and his twenty-one companions are the first martyrs from Uganda to be canonized. In the late 1800s King Mwanga began persecuting Christians. Charles was a page in the royal court under Mkasa, who was the master of the pages and a Christian. When Mkasa was killed for criticizing the king's immoral acts, Charles was baptized on the same day. He replaced Mkasa as head of the pages and encouraged them not to take part in the king's immoral acts. The enraged king separated out the Christian pages and sentenced them to death. They prayed and sang at their deaths. Most of them were under the age of twenty-five.

Themes: Resisting evil, faith in Christ

307 JUNE 5
Boniface, *Bishop, Religious, Missionary, Martyr* (MEMORIAL)

Boniface was born in England and baptized Winfrid. He became a Benedictine and went as a missionary to Frisia, which is now Holland. Because a war stopped his work there, in 716 he asked the pope where he could serve. The pope sent him to eastern Germany where Catholic beliefs had become mixed with pagan beliefs. In time the pope made him a bishop. For nearly thirty-five years, Boniface, the Apostle of Germany, preached, taught, and built monasteries and convents. In his old age, Boniface returned to Frisia. One day as he was about to confirm a group of converts, pagan natives murdered him and about fifty of the converts.

Themes: Zeal for the faith, teaching the faith

308 JUNE 6
Norbert, *Bishop, Religious Founder*

St. Norbert was born in Germany about 1080. He was the emperor's cousin and had everything he wanted. One day as he was riding in the woods, lightning scared his horse. It reared up and Norbert fell off. When he came to, he realized he should change his empty life and do good. He sold his property and became a priest. He started monasteries in pagan places and usually opened a hospice near each one for the sick, travelers, and pilgrims. Norbert founded the Premonstratensian order (or Norbertines) named for Premontre, France, where it began. Its mission was to help make priests holy. Norbert became an archbishop and worked hard to stop heresies and to encourage loyalty to the pope.

Themes: Priests, priorities in life

309 JUNE 9
Ephrem of Syria, *Deacon, Doctor of the Church*

Ephrem was born around 306 into a Christian family in a country that is now Turkey. He became a deacon and a teacher of theology. He did not think he was good enough to be a priest, but he became a monk. For a time he lived alone in a cave. Many people came to him for help with their problems. He wrote many books. He also wrote religious poems and hymns for the liturgy, sometimes putting words about the Catholic faith to popular melodies. For this reason St. Ephrem is called "harp of the Holy Spirit." A number of his talks and hymns are about the Mother of God.

Themes: Vocations, hymns, Mary

310 JUNE 11
Barnabas, *Apostle* (MEMORIAL)

Barnabas lived in the first century. He was from Cyprus. When he became a Christian, his name was changed from Joseph to Barnabas, which means "son of encouragement." Barnabas sold his property and shared the money with the community in Jerusalem. After Paul was converted, Barnabas introduced him to the apostles and defended him. For a time Barnabas and Paul were leaders of the Church at Antioch. Then they went to Cyprus and Lystra as missionaries. According to tradition, Barnabas was stoned to death, clasping a copy of the Gospel of St. Matthew.

Themes: Community, missionary work

311 JUNE 13
Anthony of Padua, *Presbyter, Religious, Doctor of the Church* (MEMORIAL)

St. Anthony was born in Portugal in 1195 and was baptized Ferdinand. He was an Augustinian priest until five Franciscans were martyred in Morocco. Their lives inspired him to be like them. He joined the Franciscans, took the name Anthony, and sailed to Morocco. When he became ill, he tried to return to Portugal, but a storm sent his boat to Sicily. While in Italy, Anthony attended a meeting of Franciscans in Assisi. He lived as a hermit, praying and studying. One day at a special Mass no one was assigned to preach. Anthony was called on, and his great gift of preaching and his outstanding knowledge of the Bible were discovered. He became a famous preacher and teacher in Italy, France, and Belgium and converted many heretics. St. Anthony also pleaded for the poor and did works of mercy. He died at age thirty-six. He is the popular patron of lost things.

Themes: Discerning a vocation, helping the poor, sacred Scripture

312 JUNE 19
Romuald, *Abbot, Religious Founder*

St. Romuald was born in Italy around 950. When his father, a duke, killed a relative over an argument about money, Romuald entered a Benedictine monastery to do penance for his father's crime. After three years his father became a monk. Romuald left the monastery because it was not strict enough. For many years Romuald lived as a hermit, fasting and praying. Then for thirty years he founded monasteries and hermitages throughout Italy. He founded the order of the Hermit Camaldolese Benedictines. Hoping to be a martyr, he traveled to Hungary, but he became ill and returned to a hermit's life in Italy. Once a nobleman falsely accused Romuald of a serious crime, and the monks punished him for six months.

Themes: Silence, solitude, prayer, suffering

313 JUNE 21
Aloysius Gonzaga, *Religious* (MEMORIAL)

St. Aloysius is the patron of youth. He was born in Italy in 1568 to a noble Spanish family. His father wanted him to be a military leader or political figure and sent him to military camp at the age of five. Aloysius, however, made up his mind to be a saint. He prayed long hours and fasted. When he was in his early teens, Aloysius became a page in the courts of Italy and, later, Spain. After reading the lives of Jesuit missionaries, he gave his share of his inheritance to his brother and joined the Jesuits. During a serious epidemic, Aloysius cared for the sick in a hospital and became ill. He died when he was only twenty-three.

Themes: Holiness for youth, prayer, penance, vocation

314 JUNE 22
Paulinus of Nola, *Bishop*

Paulinus was born in France in the middle of the fourth century. He was a successful lawyer and governor. He and his wife, a rich Spanish woman, became Christians. They had a son who died after only eight days. The couple gave their wealth to the poor and moved to Nola to live a simple life. The people in the city wanted Paulinus to be a priest. He was ordained and for twenty years was bishop of Nola. The first floor of his house was for the poor. On the second floor he and a few other men lived as monks. His wife took care of the household. Paulinus wrote letters to other saints. He also composed poems.

Themes: The simple life, helping the poor

315 also JUNE 22
John Fisher, *Bishop, Martyr*, and
Thomas More, *Married Man, Martyr*

St. John Fisher was born in 1469. As bishop of Rochester in England he led a life of self-denial and frequently visited his people. Thomas More, born in 1477, was a lawyer and the father of four children. He became the chancellor of England and a friend to King Henry VIII. To get approval for his divorce King Henry declared himself head of the Church in England. Thomas More refused to accept this decree. John Fisher was the only bishop in England who stood firm against it. Both men were imprisoned in the Tower of London. Thomas More was there for more than a year. In prison Bishop Fisher was made a cardinal. The King had both men beheaded on the charge of treason.

Themes: Loyalty to the Church, suffering for what is right

316 JUNE 24
The Birth of John the Baptist (SOLEMNITY)

John the Baptist was called to prepare the way for Christ. He led people to obey God and do what is right. At our baptism we, too, were called to be prophets and act and speak for God. Let us pray at this Eucharist to have the wisdom and courage to carry out this role of a Christian.

Universal Prayer
The response is *"Lord, hear our prayer."*

That the Church may prepare the world for the second coming of Christ, let us pray to the Lord.

That government leaders may do what is right and lead others to do what is right, let us pray to the Lord.

That people who are God's prophets today may be listened to, let us pray to the Lord.

That we may respond to God's call to be prophets and speak up for what is right, let us pray to the Lord.

Special Features
- Have incense burning at a display that has baptismal articles, such as a shell, a candle, and a glass pitcher of water.
- Invite the children to renew their baptismal promises after the homily.

Songs
Canticle of Zachary; Every Valley; On Jordan's Bank; Prepare the Way; A Voice Cries Out

Homily Ideas
Visual: A business card

Show a business card and tell the children that if John the Baptist had a business card it would read, "John the Baptizer, Prophet," and his address would be the Judean desert and along the Jordan River. John's role was to get people ready for Jesus the Savior.

. . .

Comment that most people discover what they will be as they grow into adulthood. John's life work was decided even before John existed. While his father Zechariah, who was a priest, was burning incense in the Temple, the Angel Gabriel came to him and told him he would have a son who would be a prophet. Gabriel told him to name the boy John. As a prophet John would lead people back to God.

. . .

Tell the children that the announcement of John's birth can be compared to the announcement of Jesus' birth. Gabriel also appeared to Mary and told her that she would have a son and what his name would be. Both births were miraculous, for Elizabeth was too old to have a child and Mary was an unmarried virgin. Point out that John and Jesus were related, and John was six months older than Jesus.

. . .

Explain that a prophet is someone who speaks for God. A prophet tells people what God wants them to do. Sometimes this means pointing out their sins and as a result making them angry.

. . .

Remind the children that in the first reading they heard the story of the call of Jeremiah. When God called him to be a prophet, Jeremiah argued that he was too young. God promised to be with him, and Jeremiah became one of the most important prophets, but he suffered much from people who didn't want to hear his message.

. . .

Mention that Jesus once said that there was no man greater than John the Baptist. John called people to repent and baptized them as a sign of their willingness to change their lives. He baptized Jesus when it was time for Jesus to begin his ministry. Eventually because John was a good and courageous prophet, he was killed by King Herod's command.

. . .

Tell the children that when they were baptized they were called to share Jesus' role of being a prophet. Christians are to speak up for what is right. They are to fight injustice and help other people live by God's law. Being a prophet is not an easy or comfortable mission. Ask the children how they can be prophets at their age (by not going along with others who are doing wrong, by helping their friends decide to do the right thing).

. . .

Tell about a person who has acted as a prophet: someone in the recent news, a famous prophet like Archbishop Oscar Romero, Cesar Chavez, and Dorothy Day, or a saint like Thomas More, Dominic, Teresa of Jesus, or Catherine of Siena.

---

317 JUNE 27
Cyril of Alexandria, *Bishop, Doctor of the Church*

St. Cyril was born around the year 370 in Alexandria, Egypt. He succeeded his uncle as archbishop of Alexandria. At first he was severe toward heretics and others who caused trouble, but he grew in compassion. The Nestorian heresy taught that Mary was not the Mother of God. Cyril is most known for representing the pope at the Council of Ephesus, which declared that Mary was the Mother of God. Some bishops had Cyril imprisoned for holding to this truth. He was saved by three representatives of the pope. Cyril fought bravely against the heresy and wrote many works about the Catholic faith.

Themes: The Mother of God, upholding what is right

318 JUNE 28
Irenaeus, Bishop, *Martyr* (MEMORIAL)

Irenaeus was born around 130 in Smyrna, a town in what is now Turkey. He was a disciple of his bishop, Polycarp, who had been taught by the apostle John. Irenaeus went to France, was ordained in Lyons, and became its bishop. He fought against the heresy of Gnosticism, which held that only people who had special knowledge could have eternal life. True to his name, which means "peace," Irenaeus kept peace between the pope and a group of Eastern Christians when they disagreed about the date Easter should be celebrated. Irenaeus was one of the most important writers in the early Church. It is believed that he was martyred.

Themes: The faith, peace, eternal life

319 JUNE 29
Peter and Paul, *Apostles* (SOLEMNITY)

St. Peter and St. Paul are the two giants of our Church who guided its beginning and growth. Both men were devoted to Jesus Christ. Their love for him drove them to spread the Good News about him throughout the known world. We honor Peter and Paul today and pray that God will bless the Church for which they gave their lives. May we imitate their faith and love.

Universal Prayer
The response is *"Lord, hear our prayer."*

For the Church, that its missionary spirit may grow, let us pray to the Lord.

For our Holy Father, bishops, priests, and religious, that their enthusiasm for the Lord may inspire others, let us pray to the Lord.

For civic leaders and heads of organizations, that they may have the gifts they need to carry out their responsibilities, let us pray to the Lord.

For those who are suffering for their faith today, that they may have courage and be comforted by God, let us pray to the Lord.

For ourselves, that we may always try to work for the Church, let us pray to the Lord.

Special Features
- Display statues or pictures of St. Peter and St. Paul in church.
- Have children take parts for the gospel.

Songs
Center of My Life; Do You Really Love Me?; Go; Jesus the Lord; Lord, to Whom Shall We Go?; Paul's Prayer

Homily Ideas
Visual: A pair of scissors

Show the scissors and point out that two blades are needed in order to make scissors. Explain that the Church celebrates St. Peter and St. Paul on the same day because they are like the two blades of scissors. Each man played an important role in the early Church that helped to make it what it is today.

• • •

Tell the children that Peter and Paul were both apostles. Peter was one of the twelve who were chosen by Christ to lead the Church. He was one of the favored three apostles, and the one Christ chose to be the visible head of the Church. Today's gospel told the story of Jesus declaring that he would build his Church on Peter. As an apostle, Peter lived and worked with Jesus for about three years, and then he witnessed the risen Lord. On the other hand, Paul was not a follower of Christ until after the resurrection. He was a Jewish man traveling to arrest Christians when Christ spoke to him. From that day on Paul was an apostle. He is most known for leading the Church to accept Gentiles, or non-Jewish people, as members. Paul began many churches and wrote letters that are now part of our Bible.

. . . .

Point out the love Peter and Paul had for Jesus. Peter left his family and work to follow Jesus. He had a dangerous job starting the Christian Church. He was put in prison for it, as the first reading shows. Paul had many sufferings. He made his Jewish friends angry by becoming a Christian, and Jewish Christians who had been hunted by him didn't trust him. At times Paul was whipped, imprisoned, and chased out of town. Both men risked these things because they believed so strongly in Jesus and his teachings. In the end Peter and Paul were martyred. Peter was crucified upside down, and Paul was beheaded.

. . . .

Comment that God gave his two apostles strength and courage. Sometimes God worked miracles to get them out of trouble. God's promise of eternal life inspired them not to give up.

. . . .

Ask the children to tell about people they know who do what God wants even when it is difficult. Talk about some people who are active in the Church today, famous people as well as people the children may know.

. . . .

Point out to the children that if they are really excited about their faith in Jesus, they, too, will want to share it with others.

329 JUNE 30
First Martyrs of Rome

Many Christians were brutally slain in the first persecution of Rome. The insane emperor Nero had them killed as scapegoats after the burning of Rome in 64. The historian Tacitus and St. Clement of Rome wrote the horrible story of the night when these nameless martyrs were put into animal skins and hunted in the imperial parks.

Themes: The cost of faith, witnessing today

JULY

321 JULY 1
Blessed Junípero Serra,
Presbyter, Religious, Missionary

Junípero Serra was born in 1713, the son of a farmer in Spain. He joined the Franciscans and became a priest and a teacher. His dream of being a missionary came true when he sailed for Mexico. For eight years he worked with the Pame Indians. Then he became a traveling missioner. In 1769 when he was fifty-six and had an injured leg because of an insect bite, Junípero traveled 300 miles to San Diego. There he founded the first of nineteen missions he planned. Junípero baptized about 6,000 Native Americans. He fought for the rights of the Indians when civil authorities mistreated them. Nine of the twenty-one Franciscan missions along the Pacific coast were established by Junípero. Many large cities in California, such as San Francisco, Santa Barbara, and San Diego, originated with these missions.

Themes: Missionary work, the importance of faith

322 JULY 3
Thomas, *Apostle* (FEAST)

Thomas was one of the twelve apostles who saw the resurrected Christ. He was probably a fisherman from Galilee. He is most known for doubting that the other apostles had seen Jesus on Easter Sunday evening. It is believed that Thomas became a missionary in India, where he was probably martyred. He is the patron of India.

Themes: Faith, following Christ

Special Features
- Sing We Walk by Faith, In Steadfast Faith, or Look Beyond.
- As part of the homily or after the homily have someone prepared to read their personal creed.

323 JULY 4
Elizabeth of Portugal,
Married Woman

Elizabeth, a princess of Aragon in Spain, was named for her aunt, St. Elizabeth of Hungary. She married the king of Portugal when she was twelve and had two sons. The king was not faithful to her, but she was devoted to him. As queen, she showed much love for the poor and built a hospital, an orphanage, and a shelter for poor travelers. She also worked hard to settle conflicts between her family members, including her husband and their only son. She even rode into battle to force the rulers to stop fighting. After her husband died, Elizabeth distributed her property to the poor and became a Third Order Franciscan. After making peace between her son and his son-in-law, she died in 1336.

Themes: Working for peace, serving the poor

325 JULY 5
Anthony Mary Zaccaria,
Presbyter, Religious Founder

St. Anthony was born in Italy in 1502. He became a doctor and then decided to become a priest. He founded a congregation of priests called Bamabites who preached in churches and on street comers and gave parish missions. During the Protestant Reformation, Anthony and his men worked hard to bring halfhearted Catholics back to the faith. He promoted the frequent reception of Holy Communion.

Themes: Zeal for the faith, Holy Communion

326 JULY 6
Maria Goretti, *Virgin, Martyr*

Maria Goretti was only twelve when she was stabbed to death for refusing to commit a sexual sin. She was born in Italy in 1890. Her family was poor but rich in faith. One day while Maria was in the house alone mending clothes, eighteen-year-old Alessandro, whose family lived with the Gorettis, tried to force her to sin. Maria lived for a day after the attack and forgave him. After twenty-seven years in prison, Alessandro was released and entered a monastery to do penance.

Themes: Purity, forgiveness, repentance

326A JULY 9
Augustine Zhao Rong, *Priest, Martyr,*
and His Companions, *Martyrs*

Augustine was the first native Chinese priest to be martyred. He lived in an era when the Church was persecuted in China. Augustine was a Chinese soldier who accompanied a bishop on his journey to Beijing to be martyred. Impressed by the bishop's patience, Augustine became a Christian. Five years later he was ordained a diocesan priest. In 1815, Augustine died in prison in Beijing after being tortured. Today we remember the 120 people who were martyred in China between 1648 and 1930.

Themes: Faith, courage

327 JULY 11
Benedict, *Abbot, Religious Founder*

St. Benedict was born in Italy about 480. Disgusted with the wild student life in Rome, he lived as a hermit in a cave for three years. Other men who were attracted to his holiness wanted to join him, so Benedict founded a monastery at Monte Cassino. This was the first of twelve monasteries, which were centers of learning. Because Benedict's rule was adopted throughout Europe, he is called the patriarch of Western monasticism. His monks live by the motto "*Ora et labora,*" which means "Pray and work." They live a common life centered around liturgical prayer. The name Benedict comes from the word "blessed."

Themes: Holiness, monks today, the liturgy

328 JULY 13
Henry, *Married Man*

St. Henry was born in 973, the son of the duke of Bavaria. He succeeded his father as duke and then became emperor of the Holy Roman Empire. He married St. Kunegunda, who joined the Benedictines after his death. Henry was a remarkable ruler. He built monasteries, worked to reform the Church, helped the poor, and fought rulers who tried to gain more power unjustly. He longed to be a monk, not an emperor, and even pledged obedience to an abbot.

Themes: Fulfilling responsibilities, holiness

329 JULY 14
Kateri Tekakwitha, *Virgin* (MEMORIAL)

Kateri Tekakwitha was a Mohawk Indian born in 1656 in what is now Auriesville, New York. Ten years earlier St. Isaac Jogues and his companions had been martyred there. Kateri's parents and brother died of smallpox when she was four. The disease left her face scarred and her eyes weak. A friend of her mother named Anastasia raised her and told her about the Christian God. When Anastasia left to join the Christians in Canada, Kateri's uncle, a Mohawk chief, adopted Kateri. Because Kateri wanted to love the Great Spirit alone, she refused to be married A missionary taught her more about God, and she was baptized. Because she followed Catholic practices, the others tormented her for two years. Then Kateri escaped to Canada where she freely lived a Christian life, praying and doing penance until she died at the age of twenty-four.

Themes: Valuing our faith, missionary work

330 JULY 15
Bonaventure, *Bishop, Religious, Doctor of the Church* (MEMORIAL)

St. Bonaventure was born in Italy around 1218 and joined the Franciscans. He became a professor of theology at the University of Paris, where he became friends with St. Thomas Aquinas. He wrote many books. His spiritual life was centered on the passion and death of Jesus. For seventeen years Bonaventure was minister general of the Franciscan order. Against his wish, he was made bishop and then a cardinal. He died suddenly at the Council of Lyons, which he had helped to prepare. He was greatly loved by many people.

Themes: Using our gifts, Jesus' passion and death

331 JULY 16
Our Lady of Mount Carmel

Mount Carmel is a beautiful, sacred mountain in Israel where the prophet Elijah held a contest with the pagan prophets of Baal. During the Crusades, Christian hermits lived on the mountain. They formed the Order of Carmel, or Carmelites, and dedicated themselves to Mary, who had lived nearby in Nazareth. They wear a scapular (a long piece of cloth that covers the front and the back) to show dedication to Mary.

Themes: Mountains as sacred places, Mary, scapular

331A JULY 20
Apollinaris, *Bishop, Martyr*

Apollinaris was one of the first martyrs and perhaps a disciple of St. Peter. As bishop of Ravenna in Italy, Apollinaris had a reputation as a preacher and miracle worker. This angered the priests of idols, and often he was exiled, beaten, tortured, and imprisoned. After Apollinaris escaped from prison, guards caught him and beat him badly. Christians carried him away, and he died a week later.

Themes: Zeal for the faith, patience in suffering

332 JULY 21
Lawrence of Brindisi,
Presbyter, Religious, Doctor of the Church

St. Lawrence was born in Italy in 1559 and named Julius Caesar. He joined the Capuchin Franciscans at the age of sixteen and was ordained. He could speak eight languages. This helped him in his roles of minister general of his community, missionary, and diplomat. He worked hard to preach the faith to a world shaken by the Protestant Reformation. Fifteen volumes of his writings explaining the faith

still exist. Lawrence was devoted to the Blessed Virgin and known for his goodness and simplicity.

Themes: Learning the faith, devotion to Mary

333 JULY 22
Mary Magdalene,
Disciple of the Lord (MEMORIAL)

Mary Magdalene was a disciple of Christ. She was one of those who assisted and supported Christ and the apostles as they preached the Good News. She was present at the foot of the cross. According to Mark's gospel, Mary Magdalene was the first to see the risen Lord. This made her the apostle to the apostles. In the past Mary has been identified with the sinful woman in the gospels and consequently a model of sorrow for sin, but there is no basis for this.

Themes: Love of Christ, the resurrection, spreading the Good News

Special Feature
- Have children take parts for the gospel.

334 JULY 23
Bridget of Sweden,
Married Woman, Religious Founder

St. Bridget was born into high Swedish society about 1303. She married at the age of thirteen and had eight children. She was a good wife and mother. For two years she was chief lady-in-waiting to the queen and encouraged the queen and king to be holy. Bridget was a mystic who had special gifts of prayer and revelations about Christ's passion and Church conditions. After her husband died, Bridget became a Third Order Franciscan. She planned an Order of the Holy Savior, which after her death was formed by her daughter St. Catherine. The order is known as the Bridgettines. Bridget spent her last years in poverty in Rome, praying and doing penance. Like Catherine of Siena, she urged the pope to leave Avignon and return to Rome.

Themes: Prayer, vocations in life

334A   JULY 24
Sharbel Makhluf, *Priest*

St. Sharbel was a priest of the Maronite rite. Born to a poor family in Lebanon, he became a monk at the Monastery of St. Maron and was ordained. For sixteen years he lived an outstanding monastic life. Then he was allowed to live as hermit for the rest of his life. He prayed, fasted, did penance, and kept a strict silence. Sharbel was devoted to the Eucharist and to the Blessed Virgin Mary. People recognized his holiness and asked for his prayers. Sharbel died on Christmas Eve 1898.

Themes: Religious life, prayer, silence, acts of self-denial

335   JULY 25
James, *Apostle* (FEAST)

James, son of Zebedee, is among the first apostles called by Christ. Along with Peter and John, he is one of the favored three apostles to witness the transfiguration, the raising of Jairus's daughter, and the agony in the garden. The apostles James and John were known as Boanerges, which means "sons of thunder." Tradition says that James was an apostle to Spain. Because Acts states that Herod beheaded James, the brother of John (Acts 12:1–2), it is believed that James was the first apostle martyred.

Themes: Faith, discipleship

336   JULY 26
Joachim and Ann,
Parents of the Virgin Mary (MEMORIAL)

A tradition going back to the second century names Mary's parents as Joachim and Ann. From early times these grandparents of Jesus have been honored by the Church. They are the patron saints of grandparents.

Themes: Faith in families, Mary's virtues

337   JULY 29
Martha, *Disciple of the Lord* (MEMORIAL)

St. Martha is the model of hospitality. She had a home in Bethany, where she lived with her sister, Mary, and brother, Lazarus. All three were friends of Jesus, and he visited them there. Once while Mary listened to Jesus, Martha was busy preparing a meal. When she complained about Mary, Jesus pointed out that Martha was worrying too much about the work. Another time when Lazarus died, it was at Martha's urging that Jesus brought him back to life.

Themes: Friendship with Jesus, trust in Jesus

Special Feature
- Have children take parts for the gospel.

338   JULY 30
Peter Chrysologus,
Bishop, Doctor of the Church

St. Peter was born in Italy around 480. As bishop of Ravenna, he was a good, dedicated leader. He was known for his short sermons, which were direct, warm, and effective in correcting false teachings and encouraging the Christian life. The title

Chrysologus means "golden word." Peter promoted education as a privilege and an obligation.

Themes: Christian values, education

---

339 JULY 31
Ignatius of Loyola,
Presbyter, Religious Founder (MEMORIAL)

St. Ignatius was born in 1491 at Loyola in Spain, the youngest son in a noble family of eleven children. He was a soldier until the age of thirty, when he was injured in battle. While recovering, Ignatius read the life of Christ and the lives of the saints. These books prompted him to hang up his sword at a picture of Mary. He began to write the Spiritual Exercises, a guide for the Christian life. For ten years he studied and then went to the University of Paris. Six men he met there joined him in forming a religious community, the Society of Jesus, or Jesuits. They became priests who took the vows of poverty, chastity, obedience, and an additional vow of obedience to the pope. Their teaching and missionary work helped renew and spread the Church.

Themes: Religious life, the spiritual life, reading about the saints

AUGUST

340 AUGUST 1
Alphonsus Liguori, *Bishop, Religious Founder, Doctor of the Church* (MEMORIAL)

St. Alphonsus was born in 1696 in Italy. He was a lawyer of both civil and canon law. After eleven years, he was so disturbed by the corruption in the courts that he left law and became a priest. He founded the Congregation of the Most Holy Redeemer, the Redemptorists, to evangelize the poor. He was an untiring preacher, writer, and moral theologian. Alphonsus became a bishop and wrote many sermons, articles, and books. He stressed devotion to Mary and to Jesus in the Blessed Sacrament. During the last part of his life he experienced many trials.

Themes: Goodness, religious publications, Jesus in the Blessed Sacrament

341 AUGUST 2
Eusebius of Vercelli, *Bishop*

Eusebius was born in Sardinia in Italy around the year 300. He became a priest and then bishop of Vercelli in Italy. He established the monastic life in his diocese. Because Eusebius took a stand against the heresy of Arianism, which held that Jesus was not God, he was exiled by the emperor to Palestine and Egypt for six years. When he returned, he worked to restore faith and fight Arianism. He encouraged diocesan priests to live in community.

Themes: Faith, the Creed

341A also AUGUST 2
Peter Julian Eymard, *Priest*

St. Peter lived in France from 1811 to 1839. He was ordained a diocesan priest and then joined the Marist Congregation, which fostered his devotion to Our Lady. Drawn toward the Eucharist, Peter founded the Congregation of the Blessed Sacrament. Throughout the process he struggled with ill health and financial difficulties. His new community promoted eucharistic devotion, preparation for First Communion, and the appreciation of the Eucharist as a sign of Christ's love. Peter also co-founded for women the Congregation of the Servants of the Blessed Sacrament.

Themes: The Eucharist, Mary

342 AUGUST 4
John Mary Vianney, *Presbyter* (MEMORIAL)

St. John Vianney, or the Curé of Ars, is the patron of parish priests. He was born in France in 1786. Because it was the time of the French Revolution, many people were growing up without learning the faith. John wanted to be a priest, but he had a difficult time studying. The priest who taught him persuaded the bishop to ordain John because of his holiness. John was sent to a parish in Ars, a small village where people were not very religious. John renewed the parish by his life of holiness. Soon people came from all over to consult him and to go to him for confession. He would sometimes hear confessions for sixteen hours a day.

Themes: Holiness, repentance

343 AUGUST 5
The Dedication of the Basilica of Saint Mary in Rome

At the Council of Ephesus the mother of Jesus was proclaimed as Mother of God. A church was built in Rome in the fourth century. Tradition says that Mary appeared to a nobleman and asked to have it built on the spot where he would find snow on that summer day. This church was rebuilt in 434 and rededicated to Mary, Mother of God. It is the first church in the West in honor of Mary and the largest one dedicated to her in the world.

Themes: Mary, church buildings

344 AUGUST 6
The Transfiguration of the Lord (FEAST)

The Bible says that one day Jesus was transfigured or changed before three of the apostles. His face shone and his clothes became dazzling white. The glory of God was seen in Jesus. We celebrate this mystery today in the Eucharist. Although we do not see Jesus present with us, we believe that he is here and that he will soon be with us in a special way under the forms of bread and wine.

Universal Prayer
The response is *"Lord, hear our prayer."*

The Church is Christ present on earth. That its members may always act as Christ would, let us pray to the Lord.

World leaders must follow God's laws. That they may obey God as they serve us, let us pray to the Lord.

Some people do not have faith, and some have weak faith. That all may believe in Jesus, let us pray to the Lord.

We are to know, love, and serve God. That we may listen to Jesus who tells us how to do this, let us pray to the Lord.

Special Features
- Display different pictures of Jesus.
- Have the children take parts for the gospel.
- As a communion reflection have someone pray the following prayer:

Risen Lord Jesus, we long to be with you. Touch our eyes that we may see. Touch our ears that we may hear your word. Touch our hearts that we may do your will in all things. Then you will live in us, and we will be transformed into other Christs. We will help make a new earth and live forever with you in heaven.

Songs

Alleluia! Sing to Jesus; Christ Be Our Light; Earthen Vessels; I Have Loved You; Jesus, Joy of Our Desiring; Look Beyond; Open Our Eyes

Homily Ideas

Visual: A transistor radio

State that the air is filled with sounds that we do not hear now. Show a radio and turn it on. Comment that the radio enables us to hear what is really there all the time.

• • •

Tell the children that the apostles never saw Jesus in all his glory as God until the transfiguration. Jesus looked like any other man. But one day Jesus' three favored apostles—Peter, James, and John— saw him as he really was.

• • •

Explain that the gospels of Matthew, Mark, and Luke all tell the story and the first reading from Peter's letter talks about the transfiguration. No doubt it made an impression on the apostles.

• • •

Point out that Moses and Elijah appeared with Jesus and talked with him about his coming death. These were great prophets from Old Testament times. Their presence showed the apostles that Jesus was someone they could believe.

• • •

Ask the children what else happened to strengthen the apostles' faith in Jesus. (The Father said that

Jesus was his beloved Son and told the apostles to listen to him.)

• • •

Explain that some people think that God let this event happen in order to prepare the apostles for Jesus' suffering and death. When Jesus died, they couldn't understand it; but having seen his glory, they would not give up their faith completely.

• • •

Tell the children that Jesus is in glory in heaven now, but he is with us always even though we don't see him. He is present loving us and caring for us. We can speak to him at any time.

• • •

Tell the children that God's words are meant for us, too: "Listen to him." Ask them how they can find out what Jesus is saying to them (by praying, reading Scripture, studying religion, listening to people who are in charge of them). Suggest that they ask the Holy Spirit to give them the grace to obey Jesus. Then someday they will be with him in glory. Their bodies will be transfigured.

345 AUGUST 7
Sixtus II, *Pope, Martyr,* and His Companions, *Martyrs*

Sixtus became pope in 257 and for a year guided the Church through difficult times. Then Emperor Valerius suddenly turned against Christians and began to persecute them as enemies of the government. One day while Sixtus was celebrating Mass, soldiers appeared. They beheaded Sixtus and the four deacons with him.

Themes: Faith, practicing faith

346 also AUGUST 7
Cajetan, *Presbyter, Religious Founder*

Cajetan was born in Italy in 1480. He studied theology and law. After becoming a priest he chose to serve the poor and the sick instead of serving in the Roman Curia as an advisor to the pope. He began a religious order called the Theatines who were to live the gospel and help reform the Church. Cajetan began organizations that loaned money to needy people in return for pawned objects.

Themes: Working for the poor, living the gospel

347 AUGUST 8
Dominic, *Presbyter, Religious Founder* (MEMORIAL)

St. Dominic was born in Spain around 1170. He became a priest and dreamed of doing missionary work. Instead, he worked against the Albigensian heresy by preaching and good example. He founded the Order of Preachers, Dominicans, who carried out this work with him. Their life of poverty as they walked from city to city convinced people to accept the truth they taught. The Dominicans spread devotion to Mary through the rosary.

Themes: Poverty, the rosary

347A AUGUST 9
Teresa Benedicta of the Cross, *Virgin, Martyr* (MEMORIAL)

Born Edith Stein in 1891, Teresa was originally Jewish. Her family was well known in Poland. Edith became a brilliant philosopher and taught at a university. She had stopped believing in God when she was fourteen. But the witness of Catholic friends and reading the autobiography of St. Teresa of Avila led her to become a Catholic. Then Edith became a Carmelite nun like Teresa. The Dutch bishops had denounced the Nazis, who responded by arresting all Jewish Christians. Teresa was ar-

rested while she was living in the Netherlands. She died in a gas chamber in Auschwitz in 1942.

Themes: The faith, evangelization

348 AUGUST 10
Lawrence, *Deacon, Martyr* (FEAST)

St. Lawrence was a Spanish deacon in Rome. He was martyred four days after Pope Sixtus about the year 258. It is said that a Roman official asked Lawrence to hand over the treasures of the Church. Lawrence promised to do so in three days. When the official returned, he found a large group of lepers, orphans, blind and lame people, and widows. Lawrence explained, "These are the treasures of the Church." Lawrence was martyred by being placed on a gridiron over a fire. Tradition says that as he died he joked, "I'm done on this side. You can turn me over."

Themes: Love for the poor, witnessing to the faith

349 AUGUST 11
Clare, *Virgin, Religious Founder* (MEMORIAL)

In 1193, Clare was born into a wealthy family in Assisi, Italy. When Clare was a teenager, Francis of Assisi gave up his possessions and, dressed in a peasant's robe, begged for food. Attracted by his joy and lifestyle of living for Jesus, Clare joined him when she was eighteen. Francis himself cut her long hair and gave her a rough woolen habit. She and other women formed a Franciscan community called the Poor Clares. For forty-two years St. Clare was its abbess. Twice when the city was about to be invaded by the Saracens, Clare prayed to Jesus in the Blessed Sacrament and the city was saved. Clare is the patron of television because of a story that one Christmas Eve when she was sick in bed she saw the crib and heard the singing in church as if she were there.

Themes: Poverty and simplicity, Blessed Sacrament

350 AUGUST 13
Pontian, *Pope, Martyr*; and
Hippolytus, *Presbyter, Martyr*

In the early part of the third century the priest Hippolytus thought that the Church should be strict with sinners. When Pope Callistus chose to be forgiving, Hippolytus formed a group of followers and declared himself pope. In the year 230 when Pontian became pope, Hippolytus still would not change his mind. Then a persecution broke out, and in the same year Pontian and Hippolytus were arrested and condemned to hard labor in the mines of Sardinia. There Hippolytus was reconciled to Pontian. Both men died as martyrs.

Themes: Mercy, reconciliation

351 AUGUST 14
Maximilian Mary Kolbe,
Presbyter, Religious, Martyr (MEMORIAL)

Maximilian was born in 1894 in Poland. At the age of thirteen he joined the Franciscans. He spread devotion to Mary Immaculate, even in Japan and India. He published Catholic literature and a monthly magazine that taught the gospel under Mary's protection. He founded spiritual centers called City of Mary Immaculate, including one in Nagasaki. During the Second World War Maximilian sheltered suffering people. For this he was sent to the concentration camp Auschwitz. There he was forced to do hard work and was beaten. He ministered to the other prisoners. One day because someone escaped, ten men were chosen to die by starvation in a pit. When one of

these men cried out that he had a wife and children, Maximilian offered to take his place. For two weeks in the pit he led the men in prayer until they died. When he was the only one left, he was killed by an injection. He suffered the martyrdom of charity.

Themes: Devotion to Mary, self-sacrifice

352 AUGUST 15
The Assumption of the
Virgin Mary into Heaven (SOLEMNITY)

This feast commemorates the day Mary was taken into heaven, body and soul. No one knows whether Mary died or not. The Assumption, however, was declared a dogma of the Catholic faith in 1950. Mary did not have to wait until the end of the world to enter heaven, body and soul. God gave her this privilege because of her sinlessness and role as the Mother of God. This feast is a preview of what is in store for us. Someday we, too, will be in heaven, body and soul.

Special Features
- Have children take parts for the reading of the gospel.
- Sing the Magnificat in a musical setting such as "Mary's Song" and "My Soul Rejoices."

353 AUGUST 16
Stephen of Hungary, *Married Man*

Stephen's father was leader of tribes in an area called Hungary. Both he and his father became Christian. On Christmas Day in the year 1000, the pope declared Stephen the first king of Hungary. He worked to spread the Church in his country. He invited Benedictine monks to come to Hungary, he built churches, and he shared his wealth with the poor. He ruled with justice and humility. His son Emeric, who was killed in a hunting accident, is also a saint.

Themes: Zeal for the faith, virtue

354 AUGUST 18
Jane Frances de Chantal,
Married Woman, Religious Founder

Jane was born in 1572 to a noble French family. She married Christopher de Chantal and had four children. After seven years of marriage, Jane's husband was killed in a hunting accident. Jane was called to run her bossy father-in-law's household, which she did for seven years. Then she met Francis de Sales, a bishop, who became her spiritual director. He helped her forgive the man who caused her husband's death and guided her in founding the Sisters of the Visitation of Holy Mary. These Sisters gave their lives to prayer and helping the poor.

Themes: Forgiveness, love for the poor, doing one's duty

355 AUGUST 19
John Eudes, *Presbyter, Religious Founder*

John was born in France in 1601. He joined the Oratorians and became a priest. For several years he gave parish missions. Realizing the need for holy, educated priests, John established seminaries and founded a community, the Congregation of Jesus and Mary (the Eudists), which was dedicated to forming Christlike priests. He also established the Congregation of Our Lady of the Refuge to care for wayward girls. He spread devotion to the hearts of Jesus and Mary.

Themes: Priests, meeting needs, devotion to the Sacred Heart

356 AUGUST 20
Bernard, *Abbot, Doctor of the Church*
(MEMORIAL)

St. Bernard was born in France in 1090. At the age of twenty-two he left his wealthy family to become a monk. He joined the strict Cistercians at Cîteaux, bringing thirty-one other men with him. Three years later, Bernard began another monastery at Clairvaux and became abbot. He gave spiritual advice to individuals and to church leaders and settled disputes. When two men claimed to be pope, Bernard convinced the leaders of countries to support the true pope. He preached the Second Crusade. Bernard is known for his preaching and his writings on spiritual topics.

Themes: Love of God, peace

357 AUGUST 21
Pius X, *Pope* (MEMORIAL)

Giuseppe Sarto was born in Italy in 1845, the second of ten children. He became a priest, bishop, cardinal, and then pope. His motto was "Renew all things in Christ." Because of this pope, children can now receive communion when they reach the age of reason. Pius X also encouraged the reading and study of Scripture, and he promoted justice and charity. He tried to prevent the world from going to war, but in vain. Although he was pope, Pius X remained a simple, humble man.

Themes: Holy Communion, charity, humility

358 AUGUST 22
The Queenship of the Virgin Mary
(MEMORIAL)

This feast was established in 1954 and celebrated a week after the Assumption. It is a celebration of the

Fifth Glorious Mystery of the rosary, the crowning of Mary as queen of heaven and earth. The pope asked that on this day the human race be reconsecrated to the Immaculate Heart of the Blessed Virgin Mary. The holy Mother of God brought the savior into the world. She reigns over all the angels and saints in heaven and over us, her spiritual children on earth.

Themes: Mary, resurrection

Special Feature

- Pray an act of consecration to Mary at the end of the homily or the end of Mass.

359 AUGUST 23
Rose of Lima, *Virgin*

St. Rose was born in Lima, Peru, and baptized Isabel. Because a maid commented that the baby looked like a rose, Isabel became known as Rose. Although known for her beauty, Rose also had an inner beauty. She wanted to live only for Jesus. At the age of fifteen she became a Third Order Dominican in imitation of St. Catherine of Siena, the model for her life. She lived at home in a hut where she prayed, practiced penance, and did needlework to support her parents. In their home she set up a free clinic for the poor. Rose died when she was only thirty-one. She is the first saint of the Americas.

Themes: Prayer, penance, action for the poor

360 AUGUST 24
Bartholomew, *Apostle* (FEAST)

St. Bartholomew is one of the twelve apostles who were personally instructed by Jesus and given the mission to carry on his work. He is identified with the apostle named Nathanael in John's gospel. Philip brought Nathanael to Jesus. Nathanael, who was from Cana, considered Nazareth a backward village. Jesus told Nathanael he was a man without deceit in his heart. It is believed that Bartholomew did missionary work in India and was martyred.

Themes: Following Christ, being honest and good, missionary work

361 AUGUST 25
Louis of France, *Married Man*

St. Louis was born in 1214 and became King Louis IX of France when he was only twenty-two. He married and had eleven children. A Third Order Franciscan, he was a man of prayer. He lived and ruled with justice, mercy, and love. To regain the holy places from the Muslims, he organized a crusade to the Holy Land. His soldiers admired him because he lived as one of them. St. Louis died of a fever that destroyed his army in Africa.

Themes: Justice, the Holy Land

362 also AUGUST 25
Joseph Calasanz, *Presbyter, Religious Founder*

Joseph was born in 1556 in Spain. As a tutor in Rome he ministered to suffering people and was concerned about poor children. He opened free schools for them and then founded the Clerks Regular of the Religious Schools (Piarists) to teach in them. Teachers in private schools, as well as rich people, tried to abolish his schools. Then men in his community who were jealous of him reported him to the pope. At the age of eighty-six Joseph had to stand trial in Rome. His work in the schools stopped, and members of his community became diocesan priests. Only twenty years after his death did the pope restore his order.

Themes: Patience in suffering, religious education

363 AUGUST 27
Monica, *Married Woman* (MEMORIAL)

St. Monica's feast day is the day before the feast day of her son, St. Augustine. Her prayers and fasting helped to bring about his conversion from an immoral life. Monica was born around the year 322 in North Africa. She was married to a pagan official named Patricius and had three sons. Patricius was a violent man and unfaithful to his wife. Monica's example encouraged wives who had marriage problems to consult her. Patricius eventually converted. Monica followed Augustine to Milan, where the bishop, St. Ambrose, told her, "Surely the son of so many tears will not perish." St. Ambrose converted Augustine, who went on to become a bishop and a saint. On the way back to Africa with Augustine, Monica died.

Themes: Perseverance in prayer, patience in trials

364 AUGUST 28
Augustine, *Bishop, Doctor of the Church* (MEMORIAL)

St. Augustine was born in Africa in 354. In his famous autobiography, *Confessions,* Augustine tells of his conversion to faith and morality. In Milan in Italy he was converted by St. Ambrose as a result of the prayers of his mother, St. Monica. He returned to Africa, where he became a priest and then bishop of Hippo. For thirty-six years he was a true pastor. He defended the faith against heresy and explained the faith in preaching and writings. He cared for the poor and advised bishops, popes, and councils.

Themes: Conversion, teaching the faith

365 AUGUST 29
The Martyrdom of John the Baptist (MEMORIAL)

[*Note:* See ideas suggested for June 24, the Birth of John the Baptist, page 136.]

SEPTEMBER

366 SEPTEMBER 3
Gregory the Great, *Pope, Religious, Doctor of the Church* (MEMORIAL)

St. Gregory was born in Rome around the year 540. He was the son of a wealthy senator and St. Sylvia. He was a prefect or governor of Rome, but then at the age of thirty-five, he entered a Benedictine monastery. He became the papal ambassador to Constantinople. When he returned to Rome, he became an abbot and then was chosen pope. Gregory was one of the greatest and most talented popes. He made peace with the invading Lombards and saved Rome from famine. He sent St. Augustine of Canterbury and other monks to England as missionaries. He made reforms in the Roman liturgy. Gregorian chant is named for him. He also wrote much, including a book on the role of a bishop and more than 850 letters that we have copies of.

Themes: Peacemaking, liturgy, use of talents

367 SEPTEMBER 8
The Birth of the Virgin Mary (FEAST)

No one knows when Mary was born, but that day was special. The feast of the Immaculate Conception was set nine months before this feast. Tradition gives the names Joachim and Ann to Mary's parents.

Special Features
- Have the children sing "Happy Birthday" to Mary.
- Suggest that they do something special for Mary as a gift today.

368 SEPTEMBER 9
Peter Claver, *Presbyter, Religious, Missionary* (MEMORIAL)

Peter Claver was born in Spain in 1580. He became a Jesuit and volunteered to go to South America as a missionary. For forty years he ministered to black slaves in what is now Colombia. Colombia was the great market for the slave trade. On the journey to America, one-third of the slaves died. Whenever a ship arrived, Peter would take medicine, food, and clothing to it. He nursed the slaves in the warehouses who were awaiting their sale and taught them about God. He baptized nearly 300,000 blacks. On the day of his solemn profession, he signed himself "slave of the blacks forever." After being sick from an epidemic, and worn out from his work, Peter was bedridden for four years before he died.

Themes: Compassion, evangelization

368A SEPTEMBER 12
Most Holy Name of Mary (MEMORIAL)

We honor Mary's name because it stands for the Mother of Jesus, the Mother of God. She is the ho-liest woman who ever lived, the one Gabriel addressed as blessed among women. Jesus did as Mary wished at the wedding at Cana. From the cross he gave her to us as our mother. We call on Mary to intercede for us. We pronounce her holy name whenever we pray the Hail Mary.

Themes: The Blessed Virgin Mary, prayer

369 SEPTEMBER 13
John Chrysostom,
Bishop, Doctor of the Church (MEMORIAL)

John Chrysostom was born at Antioch about the year 349. He studied law and public speaking. At the age of twenty-one he joined a group of monks. Four years later he lived as a hermit in a cave until he became sick. Then he returned to Antioch and became a priest. Famous for his powerful and lively sermons, John was called Chrysostom, which means "golden mouth." He became the bishop of Constantinople, but lived simply, giving his money to the poor. Enemies falsely accused him, and he was exiled twice before he died. He is a Greek Father of the Church.

Themes: Suffering for the faith, a simple lifestyle

370 SEPTEMBER 14
The Holy Cross (FEAST)

The cross is a symbol of God's tremendous love. After we human beings spoiled our friendship with God by sinning, God sent his Son to become man. Jesus' suffering and death on the cross made up for our sins and enabled us to be God's children once more and live forever. At every Eucharist we remember and celebrate Christ's love that healed us. We offer again with him the sacrifice he offered on the cross to save us.

Universal Prayer

The response is *"Lord, hear our prayer."*

That the Church may tell everyone about Jesus' death and rising, let us pray to the Lord.

That those who govern others may accept the suffering that comes with their job, let us pray to the Lord.

That sinners may realize how much God loves them and turn away from their sins, let us pray to the Lord.

That we may show Jesus love in return for his great love, we pray to the Lord.

That we may unite our sufferings with Jesus' and make them a gift to God, we pray to the Lord.

Special Features

- Decorate a crucifix with flowers and candles.
- During the entrance procession, stand the processional cross in the middle aisle and have everyone marching in twos bow to it.
- As a communion reflection, pray the following litany.

> *Response: Hail cross, our only hope!*
> *Jesus, the cross shows your love for me.*
> *Jesus, you carried the cross.*
> *Jesus, you were nailed to the cross.*
> *Jesus, you were lifted up on the cross.*
> *Jesus, your blood flowed down the cross.*
> *Jesus, you breathed your last breath*
>   *on the cross.*
> *Jesus, after three days you rose from the dead.*
> *Jesus, your suffering and death gave me*
>   *everlasting life!*

- Give the children a cross, a picture of a cross, or a copy of the Prayer before the Crucifix.
- Make the Stations of the Cross during the week of this feast. If possible, pray in church with children representatives going from Station to Station.

Songs

Behold the Wood; Draw Near and Take the Body of the Lord; Gift of Love; Keep in Mind; Lift High the Cross; Now We Remain; The Old Rugged Cross; O Sacred Head Surrounded; Our Peace and Integrity; Soul of My Savior; Unless a Grain of Wheat; When I Survey the Wondrous Cross; Wood of the Cross

Homily Ideas

Visual: A crucifix

Show a crucifix and ask the children where they see crucifixes (at church, in their homes, around people's necks). Tell them that a cross is the symbol of the Christian religion because Jesus' death on the cross made up for sin and gave us eternal life.

• • •

Tell the children that the purpose of Jesus' life was to die and rise. We can never separate Jesus from the thought of the cross. In American Sign Language the word "Jesus" is made by touching the palm of one hand and then the other with the index finger to signify the wounds of Jesus. After Jesus rose, his glorified body still showed the wounds. Right now Jesus in heaven has these wounds. They are like badges of honor. Through his death he won victory over sin and death.

• • •

Explain that the first reading tells the story of God's people when they were traveling in the desert and poisonous snakes attacked them. God had Moses make a bronze snake and put it on a pole. People who were bitten by a snake and looked at the bronze snake lived. This bronze snake that healed people was a foreshadowing or preview of Jesus. Years later Jesus was raised up on a wooden cross. As he explained in today's gospel, anyone who looks to him with faith will live forever.

• • •

Tell the children that Jesus' death healed the entire world of sin. The cross points in all four directions. It saved people in the north, south, east, and west.

. . .

Explain that suffering is a great mystery. Some suffering is caused by sin, but other suffering we just can't understand. Everyone suffers. Suffering makes us either bitter or better. During times of trials and hardships our faith can grow and we can become more understanding of others. Someone pointed out that only when it is dark can we see the stars.

. . .

Comment that people who are suffering in prison or refugee camps sometimes draw a cross for themselves and find strength by looking at it. They unite their sufferings with Jesus' sufferings and offer their sufferings with his. We can do this, too, when we pray the Morning Offering and when we offer Jesus' sacrifice with him at Mass.

. . .

Remind the children that Catholics make the Sign of the Cross over themselves. We do this to mean that we belong to Jesus, who was crucified for us. When we were baptized, a cross was made over us to claim us for Christ. Suggest to the children that when they make the Sign of the Cross, they should do it reverently and think of the great love it stands for.

. . .

Point out that we can bless one another with the Sign of the Cross made on the forehead.

. . .

Tell the children that in Jerusalem at the place where we think Calvary might have been, there is a large church. Millions of people go there each year to make the Way of the Cross and pray.

371 SEPTEMBER 15
Our Lady of Sorrows (MEMORIAL)

When Jesus suffered rejection and hardships, his mother Mary also suffered. At the end of his life when he made the way of the cross and was crucified, his mother shared his pain. She stood there at the cross and suffered with him. She understands our sufferings, too, and will help us. Traditionally Mary's sorrows are these seven: the prophecy of Simeon when Jesus was presented in the temple, the flight into Egypt, the loss of Jesus in the Temple, meeting Jesus on the way to Calvary, Mary at the foot of the cross, Jesus taken down from the cross, and the burial of Jesus.

Special Features
- Distribute holy cards of Our Lady of Sorrows or the Pieta.
- Sing the Stabat Mater, "At the Cross Her Station Keeping."
- Display pictures of the seven sorrows of Mary, perhaps drawn by the children.

372 SEPTEMBER 16
Cornelius, *Pope, Martyr,* and
Cyprian, *Bishop, Martyr* (MEMORIAL)

After Pope Fabian was martyred in 250, the emperor prevented the election of a new pope. In 251, while the emperor was away, Cornelius became pope. Cornelius allowed those who had given up the faith during the persecution to return. Another man disagreed with this policy and made himself pope. Cyprian, a bishop in North Africa, and other bishops supported Cornelius. After two years as pope, Cornelius was exiled by the emperor. He died in exile. Cyprian was a close friend of Cornelius. He had become a Christian at the age of twenty-five and was a holy priest and bishop. During a new persecution, Cyprian was exiled and then sentenced to death by beheading.

Themes: Courage in the faith, supporting friends in the faith

— 154 —

373 SEPTEMBER 17
Robert Bellarmine,
Bishop, Religious, Doctor of the Church

Robert Bellarmine was born into a noble family in 1542. He became a Jesuit known for his powerful sermons. For twelve years he taught theology at the Roman College and wrote books defending the faith. He also wrote two catechisms. Named cardinal against his wishes, he lived as a poor man. He became archbishop of Capua for three years. Then he was called to Rome to defend the Church against heresies.

Themes: Studying the faith, a simple lifestyle

374 SEPTEMBER 19
Januarius, *Bishop, Martyr*

Januarius was bishop of Benevento, a town near Naples in Italy. He was probably martyred about the year 305. There is a legend that he was arrested while he was visiting some Christians in prison and martyred with six companions. In Naples there is a four-inch flask that contains his blood. Ever since at least 1389 this blood liquefies on this the saint's feast day and other days.

Themes: Witness, role of bishops

375 SEPTEMBER 20
Andrew Kim Taegon, *Presbyter, Martyr,*
Paul Chong Hasang, *Catechist, Martyr,*
and Their Companions, *Martyrs*
(MEMORIAL)

Christians were persecuted in Korea between 1839 and 1867. St. Andrew Kim, St. Paul, and 111 others who were martyred were canonized. Andrew, the son of converts, was the first Korean priest. He went to a seminary in China and six years later began the dangerous job of sneaking missionaries into Korea. Paul was a forty-five-year-old seminarian. The group of saints includes a twenty-six-year-old single woman and a thirteen-year-old boy. About ten thousand Catholics were martyred before there was religious liberty in Korea.

Themes: Witness, missionary work, suffering for Christ

376 SEPTEMBER 21
Matthew, *Apostle, Evangelist* (FEAST)

St. Matthew, sometimes called Levi, is one of the twelve apostles. He was a tax collector in Capernaum until Jesus called him to follow him. Traditions say that Matthew taught in Persia, Syria, Greece, or Ethiopia. Matthew is credited with writing the gospel of Matthew. An early version of this gospel was said to be written in Aramaic for Jewish converts. Matthew was martyred in Ethiopia.

Themes: Discipleship, spreading the Good News, the gospel

376 SEPTEMBER 23
Pio of Pietrelcina, *Priest* (MEMORIAL)

Padre Pio, as he is usually called, was born in Italy in 1887. At the age of sixteen, he joined the Capuchin Order, a Franciscan branch. He was ordained a priest. Because of ill health he lived several years with his family and then returned to the friary. Padre Pio was known worldwide for the divine favors he enjoyed, his confessions, and his spiritual advice. He often said, "Pray, hope, and don't worry." Padre Pio founded two hospitals. One was called House for the Relief of Suffering. He spent long hours in prayer and suffered from the stigmata, bearing the wounds of Christ in his body for fifty years. Padre Pio died in 1968 already revered as a saint.

Themes: Holiness, sacrament of penance

377 SEPTEMBER 26
Cosmas and Damian, *Martyrs*

Tradition teaches that Cosmas and Damian were twin brothers born in what is Turkey today. They were doctors who also brought belief in Jesus to their patients. Because they never charged people, they were known as "the moneyless ones." During the persecution of Emperor Diocletian, they were martyred for being Christians along with their three brothers about the year 303.

Themes: Caring for the sick, evangelization, generosity

378 SEPTEMBER 27
Vincent de Paul, *Presbyter, Religious Founder* (MEMORIAL)

St. Vincent de Paul was born in 1580 in France. After working on his father's farm, he studied to be a priest and was ordained. He had a parish in Paris where he was made chaplain to the queen. A holy man helped him understand there was more to life than wealth and comfort. Vincent began to work for the poor: slaves, abandoned babies, prostitutes, and war victims. He formed a group of men to preach to the poor and minister to them. They became the Vincentians. St. Vincent involved the rich in his work. With St. Louise de Marillac, he organized the Ladies of Charity, which became a religious community called the Daughters of Charity.

Themes: Love for the poor, vocations

379 SEPTEMBER 28
Wenceslaus, *Martyr*

St. Wenceslaus was raised by his grandmother, St. Ludmilla. He became duke of Bohemia around 925, when he was fifteen. Under his mother's rule the country had persecuted Christians. Wenceslaus ended this. He helped the poor, acted with justice, and improved the education of his people. His brother Boleslaus hoped to be duke. One day, as Wenceslaus was on the way to Mass, the jealous Boleslaus struck him on the head with his sword, and three friends of Boleslaus killed Wenceslaus at the chapel door. He was twenty-two years old and his son was born that day. The emperor declared Wenceslaus a king after his death. The Christmas carol "Good King Wenceslaus" is about him.

Themes: Justice, serving the poor

380 also SEPTEMBER 28
Lawrence Ruiz, *Married Man, Martyr,* and His Companions, *Martyrs*

Lawrence and fifteen others were martyred in or near Nagasaki, Japan. He is the first Filipino saint. Lawrence was born about 1600 and lived in Manila in the Philippines. He became a calligrapher, printing documents, and had two sons and a daughter. One day he became involved in a murder. To escape he joined a missionary group of five, including three Dominicans. On the ship he learned that they were going to Japan where there were persecutions. All six were arrested, tortured, and killed. At his trial Lawrence declared, "I shall die for God, and for God I would give many thousands of lives. So do with me as you please."

Themes: Zeal for the faith, love of God

381 SEPTEMBER 29
Michael, Gabriel, and Raphael, *Archangels*
(FEAST)

[*Note:* Also see ideas under October 2, the Guardian Angels, page 158.]

Today we celebrate the feast of the three archangels, St. Michael, St. Gabriel, and St. Raphael. Angels are spirits who worship and serve God in heaven. The three we remember today are mentioned in the Bible. At this Eucharist we join all the angels and saints in worshiping God.

Universal Prayer
The response is *"Lord, hear our prayer."*

That the Church may become more aware of God's loving presence, we pray to the Lord.

That rulers may make laws that are in line with God's laws, we pray to the Lord.

That people who are in trouble may turn to God for help, we pray to the Lord.

That we may work against evil in our own lives and in the lives of others, we pray to the Lord.

Special Features
- Use incense, especially during the Holy, Holy.
- Distribute copies of a recent version of the Guardian Angel Prayer or the prayer to St. Michael.
- Have children do a dance of adoration as a communion reflection.

Songs
Holy God, We Praise Thy Name; Let All Mortal Flesh Keep Silence; The Lord Is Near; On Eagle's Wings (verse 4); Path of Life; Praise God from Whom All Blessings Flow; Praise the Lord, Ye Heavens; They Come God's Messengers of Love; Ye Watchers and Ye Holy Ones; You Holy Angels Bright

Homily Ideas
Visual: An angel figurine or picture

Show an image of an angel and comment that angels are very popular lately. Explain that the Church has a long tradition of believing in angels and praying to them. We believe that they are creatures made by God, but unlike us, angels have no bodies. They are spirit. When artists draw angels, they show them with bodies that have wings. Angels praise and worship God in heaven and are sometimes sent by God as messengers to earth.

. . .

Mention that according to Church tradition some angels led by Lucifer turned against God. They were conquered by angels led by Michael and thrown into hell. These bad angels are now known as devils.

. . .

Comment that according to tradition there are nine choirs or ranks of angels. An archangel is a chief angel.

. . .

Tell the children about the three archangels whose feast is today.

St. Michael was the leader in the battle against Lucifer, or Satan, according to the Book of Revelation in the Bible. His name means "Who is like God." St. Michael is described in the Book of Daniel as a heavenly prince. Artists usually show him clothed in armor. He is the patron of the Church and of police.

St. Gabriel delivers three messages from God in the Bible. He tells the prophet Daniel about his vision, he tells Zechariah that he will have a son he must name John, and he tells Mary that she will have a son who will be the Son of God. The name Gabriel means "Strength of God." St. Gabriel is the patron of postal workers and those in the field of communication.

St. Raphael in the Book of Tobit is the companion and guide of a young man named Tobias who goes on a journey to collect a debt. The name Raphael means "God has healed." St. Raphael is the patron of travelers and nurses.

. . .

Explain that angels have particular jobs. These three archangels, Michael in particular, protect the Church in a special way. Comment that the names Michael, Gabriel, and Raphael all end in "el," which means "God." Some people think that angels are really different ways that God is present to us to love and care for us.

382 SEPTEMBER 30
Jerome, *Presbyter, Doctor of the Church* (MEMORIAL)

St. Jerome was born about 345. He studied in Rome where he was baptized. For three years he and some friends lived in a monastery. He was ordained but wanted to spend his life in studying. Jerome lived for a while as a hermit in the desert where he had great temptations. Then he became advisor to the pope, who had him translate the Bible from Hebrew and Greek into Latin, the common language. This translation is called the Vulgate. Jerome was also a spiritual director for some noble ladies, including St. Paula. When he went to Bethlehem to live in a cave, these women followed and set up a monastery and a convent. In the Holy Land, Jerome spent thirty years writing commentaries on Scripture. Jerome is known for his temper, as well as for his devotion to God.

Themes: Love of Scripture, use of talents for the Church

Special Features
- Give each child a Bible bookmark that has a Scripture verse about God's word, for example: "Your word, O God, is a lamp to my feet" (Psalm 119:105).
- Discuss the readings of the day's Mass.

OCTOBER

383 OCTOBER 1
Thérèse of the Child Jesus,
Virgin, Religious (MEMORIAL)

St. Thérèse of Lisieux, called the Little Flower, was born in France in 1873. Her mother died when she was five, so she was raised by her father and four sisters. All five girls entered religious life. By special permission, Thérèse joined the Carmelites at the age of fifteen. She lived a life of simplicity and trust in God and died of tuberculosis when she was twenty-four. Thérèse is known for her Little Way.

Themes: Faith in God, little acts of love, trust in God

384 OCTOBER 2
The Guardian Angels (MEMORIAL)

Today we celebrate the feast of the guardian angels. These angels are sent by God to guide and protect us during our life on earth. We praise and thank God for the loving care that surrounds us. With our angels and all the heavenly hosts we celebrate this Eucharist.

Universal Prayer

The response is *"Lord, hear our prayer."*

For the Church, that it may be comforted by God's presence, we pray to the Lord.

For world leaders, that they may trust in God for guidance, we pray to the Lord.

For those facing problems, that they may turn to God for help, we pray to the Lord.

For those who are tempted, that they may pray for strength, we pray to the Lord.

For ourselves, that we may always believe in God's care for us, we pray to the Lord.

Special Features

- Distribute angel pins or pictures of angels.
- Give the children a copy of the traditional or new Guardian Angel prayer.

Songs

Holy God, We Praise Thy Name; The Lord Is Near; On Eagle's Wings (verse 4); Path of Life; Praise God from Whom All Blessings Flow; Praise the Lord, Ye Heavens; Wherever I Am, God Is; Ye Watchers and Ye Holy Ones; You Are Always with Me; You Are Near

Homily Ideas

Visual: A safety pin

Show a safety pin and comment that it has many uses, all of which help our peace of mind. Ask the children to name some uses. Remark that God has sent us each a friend, a guardian angel, who serves as a safeguard.

· · ·

Explain that a guardian angel, like all angels, is invisible because it is spirit. An angel has no body, although artists draw them with bodies and wings. Although we can't see or feel our guard-ian angel, we each have a personal, heavenly bodyguard.

· · ·

Ask the children what they think their guardian angel does for them (keeps them safe, guides them to do what is right).

· · ·

Tell a story about a time when an angel apparently helped someone, perhaps yourself. For instance, a sixty-year-old woman keeps a picture of a guardian angel above her bed. One day when she was a little girl something stopped her from jumping down from the school bus and running across the street. At the same time, a car came tearing down the street and would have hit her if she had crossed as usual. No one was with her to hold her back, so she concluded that it was her guardian angel. Ask the children if they can think of a time when their angel helped them.

· · ·

Comment that in the gospel, Jesus spoke about the angels of children. Scripture and Church tradition tell us that such angels exist. St. Frances of Rome supposedly could see her angel for twenty-three years. One night St. Catherine Labouré was taken to see Mary by her guardian angel.

· · ·

Explain that we believe that angels do not only watch over individual people, but over nations, cities, and buildings. All angels worship and serve God in heaven.

· · ·

Remind the children that God is always with them whether in the form of angels or not. God thinks that they are precious enough to guard and guide.

· · ·

Tell the children that they can pray to their angels, and their angels can pray for them.

· · ·

Ask the children to think of a person who has acted like an angel to them. Call on a few children to tell who they thought of and why.

385 OCTOBER 4
Francis of Assisi,
Religious Founder (MEMORIAL)

In 1182, Francis was born in Assisi in Italy, the son of a wealthy cloth merchant. After spending his teenage years having fun with his friends, Francis went to war, dreaming of being a knight. He was captured and imprisoned, which caused him to think about his life. One day while he was praying he heard a voice telling him, "Repair my house." Francis gave up his wealth, put on a peasant's robe, went barefoot, and begged. Anything extra that he received he shared with the poor. With the men who followed him, he formed the Friars Minor. With St. Clare he formed the order known as the Poor Clares. Today his followers are called Franciscans. Francis lived simply but joyfully. He is known for his love of all God's creatures. Two years before he died, he received the stigmata, the wounds of Christ in his hands, feet, and side.

Themes: God's creation, poverty and simplicity, love of God

Special Features
- Hold the blessing of animals. A rite for this is found in the *Book of Blessings*.
- Within the homily or as a communion reflection pray or sing prayers attributed to St. Francis: Lord, Make Me an Instrument of Your Peace or Canticle of the Sun. Song versions are Make Me a Channel of Your Peace, Happy the Man, All Creatures of Our God and King, and Canticle of the Sun.
- Invite a Franciscan to speak about St. Francis as part or all of the homily.
- Include a slide presentation of things in creation within the celebration of Mass.
- Take up a collection for the poor.

386 OCTOBER 6
Bruno, *Presbyter, Hermit, Religious Founder*

Bruno was born of a noble family in Germany about 1030. He was ordained and taught theology for twenty-five years. Then, desiring a life of solitude, prayer, and penance, Bruno and six friends became hermits. This was the beginning of the Carthusians. Six years later Bruno was called to Rome to be an advisor to the pope. There he founded another hermitage, where he died.

Themes: Penance, silence, solitude

387 also OCTOBER 6
Blessed Marie-Rose Durocher,
Virgin, Religious Founder

Marie-Rose Durocher was born in 1811 in a village near Montreal, Canada. After her mother died, she became a lay apostle in her brother's parish. She worked there as housekeeper, hostess, and parish worker for thirteen years. Then she founded a teaching community devoted to the poorest children called the Sisters of the Holy Names of Jesus and Mary. Marie-Rose's six years as a Sister were filled with poverty, difficulties, and sickness.

Themes: Devotion to duty, education of the poor, suffering

388 OCTOBER 7
Our Lady of the Rosary (MEMORIAL)

In 1571, the naval victory of the Christians over the Turks in the battle of Lepanto was attributed to Mary's intercession. The pope established this feast to commemorate this victory. October has since then been known as the month of the rosary.

In praying the rosary we meditate on the mysteries, which give an overview of the life of Christ.

Special Feature

- A decade of the rosary may be prayed before or after Mass, but not within the Mass.

389 OCTOBER 9
Denis, *Bishop, Martyr,*
and His Companions, *Martyrs*

According to Gregory of Tours, St. Denis was a bishop in the middle of the third century who was sent from Italy to France to become the first bishop of Paris. During a persecution he and a priest and a deacon were beheaded and their bodies thrown in the Seine River in 258. St. Denis is the patron of France.

Themes: Suffering for the faith

390 also OCTOBER 9
John Leonardi, *Presbyter, Religious Founder*

John Leonardi lived in the confused times of the Protestant Reformation. Born in 1541 in Italy, he became a pharmacist. He then became a priest and trained people to teach the faith. He founded a religious order called Clerks Regular of the Mother of God. His order was opposed and John had to leave town. In 1579, he founded the Confraternity of Christian Doctrine (CCD). He also helped establish a seminary for priests from mission countries. This work grew into the Society for the Propagation of the Faith. St. John helped to reform several religious orders. He died from taking care of plague victims.

Themes: The spread of the faith, learning more about the faith

391 OCTOBER 14
Callistus I, *Pope, Martyr*

Callistus was the slave of a Christian master. He was put in charge of a bank. Falsely accused of embezzlement, Callistus was sent to the salt mines. When he was released, the pope made him manager of the burial grounds and ordained him a deacon. In 217, Callistus became pope. A man named Hippolytus was shocked at this and declared himself pope. The Church was split for eighteen years. Callistus tried to bring peace until he was martyred in a riot. Hippolytus too was martyred and is now a saint.

Themes: Judging people, peace

392 OCTOBER 15
Teresa of Jesus, *Virgin, Religious,*
Doctor of the Church (MEMORIAL)

Teresa of Jesus was born in 1515 in Avila, Spain. She joined the Carmelites when she was twenty years old. Sisters in those days lived very comfortable lives talking with friends and going on vacations. After eighteen years Teresa began to receive visions and ecstasies and longed to love Christ more. She founded a stricter order called Discalced Carmelites. With the help of St. John of the Cross, she reformed the Carmelite friars and the Carmelite community she had left. A very intelligent woman, Teresa met with kings and popes and wrote books to help others pray and love God.

Themes: Love of God, prayer, reading of spiritual books

393 OCTOBER 16
Hedwig, *Married Woman, Religious*

St. Hedwig was born in Bavaria about 1174. The daughter of a count, she was educated in a monastery. When she was only twelve, she married Henry I, duke of Silesia in Poland. They had seven children. Hedwig was not only beautiful but virtuous. She was kind to the poor and even darned their clothes for them. She had hospitals, as well as monasteries and convents, built in the kingdom. After Henry died, Hedwig lived in a convent but did not become a Sister. She wanted to keep her possessions to help the poor.

Themes: Love for the poor, devotion to duty

394 also OCTOBER 16
Margaret Mary Alacoque, *Virgin, Religious*

Margaret Mary was responsible for spreading devotion to the Sacred Heart throughout the world. Born in France in 1647, she entered the Visitation convent. From 1673 to 1675 she received private revelations about the Sacred Heart of Jesus. Jesus appeared to her and said, "See this heart which has loved so much and received so little love in return." He told her to make the first Friday of each month a day of special love by receiving communion. He asked her to pray for those who didn't love him. The Jesuit St. Claude la Colombiere believed and helped Margaret Mary in spreading the devotion to the Sacred Heart.

Themes: The Sacred Heart, friendship

395 OCTOBER 17
Ignatius of Antioch,
Bishop, Martyr (MEMORIAL)

Ignatius followed St. Peter as bishop of Antioch. During a persecution he was put in a cart and taken to Rome for martyrdom. In town after town, local bishops and groups of Christians met him and encouraged him. On the way he wrote seven letters to his churches about the Church and Christian life.

Ignatius had a great love for Christ in the Eucharist. He said, "I am the wheat of Christ. May I be ground by the teeth of beasts to become the immaculate bread of Christ." He was devoured by two lions in the arena in the year 107.

Themes: The Eucharist, courage in the face of persecution

396 OCTOBER 18
Luke, *Evangelist* (FEAST)

St. Luke was a Gentile from first-century Antioch. A cultured man and a doctor, he became the co-worker of St. Paul. He is credited with being the author of the gospel that shows a particularly compassionate Christ. The writer Ernest Renan called Luke's gospel "the most beautiful book in the world." It has these themes: the mercy of Jesus, the importance of prayer, the poor, joy, and the Holy Spirit. Luke is also thought to be the author of the Acts of the Apostles, which is considered volume two of his gospel. Tradition says he was martyred when he was about eighty-four years old.

Themes: Gospels, evangelizing

Special Features
- Have a procession with candles and incense to take the lectionary to the lectern for the readings.
- As a response to the intercessions pray, "Kyrie eleison," the Greek for "Lord have mercy," in honor of Luke's background.

397 OCTOBER 19
Isaac Jogues and John de Brébeuf,
Presbyters, Religious, Missionaries, Martyrs,
and Their Companions, *Martyrs*
(MEMORIAL)

Six Jesuit priests and two volunteer lay helpers compose the group known as the North American martyrs. They were missionaries to the Native Americans. All were tortured and martyred by members of the Huron and Iroquois tribes from 1624 to 1649. Five died in what is now Canada, and three near Auriesville, New York. After once being captured, tortured, and kept as a slave by the Iroquois, Isaac Jogues escaped and went back to France. When he recovered, he returned to work among the Iroquois. Some Iroquois believed that an epidemic had been caused by Isaac Jogues. One of them killed him as Isaac came to a peace banquet. That man later converted, took the name Isaac Jogues, and became a martyr himself.

Themes: Missionary zeal, courage, witness

398 OCTOBER 20
Paul of the Cross,
Presbyter, Religious Founder

Paul of the Cross was born in Italy in 1694. After working as a merchant and then doing military service, he spent time praying and doing penance. He gathered men to help him care for the poor and sick. Then he was ordained and founded the Passionists, men who would preach parish missions to help people turn from sin and follow Christ. Later he founded the Passionist nuns. Paul was devoted to the mystery of Christ crucified and practiced harsh penances.

Themes: Penance, love of Christ crucified, ministry to the sick

399 OCTOBER 23
John of Capistrano, *Presbyter, Religious Founder*

St. John of Capistrano was born in 1386 in Italy. He became a lawyer and then a governor who worked to combat crime. He was sent as an ambassador to another province where he was taken prisoner during a battle. When he was released, he became a Franciscan. He traveled through Italy, Germany, Bohemia, Austria, Hungary, Poland, and Russia preaching prayer and penance, strengthening people's faith, and fighting against heresy. The pope asked him to help prevent a Turkish invasion of Hungary, which he did. At the age of seventy he died of a disease caught in battle.

Themes: Working against evil, helping others live the faith

400 OCTOBER 24
Anthony Mary Claret,
Bishop, Religious Founder

St. Anthony Mary was born in 1807 in Spain. He was a weaver until, at the suggestion of his bishop, he became a priest. Anthony Mary was a popular preacher and for a year preached in the Canary Islands. Back in Spain, he founded a missionary community called the Claretians. He was assigned as archbishop of Cuba where he did much good for the people. He also escaped assassination fifteen times. Eight years later he was called to Spain to serve as the queen's confessor. There he began a publishing house and wrote books and pamphlets. He participated in the first Vatican Council and then stayed in a Cistercian monastery in France until he died.

Themes: Spreading the gospel, reading and spreading Catholic literature

401 OCTOBER 28
Simon and Jude, *Apostles* (FEAST)

Simon and Jude are apostles. Simon came from Cana and was called Zealot. The Zealots were a

Jewish group who tried to free the Jewish nation from Roman rule. Jude Thaddeus was supposedly a fisherman. In Scripture he is called the brother of James. According to tradition, Simon preached in Egypt and Jude in Mesopotamia. Then both preached in Persia, which is now Iran. There they were martyred. St. Jude is believed to be the author of the Letter of Jude in the Bible. He is known as the saint of impossible cases.

Themes: Discipleship, witnessing to the faith

Special Features

- Display symbols of these apostles. Jude is pictured with a club, the instrument of his death, and a flame over his head to show the Holy Spirit's influence. Simon is pictured with a fish, the symbol for Christ. Jude's shield is red and shows a sailboat with a cross on the mast. Simon's shield bears two oars and a hatchet.
- Sing hymns about following Jesus.

NOVEMBER

402 NOVEMBER 1
All Saints (SOLEMNITY)

In the presence of all the angels and saints we celebrate the Eucharist. This sacred meal in memory of Jesus' death and rising binds us together in the communion of saints. Today we honor the saints who have gone before us into the next world. We ask them to pray for us who are still trying to love God and others on earth.

Universal Prayer
The response is *"Lord, hear our prayer."*

That the Church may attract others by its holiness, we pray to the Lord.
That rulers may lead people to follow God's laws of love, we pray to the Lord.
That those who live unholy lives may realize God calls them to be holy, we pray to the Lord.
That Christians who are insulted and persecuted because of their faith may have courage, we pray to the Lord.

That we may someday join all the saints in heaven, we pray to the Lord.

Special Features
- Have the children dress like saints or wear crowns or banners with a saint's name.
- Let the entire congregation join in the entrance processional and/ or the recessional.
- Display banners or posters in honor of the saints.
- Distribute holy cards of saints.

Songs
Beatitudes; Blessed Feasts of Blessed Martyrs; Blest Are They; Eye Has Not Seen; For All the Saints; Holy, Holy, Holy; Lead Me, Lord; Now Thank We All Our God; Praise God in His Holy Dwelling; Praise to the Lord; Saints of God in Glory; Sing with All the Saints in Glory; This Alone; We Are the Light of the World

Homily Ideas

Visual: A salt shaker

Sprinkle some salt into your hand or walk around the church sprinkling salt and tell the children that Jesus told us to be salt for the earth. Ask the children if they would like popcorn or potato chips without salt. Ask what salt is good for (for making food taste better, preserving food). Tell the children that when Jesus calls us to be salt, he means that we are to be the kind of person that makes life better for everyone. We are to keep life good. We are to be saints.

• • •

Tell the children that today the Church celebrates all those people who were good salt for the earth. These saints are now enjoying their reward in heaven and see God face to face. This group includes well-known saints. Ask the children to name some. Point out that in heaven are thousands whose names we don't know. Recall the first reading that describes the saints as a crowd of people beyond counting who are from every nation. The crowd includes our grandparents and great-grandparents and other people we know who have died.

• • •

Mention that in the first reading John says that the saints are praising God together. They will do this forever and ever. When we celebrate Mass we join their endless praise.

• • •

Explain that St. Paul called the early Christians who were still on earth saints. He did this because they belonged to God's family and had been redeemed by Christ. They were holy by their baptism. We, too, should be living saints. Ask the children how they could be a saint right now (by doing what is right, by praying). Point out that when they do the right thing, they too are salt for the earth.

• • •

State that the description of a saint was given by Jesus' beatitudes in today's gospel. The beatitudes are ways to be blessed, or saintly. Briefly explain each: someone is blessed who trusts God for everything, is sad because of sin and evil, is humble instead of self-centered, sets his or her heart on doing what is right, is merciful, is pure, is a peacemaker, and is treated badly as a result of doing good.

• • •

Tell the anecdote about the teacher who asked what saints were. A small boy thinking of the stained-glass windows in church answered, "They're people the light shines through." Comment that that is what we are to be like, people the light of Christ shines through. Everyone should see in us the love of Christ.

• • •

Tell the story of a favorite saint, or let children tell some of theirs.

• • •

Encourage the children to pray to their baptismal patron saint, the saint of their parish, and any favorite saints. Remind them that the Queen of All Saints is Mary, the Mother of God.

---

403 NOVEMBER 2
The Commemoration of All the Faithful Departed (All Souls)

[*Note:* See the suggestions under "For the Dead," one of the Masses for special occasions.]

---

404 NOVEMBER 3
Martin de Porres, *Religious*

Martin de Porres was born in Lima, Peru, in 1579. His father was a white Spanish nobleman and his mother was a freed black woman from Panama. Martin's father deserted the family when Martin and his sister were young. At the age of twelve, Martin became an apprentice to a barber/surgeon. He worked long hours nursing the sick and then spent long hours in prayer. He became a Dominican lay brother and was known for his humility. He was ordained nine years later. Martin was head of the monastery infirmary. He also begged for the poor, founded an orphanage and a hospital, and ministered to slaves brought from Africa. People called him Martin of Charity.

Themes: Ministry to the sick, prayer, humility

405 NOVEMBER 4
Charles Borromeo, *Bishop* (MEMORIAL)

Charles Borromeo was born into a wealthy family in Italy in 1538. By the age of twenty-one he had doctorates in civil and canon law. His uncle, Pope Pius IV, called him to Rome, made him a cardinal, and put him in charge of the papal states. Charles worked to prepare for the Council of Trent. During the Council he helped to keep peace. After he was ordained, he became archbishop of Milan. He did much good in his diocese, even caring for his people during the plague when many officials had left the town. He also tried to reform the lives of priests and religious.

Themes: Renewal, peace, care for the sick

406 NOVEMBER 9
The Dedication of the
Lateran Basilica in Rome (FEAST)

In the first part of the fourth century, Emperor Constantine gave the pope property on a hill near central Rome. The buildings there have come to be known as the Lateran. The central basilica is the cathedral of Rome, the seat of the bishop of Rome, the pope. As such it is the "mother and head of all churches throughout the world." It is named St. John Lateran for John the Baptist.

Themes: Churches, prayer

407 NOVEMBER 10
Leo the Great, *Pope, Doctor of the Church*
(MEMORIAL)

Leo was probably born in Rome. As a deacon he was looked to for advice and explanations of doctrine. He was often sent to settle arguments between leaders. The people and clergy called on him to be pope in 440. As pope, Leo helped preserve the Church's unity during a time of heresies and invasions. When Attila and the Huns marched toward Rome, Leo met them and kept them from destroying it. Then, after the Vandals attacked and pillaged Rome, Leo helped rebuild the city. He is also famous for his good sermons and his writings explaining the faith.

Themes: Use of gifts for the Church, church unity

408 NOVEMBER 11
Martin of Tours, *Bishop* (MEMORIAL)

St. Martin of Tours was born in Hungary, the son of a Roman army officer. He was raised in Italy, where he heard about Jesus. Not until he was a soldier was he able to be baptized. A legend is that one cold day Martin cut his cloak in two with his sword and gave half to a beggar he met on the road. In a dream that night he saw Jesus wearing the part of the cloak he had given the beggar. Martin resigned from the army, for he could not hurt another person. He wrote to the emperor, "I have served you as a soldier. Allow me now to become a soldier of God." The emperor called him a coward. Martin became a monk and founded the first monastery in the West. In 372 the people of Tours asked for him to be their bishop. Martin founded more monasteries and worked to spread the faith to the countryside.

Themes: Respect for life, evangelizing

409 NOVEMBER 12
Josaphat, *Bishop, Religious, Martyr*
(MEMORIAL)

St. Josaphat was born in Poland in 1580 and named John Kuncevic. He was an Orthodox Christian but became Catholic. When he was a boy, six Orthodox bishops sought union with the Roman Catholic Church. After being a merchant, Josaphat became a monk of the Order of St. Basil. Then he was ordained a priest in the Byzantine Rite. Josaphat became a bishop and then archbishop of Polotsk, where there was much unrest. He worked for church unity at a time when people feared the rule of Rome. He was assassinated by a mob while visiting his people who had named their own bishop. Now he is the patron for the reunion of the Greek and Latin churches.

Themes: Church unity, zeal for the faith

410 NOVEMBER 13
Frances Xavier Cabrini,
Virgin, Religious, Missionary (MEMORIAL)

Mother Cabrini is the first canonized United States citizen. Born in Italy in 1850, she tried to enter a convent but was turned away because of poor health. She worked in an orphanage and then began an order called the Missionary Sisters of the Sacred Heart. She hoped to go to China, but the pope told her, "No, not to the East but to the West." Many Italian immigrants in the United States needed help. With six sisters, Mother Cabrini traveled to New York where she opened an orphanage. In thirty-five years she founded nearly seventy institutions and crossed the ocean thirty times. She also founded schools in South America. In 1917, Mother Cabrini died of malaria in one of her hospitals in Chicago.

Themes: Missionary zeal, works of mercy

411 NOVEMBER 15
Albert the Great,
Bishop, Religious, Doctor of the Church

St. Albert was born in 1206 in Germany. He studied at Padua and became a Dominican. He became a teacher in Paris and taught St. Thomas Aquinas. Albert had knowledge in many fields. He spent twenty years writing a collection of knowledge. To him all of science reflected the providence of God. Albert was made provincial of his order and later was appointed a bishop. After two years as bishop he was able to return to writing and teaching. He is the patron of scientists.

Themes: Creation as revealing God, importance of knowledge

412 NOVEMBER 16
Margaret of Scotland, *Married Woman*

Margaret was born in Hungary and raised in court there while her father was exiled. When she was twelve she was sent to England. On the way back to Hungary with her mother, brother, and sister, the ship was blown off course and landed in Scotland. Margaret married King Malcolm III of Scotland and had eight children. She brought art and education to the people and showed great devotion to the poor, feeding them and washing their feet. Margaret died four days after her husband was killed in an attack on the castle in 1093. Her children carried on the progress she made in Scotland.

Themes: Caring for the poor, value of education

413 also NOVEMBER 16
Gertrude the Great, *Virgin, Religious*

Gertrude, a great mystic, was born in 1256 in Germany. As a child she went to the Cistercian

Abbey where she was educated. She became a Benedictine nun herself and spent her life studying and writing. She especially wrote about revelations she had. These centered on the love between herself and Christ. She was devoted to the Sacred Heart.

Themes: Prayer, study of religion, the Sacred Heart

414 NOVEMBER 17
Elizabeth of Hungary,
Married Woman, Religious (MEMORIAL)

Elizabeth, the daughter of the king of Hungary, was born in 1207. When she was fourteen she married Louis IV of Thuringia. They were happily married and had three children. Together the couple tried to follow the ideals of St. Francis. Elizabeth sold her possessions and gave the money to the poor. Louis supported her in this. Elizabeth also dressed simply and bore the resentment of her in-laws and the court members. After six years of marriage, when Elizabeth was expecting their third child, Louis died on the way to a war. The in-laws forced Elizabeth and her children out of the palace. They stayed with her uncle, a bishop. When Louis's friends returned from the war, they regained her rightful place. Her son was next in line to the throne. Elizabeth became a Third Order Franciscan and worked in a hospital that she had built. She died when she was only twenty-four. She is the patron of Catholic Charities and Third Order Franciscans.

Themes: Simple lifestyle, works of mercy

415 NOVEMBER 18
The Dedication of the Basilicas of the Apostles Peter and Paul in Rome

[See also June 29, Peter and Paul, page 138.]

Today we celebrate the feast of the churches named for the two great apostles Peter and Paul. Actually we celebrate the whole Catholic Church, which these two giants of the faith helped to form. Both Peter and Paul gave their lives to spreading the Good News of Jesus. For two thousand years Christians have followed them in living by the teachings of Jesus and celebrating his sacraments. During this Eucharist we join with other members of the Church all over the world.

Universal Prayer
The response is *"Lord, hear our prayer."*

For the Church, that it may grow both in numbers and in devotion to Christ, let us pray to the Lord.

For world leaders, that they may promote and protect life, let us pray to the Lord.

For our Holy Father, bishops, and priests, that they may guide the Church with the faith and love of Peter and Paul, let us pray to the Lord.

For ourselves, that we may always love the Church, let us pray to the Lord.

Special Features
- Let the children take parts for the reading of the gospel.
- Show slides of the basilicas as part of the homily.
- Distribute pictures of Peter or Paul.

Songs
Christ Be Our Light; The Church's One Foundation; Do You Really Love Me?; Lord, to Whom Shall We Go?; Paul's Prayer; Precious Lord, Take My Hand; Send Us Forth; Sing a New Church; Song of the Body of Christ; Where Two or Three Are Gathered.

Homily Ideas

Visual: A picture or blueprint of your parish church

Show the picture or blueprint of your parish church. Remark that a church is holy space. God dwells in our churches, and God's holy people worship there. Comment on the name and history of your church.

. . .

Tell the children that basilicas are large churches. Our largest basilica is the basilica of St. Peter in Rome. It and the basilica of St. Paul were completed in the fourth century. They were destroyed in wars and then rebuilt. The basilica of St. Peter is over his tomb, and St. Paul's honors the place where Paul was martyred.

. . .

Ask the children why St. Peter is so important (he was one of the twelve apostles. He was the first leader of the Church). Ask why St. Paul is so important (he spread Christianity to the Gentiles, founded many churches, and wrote letters that are in the Bible).

. . .

Comment that both Peter and Paul loved Jesus with all their hearts. They did much for him and suffered greatly for him. Explain that the first reading tells how Paul, who was arrested for being a Christian, was taken as a prisoner to Rome. Both saints were martyred in Rome for Christ.

. . .

Tell the children that Peter and Paul received courage and strength from Jesus to carry out their difficult missions. Point out that in the gospel Peter, with Jesus' help, is able to walk on the water. As long as he trusted Jesus, he could do the impossible. Explain that we, too, can do wonderful things if we trust Jesus to help us. We can do what is right when everyone else seems to be doing something else. We can go to Mass each weekend when it's easier not to. We can be nice to someone that no one likes. We can share what we have with other people.

. . .

Mention that Peter and Paul went out to spread the Good News to others. They didn't just stay at home and be glad that they themselves were saved. Tell the parable of the two seas in the Holy Land: The Sea of Galilee has good, fresh water. Fish swim in it and trees, flowers, and grass grow along its shores. The Dead Sea is like its name. Nothing lives in it, and all around it are rock and sand. The difference between the two seas is that the Sea of Galilee gives its water to the Jordan River, which carries it to the Dead Sea. The Dead Sea keeps all the water to itself.

. . .

Explain that the Holy Father, who governs and guides the Church, lives in Rome. The main government offices of the Church are also there. Rome is special because Peter and Paul died there. Sometimes it is called the eternal city.

. . .

Encourage the children to pray for the pope and bishops.

416 also NOVEMBER 18
Rose Philippine Duchesne,
Virgin, Religious, Missionary

Rose was born in France in 1769 and went to a school of the Visitation Sisters. She joined the community, but the French Revolution forced them to disband. When St. Madeleine Sophie Barat started the Society of the Sacred Heart, Rose joined them. When she was forty-nine, her dream of being a missionary in America came true. She went to St. Louis, Missouri, with four other Sisters and opened the first free school for girls west of the Mississippi. Rose founded six convents. At the age of seventy-one she resigned as American superior. She went to Kansas, where the Sisters opened a school for Native Americans. Mother Duchesne could not speak the language or teach, but she prayed for four hours each morning and evening. The people called her "Woman Who Always Prays."

Themes: Prayer, missionary zeal

417 NOVEMBER 21
The Presentation of the Virgin Mary (MEMORIAL)

This feast celebrates the apocryphal story of Mary being presented in the Temple at the age of three. It is also thought to be the anniversary of the dedication of the church of Santa Maria Nova in Jerusalem, which occurred on November 1, 543. In any case, on this feast we honor Mary, the new Temple of God.

Themes: Mary, dedication to God

418 NOVEMBER 22
Cecilia, *Virgin, Martyr* (MEMORIAL)

As far as is known, Cecilia was a martyr in Italy in the second century. A story about her is that she wanted to give her life to God, but her parents forced her to marry a nobleman. It is said that she sang to the Lord in her heart while the musical instruments sounded for her wedding. She converted her husband and his brother, and all three died as martyrs. Legend says that Cecilia was struck three times on the neck with a sword and lived for three days. She is often shown with a musical instrument and is the patron of musicians.

Themes: Love of Christ, converting others

419 NOVEMBER 23
Clement I, *Pope, Martyr*

Clement is believed to have been martyred around the year 100. He was the fourth pope. St. Irenaeus stated that Clement knew the apostles. Clement wrote a letter to the people of Corinth, a city in which the church was divided. In this letter Clement explained the role of authority and encouraged peace.

Themes: Respect for authority, peace

420 also NOVEMBER 23
Columban, *Abbot, Missionary*

St. Columban was a great Irish missionary. He was born about the year 543 in Ireland and became a monk. He led a life of prayer and study for thirty years. Then he went to France and Switzerland, where he founded monasteries and spoke out against the immorality of the times. He was exiled for his criticism of the king and complacent local bishops. On the way back to Ireland his ship was wrecked, and he went instead to Rome where he founded another monastery.

Themes: Missionary work, need for reform

421 also NOVEMBER 23
Blessed Miguel Agustín Pro, *Presbyter, Religious, Martyr*

Miguel Pro was born in Guadalupe, Mexico, in 1891. He became a Jesuit. Because of persecution in Mexico, he studied in other countries and was ordained in Belgium. He returned to Mexico at a time when public worship was banned there. Father Pro lived with his parents and secretly ministered to the faithful. He wore many disguises and delighted in playing pranks to help him escape. When an assassination attempt was made on a Mexican general, the police arrested Father Pro and his two younger brothers. With no witnesses and no trial Father Pro and his brothers were condemned to death. Although the man behind the plot confessed,

Father Pro was executed by firing squad. His last words were "Long live Christ the king!"

Themes: Christian joy, steadfastness in faith

422 NOVEMBER 24
Andrew Dung-Lac, *Presbyter, Martyr,*
and His Companions, *Martyrs* (MEMORIAL)

Vietnam has seen several persecutions of Catholics. One hundred and seventeen Vietnamese martyrs were canonized together. The group includes eight bishops, fifty priests, and fifty-nine lay Catholics. Andrew Dung-Lac was a parish priest. Eleven of the group were Spanish, ten were French, and ninety-six were Vietnamese. They died for their faith between 1820 and 1862. Andrew was beheaded in Hanoi.

Themes: Suffering for the faith, courage

422A NOVEMBER 25
Catherine of Alexandria, *Virgin, Martyr*

Catherine is one of the most famous of the early virgin martyrs. She died for the faith in the early fourth century. Tradition holds that she was beautiful and intelligent and converted many people. She was united to Christ in a mystical marriage. Supposedly the emperor tried to persuade her to give up the faith by torture and by a marriage proposal. When she refused, he sentenced her to death on a spiked wheel. This broke, and so she was then beheaded. For centuries people have turned to Catherine to intercede for them.

Themes: Evangelization, strong faith in the face of persecution

423 NOVEMBER 30
Andrew, *Apostle* (FEAST)

St. Andrew was an apostle, the brother of St. Peter, and a disciple of John the Baptist. He was a fisherman in Galilee and one of the first to be called to follow Christ. Andrew became a missionary in the area around the Black Sea. He died a martyr. Tradition says that in Greece he was tied to a cross that was shaped like the letter X. St. Andrew is especially venerated by the Eastern churches.

Themes: Discipleship, spreading the faith

DECEMBER

425 DECEMBER 3
Francis Xavier, *Presbyter, Religious, Missionary*
(MEMORIAL)

St. Francis Xavier, the Apostle of the Indies, was born of a noble family in Spain in 1506. He studied at the University of Paris, where he met Ignatius Loyola, a retired soldier who was a student. With five other men, Francis joined Ignatius, who founded the Society of Jesus, the Jesuits. They became priests. Francis went to India as a missionary; there he lived and worked with the poor. He built mission churches on the islands of Malaysia and Japan. His dream was to work in China. On his way to China he became ill while aboard the ship. He was let off on an island where he could see China, and he died there in a fisherman's hut.

Themes: Vocation, missionary work

426 DECEMBER 4
John of Damascus,
Presbyter, Doctor of the Church

John was born at Damascus around the year 675. He grew up in the court of the Muslim ruler there. His father, a Christian court official, had a monk who was a war captive educate John. After holding a government post, John became a monk in Jerusalem and then was ordained. He wrote much about the faith and is especially known for his writings on Mary. He also wrote religious poems and hymns. John opposed the heresy of the Iconoclasts, who were against religious images. He is the last Greek Father of the Church.

Themes: Religious art, love of Mary

427 DECEMBER 6
Nicholas, *Bishop*

Nicholas was the bishop of Myra, which was on the southern coast of Turkey. He lived in the first half of the fourth century, and it is believed that he participated in the Council of Nicea. There are many legends about his generosity. One of the best known is the story of the poor man who did not have dowries for his three daughters. Whenever it came time for a daughter to be married, Nicholas threw a bag of gold into an open window where the man slept. In the United States and England, St. Nicholas has come to be known as Santa Claus. He is the patron of children, brides, and sailors.

Themes: Generosity, love for the poor

Special Feature
- Present a small gift to the children after Mass.

428 DECEMBER 7
Ambrose, *Bishop, Doctor of the Church* (MEMORIAL)

Ambrose was born around the year 340, the son of a Roman who was a chief officer in the army. Ambrose became governor of Milan, Italy. When the bishop of Milan died, Ambrose was a catechumen, planning to be baptized. At the election for the next bishop, a fight broke out. Ambrose called for peace, and the people began to cry, "Ambrose for bishop." Quickly Ambrose was baptized, ordained, and consecrated bishop. As bishop he fought against the heresy of Arianism, which claimed that Jesus was not God. Ambrose was also responsible for the conversion of St. Augustine.

Themes: Acting for the right, peacemaking

429 DECEMBER 8
The Immaculate Conception of the Virgin Mary (SOLEMNITY)

On this day we celebrate that Mary was free from sin from the first moment of her existence within her mother, St. Ann. Mary under the title of the Immaculate Conception is the patron of the United States. As we join in the sacrifice of her Son, which saved the world, we ask Mary to help us be loving like her. Then we will also be like her Son, Jesus Christ.

Universal Prayer
The response is *"Lord, hear our prayer."*

That the Church may look to Mary as her best model, let us pray to the Lord.

That people in authority may lead with loving and merciful hearts, let us pray to the Lord.

That mothers everywhere may teach their children the ways of Mary, let us pray to the Lord.

That the United States may be blessed, let us pray to the Lord.

That we may show devotion to Mary by trying to imitate her, let us pray to the Lord.

Special Features

- Decorate the Mary's altar or shrine with a white Mary candle and flowers.
- Have children take parts for the first reading and the gospel.
- Give out blue ribbons to wear for the day or medals or holy cards of Mary.

Songs

Immaculate Mary; Mary Immaculate, Star of the Morning; Mary the Dawn; O Holy Mary; She Will Show Us the Promised One

Homily Ideas

Visual: A white cloth

Show a white cloth and ask the children if there is a spot on it. Explain that the cloth is spotless, or immaculate. It is pure white. Explain that Mary is called the Immaculate Conception. This means that she had no sin. She was pure from her conception, or the time she first came into being.

. . .

Recall that in the gospel the angel Gabriel greeted Mary with, "You are truly blessed. The Lord is with you." We pray, "Hail, Mary, full of grace." Explain that Mary was always completely filled with God's life. The gospel of today reminds us of the time she agreed to be the mother of Jesus.

. . .

Mention that God would want the perfect mother to raise and care for Jesus and teach him how to live as a human being.

. . .

Point out that Mary never sinned during her life on earth. She always loved God and did what God wished. She always showed love for other people. Ask for some examples (she helped Elizabeth, an older relative who was pregnant. She saved the newlyweds at Cana from being embarrassed when the wine ran out). Ask what Mary does because she loves us (she prays for us).

. . .

Assure the children that being good and doing what God wanted wasn't easy for Mary, just as it isn't always easy for us. It was hard to be the mother of Jesus and be pregnant when Joseph didn't understand. It was hard to be the mother of Jesus when people made fun of him and criticized him. It was hard to be his mother and watch him suffer and die. Because Mary was human like us, she was tempted at times, too. But her love for God made her resist sin.

. . .

Encourage the children to pray to Mary. Ask them what prayers we can pray to her (Hail Mary, the Rosary, Angelus, Memorare). Add that we can always just talk to our heavenly mother in our own words the way we talk to our mothers on earth.

. . .

Talk about the National Shrine of the Immaculate Conception in Washington, D.C., which contains shrines to Mary from many nations.

. . .

Tell the children that we are to try to imitate our mother Mary. Although we are sinners, we can always try to be pure like her. We can try to listen to God. We can let our love flow out to others. State that it would be wonderful if when we reach heaven, Jesus can say to us, "You remind me so much of my mother."

430 DECEMBER 9
Juan Diego, *Hermit*

Juan Diego was born in 1474. He was an Aztec Indian who lived near Mexico City. He and his wife were converts. When Juan was a fifty-seven-year-old widower, he saw the Immaculate Virgin Mary as he was on his way to Mass. She asked to have a shrine built there on Tepeyac Hill and promised to help people. Mary sent Juan to the bishop. The bishop asked Juan for a sign that the woman was the Mother of God. On the day that Mary promised to meet Juan and give him a sign, his uncle was ill, so Juan missed the meeting. The following day as Juan went to get a priest for his dying uncle, Mary appeared. She told Juan to gather flowers on the hill even though it was winter. Juan found roses there and picked them. Mary arranged them in his cloak and sent him to the bishop. Before the bishop Juan opened his cloak and let the roses fall to the floor. On his cloak was a life-size image of Mary as she had appeared to Juan. The bishop called her Our Lady of Guadalupe, after a shrine in Spain. Juan Diego spent the next seventeen years bringing others to the faith. It is said that through him eight million Aztec Indians became Catholic.

Themes: Our Lady of Guadalupe, missionary work, works of mercy

431 DECEMBER 11
Damasus I, *Pope*

St. Damasus was born of Spanish descent in Rome about the year 305. He was archivist of the Church and preserved records of the persecutions. As pope, he was devoted to the martyrs buried in the catacombs. Damasus had St. Jerome translate the Bible into Latin, which was the language of the people. He also had to defend himself in court when an antipope elected by a small group accused him of a serious crime.

Themes: Persecution, devotion to the saints

432 DECEMBER 12
Our Lady of Guadalupe (FEAST)

Mary appeared to Juan Diego in 1531 on Tepeyac Hill near Mexico City. She looked like a pregnant Indian woman, and she was shining. As a sign to the bishop of the reality of Juan's vision, Mary let Juan find roses in the winter to take to the bishop. He wrapped these in his cloak on which Mary left a picture of herself. Mary promised Juan she would pray for people. She asked for a shrine to be built on the hill where she appeared.

Themes: Mary as Mother, devotion to Mary

433 DECEMBER 13
Lucy, *Virgin, Martyr* (MEMORIAL)

St. Lucy was born in Sicily and was martyred about the year 304. According to a legend, Lucy had vowed to remain unmarried. When the man to whom she was engaged found out, he turned her in as a Christian. The name Lucy means light. She is a fitting saint for Advent. Her feast is celebrated in Sweden by having the oldest girl in the family bring special Lucy buns as breakfast in bed to her parents. The girl wears a white dress with a red sash. In some St. Lucy rituals the girl wears lighted candles in a crown on her head. Lucy is the patron of eyes.

Themes: Light of Christ, being persecuted for the faith

434 DECEMBER 14
John of the Cross,
Presbyter, Doctor of the Church (MEMORIAL)

St. John of the Cross was born in Spain about 1541.

He spent much of his youth in an institution for children. At the age of seventeen he worked as a nurse and went to a Jesuit college. He entered the Carmelite Order and became a teacher at a university. John helped Teresa of Avila as she reformed the Carmelite Order, and he also worked to reform the Carmelite men. He began to live very simply in prayer and solitude. Misunderstood, John was once imprisoned in a cell for nine months. During this time he had beautiful prayer experiences. When he escaped, he became a leader in Carmelite communities. His writings describe the spiritual life and union with God.

Themes: Prayer, union with God, reform

435 DECEMBER 21
Peter Canisius, *Presbyter, Religious, Doctor of the Church*

Peter was born in Holland in 1521 and became a Jesuit priest. He was sent to Germany. It was the time of the Protestant Reformation. Peter rekindled the faith in people. He wrote to defend the faith and advised popes. He attended the Council of Trent and wrote a catechism that was translated into fifteen languages. He also founded seminaries and colleges. Peter died in Switzerland.

Themes: Spreading the faith, Catholic literature

436 DECEMBER 23
John of Kanty, *Presbyter*

St. John Wacienga was born about 1390 in Kanty, Poland. He became a priest and a teacher at the University of Cracow. He led a life of penance and was known for his generosity. When jealous faculty members caused him to be transferred to parish work, he was not successful. He returned to the university where he was much loved by the stu-dents and remembered for his holiness. John gave everything to the poor and kept only the clothes he most needed.

Themes: Penance, generosity

437 DECEMBER 26
Stephen, *First Martyr* (FEAST)

St. Stephen, who lived in Palestine during the first century, was one of the first deacons. He served the needy and preached. When he was falsely accused, he defended himself in court. His words angered the people, who then dragged him outside and stoned him to death. As he suffered, Stephen prayed that the Father forgive his persecutors. In this act he imitated Jesus. Stephen was the first martyr. He died in Jerusalem about the year 36. St. Paul, who was not yet converted, was present. The account of Stephen's death is found in the Acts of the Apostles.

Themes: Deacons, dying for the faith

438 DECEMBER 27
John, Apostle, *Evangelist* (FEAST)

St. John, the brother of James, was one of the three favored apostles. He was called by Jesus as he was mending nets with his father, Zebedee. According to Scripture, John was the only apostle at the foot of the cross. Jesus entrusted to him his mother, Mary. It is said that when John was old, he always gave the same homily: "Little children, love one another." John is credited with having written one of the gospels, three letters, and the Book of Revelation. The only apostle not to be martyred, he was exiled to the isle of Patmos, where he died.

Themes: Discipleship, gospels, love

439 DECEMBER 28
The Holy Innocents, *Martyrs* (FEAST)

This feast is in memory of those infants who were killed by King Herod's soldiers when they were seeking Jesus. They are boys two years old and younger who lived in Bethlehem. No one knows how many were killed.

Themes: Infancy narratives, dying for Jesus

Special Feature
• In the Prayer of the Faithful, include a petition for children who are not allowed to live.

440 DECEMBER 29
Thomas Becket, *Bishop, Martyr*

Thomas lived in the twelfth century. He was a young legal clerk who was an excellent speaker and businessman. At the archbishop of Canterbury's recommendation, he became chancellor of England for eight years. He loved a life of fine clothes, entertainment, hunting, and good times. He also became a close friend of King Henry II. This king wanted to take some powers from the Church and needed the help of an archbishop, so he appointed Thomas archbishop of Canterbury. This appointment changed Thomas completely. He sold his be-longings and gave the money to the poor. He went to live in a monastery. Moreover, he stood firm in protecting the Church, even when it meant going against Henry. The king threatened Thomas, who fled to a monastery in France for six years. Thomas returned and there was peace until the pope angered Henry, and Thomas upheld the pope. Henry exclaimed, "Will no one rid me of this troublesome priest?" Four knights murdered Thomas while he was praying in the cathedral. Henry did public penance.

Themes: Following your conscience, supporting the Church

441 DECEMBER 31
Sylvester I, *Pope*

St. Sylvester became pope in 314 and governed the Church for twenty-one years. He fought against Arianism, the heresy that denied that Jesus was God. Although persecutions were ended, Sylvester had to deal carefully with the emperor, who oversaw the Church. Sylvester built churches in Rome. He was a humble man who led a hidden life, and he was the first person to be honored as a saint who was not a martyr.

Themes: Church leaders, devotion to duty, humility

Commons

Common of the Dedication of a Church

(PAGE W263) ISAIAH 56:1, 6–7 or EPHESIANS 2:20–22 or REVELATION 21:1–4 • LUKE 19:1–10

We celebrate today that God is with us in a special way in our churches, in particular in (name of church being celebrated). *When we are in church, we are in God's presence no less than Moses was on Mount Sinai or in the Meeting Tent, no less than Zacchaeus was when Jesus came to his house. A church is God's house where we, God's people, gather to worship. Let us sing and pray joyfully to our good God, who is here in this church with us today.*

Universal Prayer

The response is *"Lord, hear our prayer."*

That church members may be aware that God dwells in them and strive to be holy, we pray to the Lord.

That those who worship in the church that we celebrate today may come closer to God, we pray to the Lord.

That all people may come to know the one true God, we pray to the Lord.

That people who feel hurt or rejected by the Church feel at home again in the Church through the love of others, we pray to the Lord.

That those who build churches and those who take care of churches may be blessed, we pray to the Lord.

Special Features

- Include the whole assembly in the entrance procession and recessional.
- Give each child a booklet about the parish church.
- As a communion reflection, show slides of different churches. Conclude with pictures of people who are temples of God.
- Have a special collection for the upkeep of your church.
- Decorate the church with banners.

Songs

Christ Be Our Light; The Church's One Foundation; Father, We Thank Thee; I Rejoiced; Into the House of God; Out of Darkness; Sing a New Church; Sing of the Lord's Goodness; Song of the Body of Christ; We Have Been Told; Where Two or Three Are Gathered

Homily Ideas

Visual: A tabernacle lamp

Comment that the Catechism calls God not only God Most High but God Most Near. God is near us by being with us in churches in a special way. Explain that people long ago considered mountains to be holy places where God was. They went up a mountain to meet God and to offer sacrifice. We do not have to go up a mountain to meet God. Today a church is sacred space, for it is God's house.

. . .

Point out the tabernacle lamp, which is a sign of God's presence. The ever-burning light is a symbol of God's glory and love. In church we can find strength, comfort, peace, and joy.

. . .

Discuss church etiquette: genuflecting reverently, taking holy water and blessing ourselves reverently when we enter and leave the church, keeping quiet and being silent in the sacred space.

. . .

Mention that church is a foretaste and reminder of our eternal home where we will be with God forever. The church is not only God's house, but our house too, for we are God's children.

. . .

Encourage love for the church by reminding the children that important events in our lives are celebrated there: baptisms when we become children of God and members of the faith community, wed-

dings, and funerals. Explain that the greatest act we can perform takes place in church: the offering of Jesus to the Father in the sacrifice of the Mass.

. . .

Refer to how happy Zacchaeus was when Jesus said he would come to his house and eat with him. Remind the children that we can also be with Jesus when we come to church. Jesus is Emmanuel, God with us, in the Blessed Sacrament. At Mass we express sorrow for our sins, as Zacchaeus did, and we share a sacred meal.

. . .

Point out that some people say they don't have to pray in church. They can pray anywhere. Tell the story about the priest who visited a woman who asked why she should go to church. As they talked, a live coal fell out from the fireplace onto the floor. Apart from the other coals, it soon cooled off and died. The priest said, "That is why you need to worship with other members of the Church."

. . .

Talk about the church whose dedication is being commemorated. Point out features of the parish church. Explain that people make sacrifices so that their church is a fitting dwelling for God.

. . .

Explain that God dwells in us, too, and that is why Paul tells us in the letter to the Ephesians that we are like a holy temple. Together all the church members are a building, and Christ is the most important stone.

Common of the Blessed Virgin Mary

(PAGE W267) ISAIAH 9:2–3A, 6–7A or ZECHARIAH 2:14–15 or ACTS 1:12–13A, 14 or EPHESIANS 1:3–6
LUKE 1:26–38 or LUKE 2:41–51 or JOHN 19:25–27

Because Mary agreed to be the mother of Jesus, she became the holy mother of God. She is honored above all people on earth. Mary is also our mother. We look

to her for help. Mary is our model of how to live like Christ. We try to imitate her faith in God, her obedience, and her love. During this Eucharist we think of

Mary and honor her as we offer the sacrifice of her Son, who redeemed us.

Universal Prayer

The response is *"Lord, hear our prayer."*

For the Church, that its members may resemble their mother, Mary, we pray to the Lord.

For mothers everywhere, that they may truly love their children and be willing to sacrifice for them, we pray to the Lord.

For sinners, that they may turn again to God, we pray to the Lord.

For ourselves, that we may have the faith of Mary, we pray to the Lord.

Special Features

- Arrange flowers and candles around the image of Mary.
- Use a musical setting for the second responsorial psalm provided, which is the Magnificat. Accompany it with a dance by a few students.
- Display banners with the titles of Mary.
- Distribute holy cards of Mary to the children, perhaps Our Lady of Perpetual Help.

Songs

Blest of the Lord; Hail Mary: Gentle Woman; Hail, Holy Queen; Hail, Mary; Holy Is His Name; Immaculate Mary; Mary Full of Grace; Mary's Joy; Mary's Song; My Soul Rejoices; Sing of Mary

Homily Ideas

Visual: A picture of Mary and Jesus

Comment that most pictures of Mary show her with Jesus. Explain that because Mary is Jesus' mother, she is very important. When God asked her to be the Mother of God, Mary said yes. As a result, God came into the world as a human being, like one of us. Jesus was born, and we were saved from sin and death.

. . . .

Elaborate on what it meant to be the Mother of Jesus. Mary gave birth to him, fed him, taught him to speak and walk, washed his clothes, and taught him to pray. Recall how frightened she must have been when he was missing for three days. Point out that when Jesus was found in the Temple, she reacted as their parents would have by asking, "How could you do this to us?"

. . . .

Refer to the picture of Our Lady of Perpetual Help to reinforce the relationship between Mary and Jesus. Tell the children that this picture shows Jesus with a shoe partly off. It is said that in Jesus' hurry to run to his mother's arms, it came loose.

. . . .

Explain that because Mary was the Mother of God, she had the privilege of being free from sin from the first moment she existed. She is the greatest Christian.

. . . .

Ask the children what they think Mary was doing when the angel appeared to her in Nazareth. Explain that Mary was like us, but she is a model for us to follow. Ask the children for examples of Mary's love for God and others (the Annunciation, the visitation, the wedding feast of Cana, standing at the foot of the cross).

. . . .

Explain that Mary is our mother, too. Jesus said on the cross, "Behold your mother." In the early days of the Church she was with the apostles and first Christians to help them. Mary loves and cares for us today. Recall her appearances at Guadalupe, Lourdes, and Fatima. Mary prays for us.

. . . .

Tell the story of someone who experienced Mary's help, for instance, Father Patrick Peyton, who was cured of tuberculosis by praying to her.

. . . .

Comment on titles for Mary from the Litany of Loreto, such as Gate of Heaven and Mystical Rose.

. . .

Encourage the children to pray the Hail Mary and the rosary.

Common of the Apostles

(PAGE W274) ACTS 3:1-10 or EPHESIANS 2:20-22 • MATTHEW 20:26B-28 or LUKE 6:12-16

The twelve apostles were privileged to be with Jesus and to be taught by him. They were witnesses to his resurrection and became the leaders of the early Church. What we believe about God can be traced back to the apostles. Today we celebrate Mass in honor of _____ . We pray that we may have his (their) courage as we live like Jesus and witness to him.

Universal Prayer
The response is *"Lord, hear our prayer."*

For our church leaders, especially our Holy Father, and our bishop, *(name)*, that they may be true representatives of Christ on earth, servants of people, we pray to the Lord.

For all nations, that they may be open to the Good News of Christ, we pray to the Lord.

For church members, that they may be loving, grateful, and obedient to church leaders, we pray to the Lord.

For those who have not yet heard or understood the Good News of Christ, that they may have the gift of faith, we pray to the Lord.

Special Features
• Set up a display with a net and paper fish.
• If the first reading is #1, help students panto-
mime the story.
• As a communion reflection have students dance or add gestures to a song about following Jesus, such as Follow Me or Lord, You Have Come *(Pescador de Hombres)*.

Songs
Bring Forth the Kingdom; I Say "Yes" Lord; For All the Saints; Go; Lord, You Gave the Great Commission; Lord, You Have Come; Sent Forth by God's Blessing; Silver and Gold Have I None; Wherever He Leads, I'll Go

Homily Ideas
Visual: A fishhook or fish

Tell the children that the word "apostle" means sent. Jesus chose twelve men to be his close companions and to carry on his work. Before he chose them from among all his disciples, he prayed all night. The apostles lived with Jesus, watched and heard him, and were taught by him. Ask the children what were some of the things the apostles learned from Jesus.

. . .

Show the fishhook or fish and explain that some of the apostles were fishermen. When Jesus called Peter, Andrew, James, and John, he told them he would make them fishers of people. Ask the children what Jesus meant by this. (They would catch people to be followers of Jesus. They would help save people.)

• • •

Explain that the apostles were the first leaders of the church. They did the same things Jesus had done. They were filled with his power. Refer to the first suggested reading, in which Peter and John healed a lame beggar in the name of Jesus. The apostles also taught people the news of God's love shown in sending Jesus to save us. Because of the apostles, even though we live two thousand years after Jesus did, we know about him and love him. We are some of the fish caught by the apostles. Their Good News spread throughout the world and was handed on from generation to generation. The apostles also presided over the Eucharist in which Christ is made present again among us in a special way.

• • •

Point out that these leaders were to be servants just as Jesus was. They were to catch people by ministering to their needs, by being loving and compassionate. Tell the children that one title for the pope is "the servant of the servants." Ask the children who their church leaders are today.

• • •

Point out that the apostles had left everything to follow Jesus. They gave their lives to him and his Church, and all of them were martyred except John. Conclude that it is not easy to follow Jesus. Ask the children when it is hard for them to follow Jesus and live as he taught.

• • •

Tell about the apostle(s) honored on this feast day.

• • •

State that we are Christians today because we are standing on the shoulders of giants. These giants are the apostles who are the foundation of the Church.

Common of Martyrs

(PAGE W278) 2 MACCABEES 7:1, 20–23 or ACTS 7:55–60 or 2 CORINTHIANS 6:4–10 • JOHN 12:24–26

Today we celebrate the life and death of St. _____ , a martyr. Martyrs are people whose faith and love are so strong that they suffer and die for Jesus and his teachings. The thousands of martyrs come from every age and nation. They inspire us to be better Christians. At this Eucharist let us pray that we may be as committed to Jesus as the martyrs were and are.

Universal Prayer

The response is *"Lord, hear our prayer."*

That the Church may continue to proclaim the love and message of Jesus, let us pray to the Lord.

That people may be able to practice their religion freely in all countries, let us pray to the Lord.

That Christians may have the courage to live the faith and die for it if necessary, let us pray to the Lord.

That people who are suffering right now because of their faith may find strength, let us pray to the Lord.

That we may accept the crosses in our lives, let us pray to the Lord.

Special Features

• Display a banner with a cross and a crown or with a seed and a plant.

- Give the children a small cross or a seed to remind them to be witnesses.

Songs

Be Not Afraid; Blessed Feasts of Blessed Martyrs; Faith of Our Fathers; For All the Saints; This Day God Gives Me; Unless a Grain of Wheat; Witnesses

Homily Ideas

Visual: A seed or packet of seeds

Tell the children that the word "martyr" means witness. A witness is someone who knows something and claims that it is true. Martyrs are those who give their lives for something they believe is true. Life is the most precious thing we own, so to give it up convinces people that we really mean what we say. Martyrs imitate Jesus because they die as a result of the way they lived. Many of them were happy to die for Christ. Their death makes our faith stronger.

• • •

If the first suggested reading was chosen, explain that the Jewish people had martyrs before Jesus lived. When a pagan king tried to make the Jewish people break the law of the one true God, many of them refused. In the Bible there is the story of a mother and seven sons who were whipped and killed because they would not give in. They chose to obey God rather than the king.

• • •

Tell the children that the first person who died for Jesus was St. Stephen. Because he was teaching belief in Jesus, people dragged him out of the city and stoned him to death. He died asking God to forgive those people, just as Jesus died asking God to forgive those responsible for his death. Since then there have been thousands of martyrs. A famous martyr was Paul, an enemy of Christians who was present at the death of Stephen. After Paul became a Christian, he suffered much for Jesus and was martyred.

• • •

If the second New Testament reading was chosen, ask the children to tell some things Paul suffered for Christ (he was beaten, put in jail, hurt in riots, and went without sleep or food).

• • •

Show a seed and refer to the gospel in which Jesus said that if a grain of wheat falls on the ground and dies, it will produce much fruit. Point out that a planted seed is no longer a seed. It dies as a seed but becomes something entirely new. Jesus promised that if we give up our life in this world, we will be given eternal life. The martyrs believed this.

• • •

Tell the children the quotation "The blood of martyrs is the seed of Christians." Ask them what it means. Comment that perhaps Stephen's death led to St. Paul's believing in Christ.

• • •

Tell the story of the saint of the day and possible results of his or her death.

• • •

Mention that martyrs are not only popes and priests, but laypeople and even children. There have been martyrs from all countries and in all ages. Name some recent martyrs, such as Archbishop Oscar Romero and other El Salvador martyrs. What they have in common is a great love for Christ.

• • •

Point out that Christians have to be brave and tough, for living according to Jesus' teachings is sometimes difficult and painful. It doesn't always make us popular. Only those who love Jesus very much are able to suffer what being a Christian means. It might mean having people make fun of us. It might mean not doing something we really want to do, or doing something we don't want to do. It might mean not having something we want to have. Jesus did not promise us a rose garden; he told us to take up our cross. The cross leads to the crown of glory.

Common of Pastors

(PAGE W283) EZEKIEL 34:11–16ABCE • MATTHEW 28:16–20 or MARK 1:14–20 or JOHN 21:15–17

Jesus cares for his Church through people he has chosen and called. These pastors teach and guide us. They go about doing the work of Jesus in every age. We remember today St. _____ , who kept alive the faith in the hearts of people. He is with us today as we gather around the altar to give God thanks and praise.

Universal Prayer

The response is *"Lord, hear our prayer."*

That our Holy Father, bishops, and priests may shepherd Christ's Church with wisdom and love, let us pray to the Lord.

That more people may hear and respond to the call to serve as priests and bishops, let us pray to the Lord.

That the Church may follow the leaders that Jesus has given it, let us pray to the Lord.

That people who have left Christ's flock may return, let us pray to the Lord.

Special Features

• Display a picture or a statue of the Good Shepherd or a picture of the pope or your diocesan bishop.

• After communion pray the following litany of thanksgiving with the response *"We thank you, Lord."*

  For being a Good Shepherd…

  For caring for us through church leaders you have chosen…

  For giving us a Holy Father to guide us in this century…

  For raising up good people to be our bishops and priests…

  For teaching us the truths of the faith…

For feeding us with the sacred bread and wine of the Eucharist…

For calling us to eternal life…

Songs

Faith of Our Fathers; Gentle Shepherd; Go; God Is So Good; Jesus, Shepherd; Like a Shepherd; My Shepherd, Lord; The King of Love My Shepherd Is; The Lord Is My True Shepherd; Trust in the Lord; Your Way, O God

Homily Ideas

Visual: A lamb from a Nativity set or stuffed lamb

Show a lamb and tell the children that we are like God's sheep. Jesus called himself the Good Shepherd because he cared for us well. He even died to save us. Before Jesus returned to heaven, he put other people in charge of caring for his sheep. Ask if the children know who these shepherds were (apostles, popes, bishops, priests). These people are called pastors because they care for Christ's flock. The pope is the chief shepherd of the sheep. Mention that the pope and all bishops carry a staff called a crosier. This is like a shepherd's staff that the shepherd uses to guide and protect his sheep.

• • •

Explain that the first reading tells how God cares for the sheep. God looks for lost sheep and rescues them, protects them, gives them good places to rest and eat, heals them when they are hurt, and helps them when they are weak. Pastors do these same things for people. They teach them about God and how to live a good life. They try to help them solve their problems. They provide God's love and mercy when the people have sinned. They administer the sacraments to make them strong. They also nourish them with the body and blood of Christ in the Eucharist.

. . .

Tell the children that pastors are specially chosen by Christ for this work. Recall that Jesus called the apostles to catch people instead of fish. Before he returned to heaven, he gave the apostles the mission of going to all nations and teaching the Good News. He was with them as they carried out this mission. If the saint of the day is a missionary, tell the story of how he or she carried out this mission.

. . .

If the saint of the day is a pope, recall that Jesus made Simon Peter head of his Church. He told Peter to feed his lambs and sheep and take care of them. Explain how the day's saint, the successor of Peter, accomplished this.

. . .

Ask the children to name their shepherds. Tell them about the current pope and their own bishop. Suggest that the children pray that their shepherds may be good shepherds like Jesus. Encourage them to go to a priest whenever they need help.

Common of Doctors of the Church

(PAGE W288) 1 KINGS 3:11–14 or EPHESIANS 4:1–7 or EPHESIANS 4:11–13 • MARK 4:1–9

Of all there is to know in the world, the most important thing is to know Jesus Christ and his love for us. Certain people in the history of the Church have studied and written about our faith in an outstanding way. They have helped the rest of us know more about God. Today we honor one such person, St. _____ . We praise and thank God for giving us saints who shed light on our way as we journey to heaven. We pray to have a greater knowledge of our faith ourselves.

Universal Prayer

The response is *"Lord, hear our prayer."*

That the Church may be successful in offering the world the faith, let us pray to the Lord.

That people may realize the importance of knowing more about the faith, let us pray to the Lord.

That all people may come to know the truth about God and life, let us pray to the Lord.

That those who teach, preach, and write about God today may be blessed and kept from error, let us pray to the Lord.

That we may come to know Jesus more and more, let us pray to the Lord.

Special Features

- As part of the homily the celebrant might bless the children's religion books.
- The homily or communion reflection might include a brief reading from a doctor of the Church, especially the one whose feast day is being celebrated.
- At the Mass pray the Apostles' Creed, a summary of truths we believe.

Songs

Faith of Our Fathers; Keep in Mind; O God, Our Help in Ages Past; Sent Forth by God's Blessing; We Thank You, Father

Homily Ideas

Visual: A light bulb

Show a light bulb and comment that it is a symbol for knowing something. In comics it is used to show that someone has a bright idea. Comment that a light bulb is a symbol for the saint celebrated today, for he or she is a doctor of the Church. Explain that this is not a medical doctor, but more like the kind of doctor who has a PhD, someone who is an expert in a particular field of knowledge. Have the children guess what a doctor of the Church has great knowledge of (God, the faith).

• • •

Recall that when King Solomon was given the chance to have anything he wanted, he asked for wisdom. Tell the children that each of us was given the gift of wisdom when we were baptized. It is one of the gifts of the Holy Spirit. True wisdom means to love God and to want to know more about God.

• • •

Explain that some saints knew so much about God that they were experts in the faith. They preached and wrote so that others would know about the faith, too. St. Paul wrote in letters that people have different roles in the Church. Being a doctor of the Church is a very important role.

• • •

Tell what the saint of the day did to merit the title doctor of the Church.

• • •

Encourage the children to learn more about their faith. Ask them how they can do this (studying religion, reading, listening to homilies, going to talks, talking about it, thinking about it, praying). Tell them that they can be smart about many things, but if they are not smart about God, they will fail their biggest test, life.

• • •

Point out that Jesus told a story that shows it is not enough just to hear the truth of God's word. We must take it in and let it affect our hearts and our lives. If our knowledge of God stays just in our minds and doesn't sink down into our hearts, it isn't much use. Some seeds in Jesus' story fell on good ground and grew to produce much fruit. Similarly, what we learn about the faith should sink into us and make us people who produce good fruit. Ask the children for examples of fruit our lives should show if we were truly wise (love, forgiveness, patience, goodness, joy, peace).

• • •

Tell the children that our knowledge of our faith should never stop growing. We never graduate from the school of faith.

• • •

Remind the children that as baptized Christians we have the responsibility to share our knowledge of the faith with others. Ask how we can do this (talk to others about it, invite others to church with us, give others good books on the faith to read). Point out that Jesus was known as a great teacher. We are to be like him.

Common of Saints

(PAGE W292) ACTS 4:32-35 or 1 CORINTHIANS 1:26-31 or 1 CORINTHIANS 13:4-13
OR PHILIPPIANS 4:4-9 or 1 PETER 4:7B-11 or 1 JOHN 3:16-18 or 1 JOHN 5:2-5
MATTHEW 18:1-4 or [FOR THOSE WHO WORK FOR THE UNDERPRIVILEGED] MATTHEW 25:31-40
or [FOR EDUCATORS] MARK 9:33-37 or [FOR RELIGIOUS] LUKE 12:32-34

The saints show us that it is possible to live like Christ. They followed him and used their gifts to bring others to him. They showed his love to all, especially those in need. Now they are with Jesus in heaven praising and glorifying God. We join them as we praise and glorify God in this eucharistic celebration. Through their prayers someday we may be with them.

Universal Prayer

The response is *"Lord, hear our prayer."*

That our church leaders may be saintly and guide us to be saints, let us pray to the Lord.

That the Church may remember and be inspired by the lives of the saints, let us pray to the Lord.

That those who die today may have the grace to be saints, let us pray to the Lord.

That we may respond to the needs of the poor as saints do, let us pray to the Lord.

That we may be grateful for all who love us and show us God's love, let us pray to the Lord.

Special Features

- Give the children crowns cut from aluminum foil as a reminder to be a saint.
- Display memorabilia of the saint whose day is celebrated.

Songs

All That We Have; Beatitudes; Blest Are They; Eye Has Not Seen; For All the Saints; Holy, Holy Holy; Litany of Saints; Now Thank We All Our God; Praise God in His Holy Dwelling; Praise to the Lord; Saints of God in Glory; Sing a Song to the Saints; This Alone; We Are the Light of the World; What You Hear in the Dark; Where There Is Love; Lead Me, Lord

Homily Ideas

Visual: A crown

[The lectionary offers a number of readings that can be chosen to best match the life of a particular saint. In one way or another these readings focus on love and how it is manifested: humility, service, faithfulness. The following suggestions fit any of the readings.]

Show a crown and explain that we sometimes say that saints now wear a crown of glory. We mean they are in heaven, a reward for their life on earth.

• • •

Remind the children that Jesus told us how to win eternal life. Ask them what he said to do (follow the commandments, love God, love others, accept the cross, receive him in holy communion).

• • •

Explain how the saint of the day lived up to the challenge of Jesus.

• • •

Tell the children that the saints lived in their situations the way Jesus would have lived. They showed the same love, the same care, the same mercy as he showed. Invite them to imagine how Jesus would act in their own situations: at home, in school, in their neighborhoods.

• • •

Point out that saints make God number one in their lives: not money or power or fame. They pray much because they enjoy being with God and they want to know God better. They live for God and try to follow God's laws.

．　．　．

Comment that the saints had gifts that they used for God. Mention the gifts of the saint of the day. Ask the children to think of gifts they have and how they can use them for God and the Church.

．　．　．

Mention that saints had a heart for the poor and that Jesus considers anything done for others as done for himself. Ask the children what opportunities they have to do things for the poor. Review the works of mercy.

．　．　．

State that we are united to the saints in the Communion of Saints. Their good deeds helped all of us, just as our good deeds can help others. The saints are our friends in high places who can pray for us if we ask them. Some of them are patrons of particular places or occupations.

．　．　．

Explain that not all saints had miraculous gifts and powers. Some of them were as ordinary as most of us are. They had to work hard to do good. They were tempted and had to fight against evil. They had trials and sufferings in their lives. Some saints just did ordinary things in an extraordinary way.

．　．　．

Ask the children if they would consider themselves saints yet. If they say no, ask why not. Point out that the only failure in life is not to be a saint.

Sacraments

Baptism

(PAGE W303) EZEKIEL 36:24-28 or 1 CORINTHIANS 12:12-13 or GALATIANS 3:26-28
MATTHEW 22:35-40 or MARK 10:13-16 or JOHN 15:1-4 or JOHN 15:5-8 or JOHN 15:9-11

At this Eucharist we celebrate the sacrament of baptism when we become children of God and members of the Church. Through baptism, God fills us with the divine life of grace, and we become joined to Christ. We make an agreement with God to live as children of God in faith and love. Today let us pray to be true to our baptismal promises. [If someone will be baptized during the Eucharist, add: Let us pray especially that (Name) will live up to the call to be a Christian.]

Universal Prayer

The response is *"Lord, hear our prayer."*

For the Church, that the members may teach and baptize people of all nations, let us pray to the Lord.

For world leaders, that they may govern with Christlike love and justice, let us pray to the Lord.

For the newly baptized, especially *(Name)*, that they may realize how much Christ loves them and live out their baptismal promises faithfully, let us pray to the Lord.

For ourselves, that we may draw others to Christ by our lives of love, let us pray to the Lord.

Special Features

- Display a banner with a fish and water or other symbols of baptism.
- Begin Mass with the sprinkling rite.
- After the homily have the children renew their baptismal vows.
- Distribute buttons or badges with an image of a fish and the Greek acronym for Christ: ICHTHYS.

Songs

All My Days; Awake, O Sleeper; Center of My Life; Christ Is Here; Church of God; God's Holy Family; The Goodness of God Cries Out; I Am the Vine; If You Belong to Me; In Christ There Is No East or West; In Him We Live; The Lord Is My True Shepherd; New Life; Out of Darkness; Sing a New Church; Song of Baptism (at a baptism); We Are Many Parts; We Have Been Told; You Have Put on Christ

Homily Ideas

Visual: A basin and water in a pitcher

Pour water into a basin in a long, visible stream. Tell the children that St. Francis wrote a song in which he called water "Sister Water, who is so useful and precious and pure." Ask the children what is so wonderful about this creation of God (water has no color. It fits its container. It sparkles in the sun. It's fun to play in. It washes and heals. It gives life).

•   •   •

Elaborate on the relationship of water to life. Early life forms came from water. We cannot survive if we go many days without water. All living things, all plants and animals, need water to live. When we were babies still inside our mothers, we were surrounded by water. Seventy percent of our weight is water.

•   •   •

Comment that because water is necessary for life it is a good symbol for the sacrament of baptism. At baptism we receive new life, God's life. We are born again as God's adopted children. This is awesome. It is somewhat like becoming princes and princesses. We are royal people who can someday live in God's kingdom of heaven.

•   •   •

Tell the story of a man whose baby son was brought home after being baptized. The man knelt down and prayed before the baby because he knew that God, the Father, Son, and Holy Spirit, were now living in the heart of his son.

•   •   •

Point out that if we are all children of God, then we are all brothers and sisters. We must love and care for one another, even our brothers and sisters on the other side of the world.

•   •   •

Explain that at baptism we become Christians, members of Christ's body. After baptism we are as close to Christ as branches on a vine. We are filled with Christ's life. We can live good lives as long as we stay connected to him. We do this by trying to be like Christ, by following Christ's commandment of love. Then Christ will love us. If we separate ourselves from Christ by sin, then we will not be able to bear fruit. We will be like a branch that is cut off from the vine. Ask what happens to that separated branch (it shrivels up and dies).

•   •   •

Point out that the members of families sometimes have things in common. For instance, the members of the Smith family might all be fun to be with, or the members of the Ling family might all like to keep things neat and clean. People should be able to tell we are members of the Christian family, God's family, because of how loving we are.

•   •   •

Explain that the early Christians used a fish as a secret way to identify themselves when they were being hunted and killed for being Christian. They chose a fish because in Greek each letter of the word "fish" (ICHTHYS) begins a word in the phrase "Jesus Christ, Son of God, Savior." Also, when we are baptized, we become like little fish in the big ocean that is Christ. We are surrounded by his love and care.

•   •   •

Tell about Martin Luther King, Jr., who worked for civil rights for all. One day in a march through an all-white neighborhood, he was pelted with tomatoes and eggs. People screamed and cursed him and the other marchers. Later a reporter asked him whether he was afraid and what he was thinking during the march. Martin Luther King answered, "Yes, of course, I am always afraid, but I keep thinking, 'I'm baptized. I'm baptized.'" Ask what he meant. (He had courage to witness from the grace of his baptism. God was with him.)

•   •   •

Explain the symbolism of the candle (the light of faith) and the white garment (the new life of Christ) which are presented to the baptized.

•   •   •

Tell the children that at baptism, in return for all that God does for us, we promise to believe in God, try to do good, and stay away from evil.

Confirmation (Holy Spirit)

(PAGE W310) EZEKIEL 36:24-28 or JOEL 3:1-3A or ACTS 2:1-6, 14, 22B-23, 32-33
OR ROMANS 8:14-17 or 1 CORINTHIANS 12:4-13 • JOHN 14:15-17 or JOHN 14:23-26

The Holy Spirit, the Spirit of Jesus, was sent to us by the Father. At our baptism the Holy Spirit came to live in us. At our confirmation the life of the Holy Spirit increases in us. We are able to be better witnesses to Jesus Christ and to show forth more strongly the seven gifts of the Spirit in our lives. At this Eucharist we celebrate the presence of the Holy Spirit within us. We thank God for the gift of the Holy Spirit.

Universal Prayer

The response is *"Create a new spirit in us, O Lord."*

That the Church may always be open to the Holy Spirit, we pray to the Lord.

That the Holy Spirit may fill the hearts of people all over the world, we pray to the Lord.

That those who have been recently confirmed may grow in enthusiasm and love for their faith, we pray to the Lord.

That we may show in our lives the gifts and fruits of the Holy Spirit, we pray to the Lord.

That when we are in need we may turn to the Holy Spirit, our good friend, we pray to the Lord.

Special Features

- Decorate the church with a banner or a mobile showing a dove and flames, the names of the gifts or the fruits, or names of the Holy Spirit.
- In the entrance procession have children carry seven red vigil lights and place them in a display in the sanctuary.
- Include dancers with red streamers in the entrance and/ or recessional procession.
- At the end of Mass distribute red ribbons to wear or Holy Spirit pins or pictures.

Songs

Bring Forth the Kingdom; Center of My Life; Come, Creator Spirit; Come, Holy Ghost; Come, O Holy Spirit; Everyone Moved by the Spirit; Holy Is the Spirit of the Lord; Holy Spirit; Like Cedars They Shall Stand; O Breathe on Me, O Breath of God; O Holy Spirit, by Whose Breath; Send Us Your Spirit; Song of the Holy Spirit; The Spirit of God; Witness Song; You Have Anointed Me; You Have Chosen Me

Homily Ideas

Visual: A hand fan

Wave the fan so that it moves something, or have the children blow on their hands. Ask them what is causing the movement or what they feel (air). Although it is invisible, moving air can be very powerful. Ask what strong winds can do (move sailboats, turn windmills, make waves, destroy property). Ask why wind is a good symbol for the Holy Spirit (it is invisible and powerful).

. . .

Explain that Jesus promised to be always with us. His Holy Spirit came to the Church on Pentecost when Mary and the apostles were gathered together in prayer. At our baptism the Holy Spirit came to live within each one of us. At our confirmation we celebrate the Holy Spirit within us. We cannot see the Holy Spirit, but we can see the result of the Spirit's action in us.

. . .

Tell the children what the Holy Spirit does for us. Jesus told the apostles that the Holy Spirit would teach the Church and remind it of what he had taught them. The Holy Spirit gives special powers to the Church, sometimes helping its members work miracles. Refer to the third New Testament reading whether or not it was selected. It explains that the Holy Spirit gives each of us different gifts to serve God and helps us to use these gifts. Ask or tell what some of these gifts are (wisdom, knowledge, faith, healing the sick, working miracles, being prophets, speaking in different languages as the apostles did on Pentecost). Give examples of people in the parish who manifest these gifts. Conclude by stating that the Holy Spirit is the Giver of Gifts.

• • •

Introduce some other names for the Holy Spirit. The Holy Spirit is the Paraclete or Advocate. These strange words mean that the Holy Spirit is like a lawyer who works on our behalf or a friend who stands by us. The Holy Spirit is our Helper who helps us know what is right and do it. The Holy Spirit is our Comforter who helps us realize God's

love. The Holy Spirit is our Teacher who shows us what is true.

• • •

Explain that what we call the fruits of the Holy Spirit are the result of being open to the Spirit. Name these, tailoring the list to the age level of the children: love, joy, peace, patience, kindness, goodness, long-suffering, gentleness, faith, modesty, self-control, and chastity.

• • •

Tell the children that above all the Holy Spirit makes us more like Christ. The Holy Spirit is the Love of God alive in us. That is why another symbol for the Spirit is fire.

• • •

Encourage the children to pray to the Holy Spirit within them when they do not know what to do or when they are faced with temptation. The Spirit will prove to be their helper.

Holy Eucharist

(PAGE W317) ACTS 2:42-47 • MARK 14:12-16, 22-26 or JOHN 6:51-58

Jesus' wonderful gift of the holy Eucharist binds us together as the people of God. At Mass we join in Jesus' sacrifice to God. We share the meal in which we remember Jesus and what he did for us. We are fed with the sacred bread and wine that are his body and blood. Then strengthened with the life of Jesus, we can go out to show love for one another and for the world.

Universal Prayer

The response is *"Lord, hear our prayer."*

That the Church may treasure Christ's gift of the Eucharist, let us pray to the Lord.

That governments everywhere may allow people to worship, let us pray to the Lord.

That those who are receiving Holy Communion for the first time this year may know the wonder and joy of this gift, let us pray to the Lord.

That all of us may come closer to Christ and to one another through the Eucharist that we receive, let us pray to the Lord.

Special Features

- For a First Communion Mass, let the children sit with their families.
- For a First Communion Mass, have parents go up with any child who has a special part in the liturgy.
- Decorate the church with banners about the Eucharist. Set flowers around the altar.

- In the homily include a witness talk in which someone tells what the Eucharist means to him or her.
- Offer communion under the forms of both bread and wine.
- Review the correct way to receive communion reverently.
- As a communion reflection, let dancers interpret a song about the Eucharist.

Songs

As Grains of Wheat; Blessed Are You, Lord; Bread, Blessed and Broken; Christ Is Our Light; Eat This Bread; Gift of Finest Wheat; I Am the Bread of Life; I, the Lord; In Memory of Jesus; I Received the Living God; Jesus, the Bread of Life; Jesus, You Are Bread for Us; Look Beyond; Love Divine, All Loves Excelling; A Meal to Remember; Thank You, Jesus; The Bread That We Break; We Come to Share God's Special Gift; We Remember

Homily Ideas

Visual: A menu

Show a menu and read some items. Tell the children that restaurants usually offer appetizers, soup or salad, a main dish, desserts, and beverages, but our most wonderful meal, the Eucharist, has only two simple things: bread and wine. Ask why the bread and wine at the eucharistic banquet are special (they are the body and blood of Christ).

· · ·

Explain to the children that the night before Jesus died, he gave us a farewell gift. He gave us the gift of himself in the Eucharist. In this way Jesus is able to be with us forever. Most amazingly, in the form of food, Jesus is able to come right into us and become a part of us. Comment how much Jesus must love us.

· · ·

Tell the children that in the Bible Jesus talked about this gift before he gave it to us. He promised that if we ate his flesh and drank his blood we would live forever. People didn't understand then what he was saying, but after the Last Supper, they understood better. At the Last Supper, Jesus and his disciples were possibly celebrating a special Jewish meal called the Passover meal. Jesus took the bread and said, "This is my body." He took the wine and said, "This is my blood." Everyone shared the bread and wine. Jesus told his disciples to do that in memory of him.

· · ·

Explain that each time we celebrate the Eucharist, the sacrifice of Jesus, which saved us, is re-presented. We offer this sacrifice with Jesus and offer ourselves, too, just as we bring up the bread and wine and offer it to God. Suggest to the children that whenever they see the bright, round, rising sun they think of the host being offered to God somewhere in the world.

· · ·

Point out that the Bible lets us know that ever since the Last Supper the first Christians celebrated this meal in memory of Jesus. They called it the breaking of bread. For the past two thousand years, Christians all over the world have celebrated the Eucharist.

· · ·

Comment that whenever we gather to celebrate this meal, Jesus is with us. When we receive communion, he is within us in a special way. We tell him of our love, praise and thank him for his love, and speak to him about anything we wish. The Eucharist changes us into people who serve as Jesus served and love as he loved. Because we all share the same bread and wine, the same Jesus, we are united with one another. We reverence and serve the body of Christ in others by being kind to them, helping them, and speaking about them in a nice way.

· · ·

Tell the children that we are all on a journey together to the next world. Jesus gave us the Eucharist as food for this journey. It strengthens us to keep going on the road to heaven. It helps us do good and avoid evil. It makes our hearts love Jesus more and desire to please him.

. . .

State the comment that author Annie Dillard made about the Eucharist. She said that if we realized the divine power that comes from the Mass, we would all come to church wearing crash helmets.

. . .

Mention that heaven is sometimes referred to as a banquet. The Eucharist that we share on earth is a foretaste of the meal we will share someday in heaven. Then we will see God face to face and be with Jesus forever.

Reconciliation

(PAGE W323) EPHESIANS 5:1–2, 8–10 or JAMES 2:14–17 or REVELATION 21:1–8
MATTHEW 5:13–16 or LUKE 15:1–3, 11–32

Deep in our hearts, we all want to be good. Sometimes, however, we are weak and do not do what we know we should do. We fail to love, and we separate ourselves from God and others. Whenever we are sorry, God offers us loving forgiveness. God welcomes us back into the circle of love. Christ's sacrifice made it possible for us to be forgiven. At this Eucharist we ask for and receive forgiveness. We celebrate God's love.

Universal Prayer

The response is *"Lord, have mercy."*

For the members of the Church, that they may always trust the loving forgiveness of God, we pray to the Lord.

For government leaders, that their laws may show not only justice but mercy, we pray to the Lord.

For great sinners, that they may return to God, we pray to the Lord.

For ourselves, that we may seek God's forgiveness as soon as we realize we have sinned, we pray to the Lord.

Special Features

- Make the penitential rite especially meaningful. (See page 10 for ideas.)
- If the parable of the prodigal son is selected, have it read with children taking the parts, or accompany it with overhead transparencies or homemade slides.
- Introduce the sign of peace with a few words about its being a sign of forgiveness and acceptance after we have hurt one another by our sins.

Songs

Amazing Grace; Bless the Lord, My Soul; Forgive Our Sins; Forgiveness Prayer; Glory and Praise to Our God; Loving and Forgiving; More Joy in Heaven; Pardon Your People; Remember Your Love; Seek the Lord; Song of Forgiveness; Though the Mountains May Fall; Turn to Me; We Come to Ask Forgiveness; You Forgive All Wrong

Homily Ideas

Visual: A roll of masking or mending tape

Show the masking or mending tape and ask what it is used for (to repair things, to hold things together that have been separated). Explain that sin separates us from God and from others. Jesus' death on the cross mended our separation from God. It made us one with God again.

· · ·

Have the children recall the story *Beauty and the Beast*. The beast was mean and wicked. But the love of the girl named Beauty changed him into a prince. Tell the children that sin made human beings somewhat like beasts. We were not the god-like people God meant for us to be. The love of Jesus changed us back into children of God. Jesus made us friends with God again. We should always try to act like friends of God.

· · ·

Explain that, as Christians, we are called to be children of light not of darkness. This means we are to be loving like Christ and shine forth love on the world. Then others, too, will be more loving. When we do not live out our faith, when we are not a light to others, then we are not the real human beings we were meant to be.

· · ·

Tell the children that everyone sins, but we can come back to God just as the boy in Jesus' parable of the prodigal son realized he had done wrong and returned to his father. After we have sinned, God is always ready to take us back. God longs for our return. Ask the children what we can do to be forgiven by God (tell God we are sorry in our heart, celebrate the sacrament of reconciliation, celebrate the Eucharist, do acts of charity).

· · ·

Point out that at the beginning of the Eucharist, there are prayers in which we ask God's forgiveness. Being forgiven makes us ready to celebrate the holy Eucharist, which is a feast of love.

· · ·

Ask the children how they feel when they apologize to someone and hear the words "I forgive you." Tell them that they can feel the same way when they express forgiveness to God. In the sacrament of reconciliation the priest even says the words for God so that we can hear them. Comment that the children ought to be quick to extend forgiveness to anyone who apologizes to them. If the gospel of the parable of the prodigal son was selected, point out that the boy's brother did not accept him back with mercy and love.

· · ·

Remind the children that the Holy Spirit who lives in them guides them to do what is right and helps them to be sorry after they have done wrong. Suggest that they pray to the Holy Spirit to be a child of light.

· · ·

Encourage the children to begin the practice of examining their conscience briefly each night before going to bed and asking God to forgive them for any sins.

Masses for Various Needs and Occasions

Beginning of the School Year

(PAGE W333) 2 THESSALONIANS 3:6–12, 16
MATTHEW 13:44–46 or MATTHEW 25:14–30 or JOHN 14:23–26

Today we celebrate the beginning of the school year. Together this year we will grow in many ways and learn many things. Most importantly, we will learn more about Jesus Christ and his teachings. At this Eucharist in which Jesus is present with us, let us ask him to open our minds and hearts to all that is true, good, and beautiful. Let us ask him to help us know him.

Universal Prayer

The response is *"Lord, hear our prayer."*

That the Church may grow in the gifts of wisdom, knowledge, and understanding, let us pray to the Lord.

That our leaders may govern us with true wisdom, let us pray to the Lord.

That those persons who work at *(Name)* School may help the children be better people, let us pray to the Lord.

That the children of *(Name)* School may be good students and not waste their talents, let us pray to the Lord.

That children who do not have the opportunity to learn in fine schools may be helped, let us pray to the Lord.

Special Features

- In the entrance procession have children carry objects from school life and add them to a display, for instance, a globe, textbooks, a basketball, a pencil case, a DVD, a notebook, a school jacket, and crayons.
- If the gospel about the parable of the talents is chosen, children might pantomime it.
- Pray the following as a communion reflection:

Teach me, Jesus, to be like you: to use my talents, to work hard, and to do my best. Teach me the lessons that will help me live a good life: the lessons of hope, kindness, and love. Teach me to be unselfish and generous, to make friends, and to be a good friend. Teach me to be patient with myself and others. Teach me to forgive and to be a peacemaker. Teach me to choose what is right. Above all, teach me, Jesus, to do the will of our Father in heaven.

Songs

All That We Have; Bloom Where You're Planted; City of God; Come, Holy Ghost; I Say "Yes," Lord; If the Lord Does Not Build the House; I Want to Walk as a Child of the Light; Lead Us On; Seek Ye First; They'll Know We Are Christians; We Are the Church; We Are the Family; We Have Been Told; Living and Loving and Learning

Homily Ideas

Visual: A textbook

Ask the children what they learned during the summer. Tell them that we never stop learning. Show a textbook and explain that with the help of teachers, other students, books, and computers, they learn in school. Comment that in the first reading, Paul tells us not to waste time loafing but to work. Ask the children what their work is (to learn in school).

. . .

Comment that Jesus had to learn. He learned how to walk and talk. He learned the history of his people and how to read Scripture. He probably learned the trade of carpentry. The gospels tell us that Jesus lived in Nazareth with Mary and Joseph and grew in wisdom, age, and grace. He is an example for us.

. . .

Tell the children that our minds make us like God instead of like the animals and other created things. Ask what we can do with our minds (think, learn, create, solve problems, make decisions). God wants us to develop our minds and use our talents. Quote the saying "A mind is a ter-

rible thing to waste." Ask the children how a mind can be wasted. Encourage them not to be like the lazy, good-for-nothing servant who buried his money.

. . .

Point out that knowledge is like the treasure or pearl in Jesus' parables. We must work hard to obtain it. We must read books, think, do homework, make reports, discuss. If we do these things, we will have a wonderful treasure that no one can take from us.

. . .

Tell the story of St. Isidore of Seville. When he was a boy, he often didn't do his homework and skipped his studies. One day when he should have been studying, he was out walking and saw an old stone well. In its walls were grooves that had been worn by thin wet ropes. By constant rubbing over a long time, rope had changed stone. Isidore realized that if he kept at his studies the way the rope had kept rubbing, he would someday be smart. Isidore began to study hard and became known and highly respected for his intelligence. Urge the students to study even when it's hard, even when they don't feel like it.

. . .

Explain to the students that the Holy Spirit in them will help them learn what is more important than arithmetic, history, or science. The Holy Spirit will help them learn more about Jesus and his teachings. Ask how the children will learn about Jesus this year (through religion class, Masses, the Bible). Comment that Jesus is called the master teacher. Those who followed him were called disciples. Suggest that the children try hard to be good disciples of Jesus.

End of the School Year

(PAGE W338) ISAIAH 63:7 or COLOSSIANS 3:12, 15B-17 • MATTHEW 13:31-32 or MARK 5:18-20

We bring this school year to a close by remembering the good things God has done for us during it. We give thanks for these things through the Eucharist, our best way to give thanks to God. We offer our year and what we have become to the Father with the sacrifice of Jesus.

Universal Prayer

The response is *"Lord, hear our prayer."*

For the Church, that the members may always have grateful hearts, let us pray to the Lord.

For leaders of countries, that they may look to God for strength and guidance, let us pray to the Lord.

For those who have helped us during this school year, that they may be rewarded for their goodness to us, let us pray to the Lord.

For all of us, that we may have a safe, happy summer, let us pray to the Lord.

Special Features

- After communion allow quiet moments when everyone can reflect on the good things the Lord has done for them during the past year.
- After communion show slides of school activities accompanied by a litany with the response "Lord, we praise and thank you."

Songs

Bring Forth the Kingdom; City of God; Companions on the Journey; Lead Us On; Lift Up Your Hearts; May God Bless You; Send Us Forth; Song of the Body of Christ (verse 5); Take Christ to the World; Walk On; We Are the Light of the World

Homily Ideas

Visual: A suitcase

Tell the children that the readings of the Mass center on giving God praise and thanks. Mention some things the school has experienced during the year for which you can give praise and thanks. Ask the children to add ideas of what the Lord has done for them (for instance, the first graders learned to read, the second graders received First Communion, the eighth graders went on a field trip, certain students won awards). Point out that after Jesus cured a man, Jesus told him to go to his family and tell them how good God was to him. Encourage the children to talk about the school year at home with their families.

· · ·

Show a suitcase and comment that the people at your school are at the end of a journey together. Together they learned more about what a Christian is and how to live as God's children, a Christian community. Now each one is going out to share with others what was learned. Each person will spread the news of God's love so that God's kingdom will grow like the tree that grows from the mustard seed. No matter where each person will travel during the summer, every one will proclaim the Good News by the way he or she lives.

· · ·

Open the suitcase and tell what the children are taking into the world from school. They have knowledge of God that they can share with their families and friends. They have a sense of right and wrong that they can use to help their friends make decisions. They learned things and developed skills that they can use to help out at home. They have a heart for the poor that can inspire others to do good for the poor.

· · ·

Tell the children that summer vacation is a time for them to use what they learned in school. Remind them that it is not meant to be a vacation from God. God will still be caring for them and wanting them to love in return. They should pray every day and celebrate the Sunday Eucharist. They should try to live as God's children.

• • •

Quote Dag Hammarskjöld's prayer: "For all that has been, thanks; for all that will be, yes." Explain that God will send us joys and sorrows during the summer as well as surprises. Like Mary, we can say yes to, or accept, all that God sends us, trusting that God does what is best for us. We have seen God's love for us in the past, and so we can trust it for the future.

In Thanksgiving

(PAGE W342) SIRACH 50:22-24 • LUKE 17:11-19

God has given us many wonderful gifts: our life and talents, the world and everything in it, and the promise of a life in heaven that will never end. Often we take these gifts for granted. Today, however, let us thank God for being so good to us. We offer in return the gift of the Eucharist, the greatest gift we can offer God because it is the sacrifice of God's Son Jesus.

Universal Prayer

The response is *"Lord, hear our prayer."*

That the Church may be a people of thankful hearts, let us pray to the Lord.

That rulers of nations may recognize that all gifts come from God, let us pray to the Lord.

That people who are sad may open their eyes to the good things they have, let us pray to the Lord.

That we may show that we are grateful for all the good things God has done for us, let us pray to the Lord.

Special Features

• Display a banner that says thank you in different languages.

• As a communion reflection pray the following prayer:

O God, if you had given us only one gorgeous sunrise, it would have been enough. If you had given us only one of our five senses, it would have been enough. If you had given us only one day to walk in this world, it would have been enough. If you had given us only one person to love and care for us, it would have been enough. If you had sent Jesus to share our life for only one day, it would have been enough. If you had given us communion only once in our life, it would have been enough. For your overflowing gifts and your great love, we give you thanks, O God.

Songs

All Creatures of Our God and King; All Good Gifts; All My Days; All Praise and All Thanksgiving; Come, Ye Thankful People, Come; Father, We Thank Thee; For the Beauty of the Earth; For the Fruits of This Creation; Give Thanks to the Lord; Let All Things Now Living; Sing with Joy; Thank You Very Much; We Are Grateful

Homily Ideas

Visual: A stone

Show a stone and tell the children that the stone can't think or speak. It can never thank God for making it or praise God for things like beautiful sunsets and spring rain. We, on the other hand, can tell God thank you for everything we are and have.

. . .

Refer to the gospel in which the lepers were cured. Jesus gave them a new life. They could go back to their families and friends and their jobs. Nine of these lepers were like stones. They did not thank Jesus for the miracle he worked for them. Jesus missed their thanks.

. . .

If the Mass is being celebrated in thanksgiving for some particular gift, elaborate on it. Otherwise, enumerate some of the things that God has done for us.

. . .

Have the children name gifts that begin with each letter of the expression "thank you."

. . .

Mention that even when we sin and disappoint God, God still cares for us and gives us gifts. One of God's greatest gifts is forgiveness.

. . .

Point out that God didn't have to create us or give us any gifts at all. The least we can do is say thank you. Ask the children how else they can show thanks (taking care of the gifts, doing as God wishes).

. . .

Ask the children how they feel when someone tells them thank you.

. . .

Suggest that when the children wake up they express thanks to God for each new day. Then at night they could think back over the day and thank God for the gifts and blessings of that day.

. . .

Point out that bad things can be blessings in disguise. God draws good out of suffering and evil. For one thing, suffering can make us better persons just as a lot of pressure turns coal into a diamond. So we can even thank God for our crosses.

. . .

Encourage the children to express thanks also to people who do things for them. Ask them for different phrases that let people know we are grateful (I appreciate, I thank you, Thanks a lot, Thanks a million, I'm grateful, Many thanks).

. . .

Tell the children they should try to have grateful hearts, not stony hearts.

For Vocations

(PAGE W345) EXODUS 3:1–6, 9–12 or 1 SAMUEL 3:1–10 or JEREMIAH 1:4–9
MATTHEW 9:35–38 or MARK 10:28–30 or LUKE 5:1–11

God calls some people to serve the Church in a special way as priests, deacons, and religious brothers and sisters. We need people to devote their entire lives to the Church. Jesus told us to pray that more laborers may be sent to harvest the crops. Today we do as Jesus said. We pray at this Mass for more men and women to give their lives to working for the Church.

Universal Prayer

The response is *"Lord, hear our prayer."*

That many good men and women may be called to serve the Church as priests, deacons, and religious brothers and sisters, let us pray to the Lord.

That those who are called to be priests, deacons, or religious may respond to their call with faith and love, let us pray to the Lord.

That priests, deacons, and religious may have the grace to live their vocation wholeheartedly, let us pray to the Lord.

That married couples and single people may use the graces of their state in life to serve God well, let us pray to the Lord.

That we may know and follow the vocation God wants us to follow, let us pray to the Lord.

Special Features

- Drape a net over the lectern or make it part of a display.
- At the Prayer of the Faithful, let the children pray for priests, deacons, or brothers and sisters whom they know.
- As a communion reflection pray a prayer about following Christ that is composed by a student or person who works at the school.

Songs

Be Not Afraid; Come with Me into the Fields; Here I Am, Lord; I Long for You; I Say "Yes," Lord; Lord, You Have Come; Take, Lord, Receive

Homily Ideas

Visual: A container of oil

Show the oil and explain that long ago people who served God and the chosen people as kings and priests were anointed with oil. This ceremony marked them and set them apart from other people. Tell the children that today during the ceremony when priests become consecrated, or set apart for God, they are anointed with oil.

. . .

Comment that God often called certain people for special work. Depending on which first read-ing was picked, elaborate on the life and work of Moses, Samuel, or Jeremiah. Point out such things as the chosen person was not perfect, he was surprised that God would call him, he was called to do a difficult task, he didn't particularly want to do it, and God promised to be with him.

. . .

Explain that the apostles who followed Jesus' call to become his followers in a special way were chosen to carry on his work. They were to teach God's people and care for them. Jesus compared them to shepherds who led and cared for sheep and said they would be fishermen who catch people instead of fish.

. . .

Point out that it is difficult to follow Jesus today as a priest, deacon, or religious. Ask the children what might be hard for a priest, deacon, or religious (not having a family, not having a lot of money, living a life of service like Jesus). Remind them that Jesus promised those who left everything for him that they would be rewarded in the next world.

. . .

Tell the story of your own vocation or someone you know.

. . .

Invite a priest, deacon, or religious to speak about his or her vocation.

. . .

Tell the children the kinds of things that priests, deacons, brothers, and sisters do. Point out that they usually have more time to pray than other people.

. . .

Explain that in addition to praying for more vocations, the children should consider whether God is calling them to serve him in one of these special ways. God will not appear to them. They will not hear God's voice. Rather, in their hearts they will feel a pull toward the life of a priest, deacon, or religious. They will notice that the gifts God has given them are those needed for the life of a priest or religious. Encourage the children to pray to know the vocation that God plans for them.

For Unity of Christians

(PAGE W352) EZEKIEL 36:24-28 • MATTHEW 5:1-12AB or MATTHEW 18:19-22

At the Last Supper, Jesus prayed that all of his followers may be one. Today there are separate Christian faith traditions. Also within the Catholic Church there are divisions. At this Eucharist we echo Jesus' prayer. We pray that all Christians may be one in faith and love.

Universal Prayer

The response is *"Lord, hear our prayer."*

That the Church may be one with all Christians united in love, let us pray to the Lord.

That government leaders may respect all religions, let us pray to the Lord.

That all Christians may show forth the love of Christ, let us pray to the Lord.

That we here may work for church unity in any way we can, let us pray to the Lord.

Special Features

- Display a banner with the names of different Christian faith traditions written within a profile of Christ.
- Pray a prayer from the Church Unity Octave prayers after the homily or as a communion reflection.

Songs

Gather Us In; In Christ There Is No East or West; Lord, Who at Thy First Eucharist; One Bread, One Body; One Lord; See Us, Lord, about Your Altar; Sing of the Lord's Goodness; Song of Gathering; They'll Know We Are Christians

Homily Ideas

Visual: A rubber band

Show a rubber band and ask what it does (holds things together). Explain that the first reading is about God's chosen people, the Israelites, who lived in different countries. God brought them all together into their own country. God united them together so that they could pray and worship as God's very own people.

· · · ·

Tell the children that Jesus wants us to be one flock. He wants all Christians to be united. At the Last Supper he prayed that all may be one. A mark of the Catholic Church is that it is one. Sadly, today groups of Christians sometimes even fight each other. Ask the children to name some groups of Christians.

· · · ·

If the first suggested gospel is read, explain that it gives us the blueprint for being people who can be joined together in love. The beatitudes tell us how to be children of God and form God's holy people. Review the kind of people the beatitudes call blessed (those who depend on God, who grieve, who are humble, who obey God, who are merciful, whose hearts are pure, who make peace, who are treated badly for doing right). If the second suggested gospel is read, explain that Jesus tells us one secret to being a united people: forgiving over and over again. This is the kind of forgiveness that is practiced in any family. It needs to be practiced in God's family. Love would bind us all together like a rubber band.

· · · ·

Stretch the rubber band and ask the children how different groups of Christians can be brought together again. (By learning about one another, by speaking to one another, by praying and working together, by praying for this intention.)

· · · ·

Mention that Christians have more things in common than we have differences. Ask the children to give examples (belief in God and in Jesus, the ten commandments, the Bible, desire for God).

. . . .

Recall for the children that the Church is Christ's body. As long as the members are separated, Christ's body is broken.

. . . .

Tell the children that the Church has a custom of praying for church unity each year for eight days: from January 18 to January 25. This is called the Week of Prayer for Christian Unity.

. . . .

Tell about the Society of the Atonement founded in 1898 at Graymoor, New York, to work for Christian unity. Originally an Episcopal Franciscan community, the Friars and Sisters became Catholic in 1909.

For Peace and Justice

(PAGE W357) ISAIAH 32:15-20 or PHILIPPIANS 4:6-9 or COLOSSIANS 3:12-15 • MATTHEW 5:1-12AB

Everyone wants to live in peace. We want no more wars or arguments. We want peace among nations and among family members. We want to have peace within ourselves. Jesus is the Prince of Peace. He came to bring us peace. During this Mass let us pray for the gift of peace. Let us ask to become peacemakers.

Universal Prayer

The response is *"Lord, hear our prayer."*

For the holy Church, that it may be a peacemaker throughout the world, let us pray to the Lord.

For the leaders of nations, that they may work to make peace, not war, let us pray to the Lord.

For countries where there is war, *(Names)*, that they may soon be blessed with peace, let us pray to the Lord.

For ourselves, our families, and friends, that we may be filled with peace, let us pray to the Lord.

Special Features

• In the presentation of gifts, include letters written by the children about peace or justice.

• For the presentation song or as a communion reflection, have a group of children do interpretive dance to a song about peace.

• Introduce the sign of peace by referring to one of the readings.

Songs

All the Ends of the Earth; Beatitudes; City of God; Feed My Lambs; For the Healing of the Nations; Let Justice Roll like a River; Let There Be Peace on Earth; O God of Love, O King of Peace; Peace Prayer; Prayer of Peace; Prayer of St. Francis; Proclaim the Good News; Shalom; Take the Word of God with You; That There May Be Bread; We Shall Overcome; What Shall I Give?; World Peace Prayer

Homily Ideas

Visual: A piece of gravel

Show the piece of gravel and ask the children if they have ever had a stone in their shoe. It makes walking difficult, even painful. If the stone is sharp, it can cut. Tell the children that there are situations that are unfair to people. They deny people their rights and are unjust. For example, in some countries wealthy people make poor people work hard and then pay them very little. Situations like these are like stones in a shoe. They cause pain. They take away peace.

* * *

Tell the children that unjust practices and unjust laws keep us from having peace. Give the example of a family in which the middle child was the only one who had to do housework. That would not be fair to that child. There probably would not be peace in that family. We must work so that everyone can have a good life. Mention places in the world where there is a lack of peace because of injustice.

* * *

Explain to the children that in some countries children have to work hard in factories instead of being able to go to school or play, and they are paid only a few pennies a day.

* * *

Point out that many problems in the world today are the result of greed. Ask the children what they see when they look out a window (the world, other people). Ask what they see when they look in a mirror (themselves). Tell them that both a window and a mirror are glass, but the glass of a mirror is backed with silver. Explain that people who make silver or money the focus of their lives only think about themselves. People who focus on God and God's laws see the whole world.

* * *

Ask the children what the Bible says the angels sang when Jesus was born (peace on earth, good will to all). Explain that God wants us to be at peace. Jesus came to bring peace between us and God. After he rose from the dead, he visited his apostles and greeted them, "Peace be with you." Point out that we can turn to Jesus and ask for peace.

* * *

Comment that each one of us can help bring peace to the world. Ask the children how they can do this (by treating their own friends and family members fairly, by not starting fights and arguments, by being a peacemaker).

* * *

To show how each person can make a difference, tell the story of the snowflake. A bird was counting snowflakes as they settled on a tree limb. Just as number 1,999 landed on the limb, the limb cracked and fell to the ground. All that was needed to break the limb was that last snowflake. Sometimes all that is needed to stop an injustice is for one more person to speak up against it. That person could be one of us.

* * *

Tell the children about someone who is a peacemaker, such as former president Jimmy Carter or St. Elizabeth of Portugal.

* * *

State that God's kingdom is a kingdom of justice and peace. Whenever we pray in the Our Father, "Thy kingdom come," we are praying for justice and peace. Explain that in the gospel, Jesus described what kind of people belong to that kingdom: those who depend on God, who grieve, who are humble, who obey God, who are merciful, whose hearts are pure, who make peace, who are treated badly for doing what is right.

For Productive Land and after the Harvest

(PAGE W362) GENESIS 1:11–12 • DEUTERONOMY 8:7–10 or 2 CORINTHIANS 9:8–11 • LUKE 12:15–21

God designed our earth-home to provide food for us. Sun, good soil, and rain make our crops grow. These crops in turn nourish us and make us grow strong. We look to God to send us good weather and to protect our crops from disease and insects. Today we thank God for the gifts of bread and wine as well as for all the food on our tables each day.

Universal Prayer

The response is *"Lord, hear our prayer."*

That the Church may work to persuade people to share with the poor, let us pray to the Lord.

That government officials may make laws that enable the hungry to be fed, let us pray to the Lord.

That men, women, and children who do not have enough to eat may be provided with food, let us pray to the Lord.

That farmers who grow our food may have good crops and receive just pay for them, let us pray to the Lord.

That we may be generous and share our food with hungry people, let us pray to the Lord.

Special Features

- Before or after Mass conduct a blessing of fields and flocks, or a blessing of seeds at planting time, or a blessing on the occasion of thanksgiving for the harvest. Rites for these are found in the *Book of Blessings*.
- Have a special collection to provide food for the poor.
- As a communion reflection show slides of wheat fields, orchards, markets, and other pictures of food. Pray a litany of thanksgiving as the slides are projected.

Songs

All Good Gifts; Bread of Friendship; Come, Ye Thankful People, Come; For the Beauty of the Earth; For the Fruits of This Creation; Glory and Praise to Our God (verse 4); I Am the Bread of Life; O Father, Whose Creating Hand; That There May Be Bread; We Plough the Fields and Scatter

Homily Ideas

Visual: A vegetable or piece of fruit

Show a vegetable or piece of fruit and ask the children where it came from. Ask them what their favorite vegetable or fruit is. Comment that God is good to give us such a rich variety of foods. When God created the world, it was filled with all kinds of good things to eat. This food keeps us and the animals alive.

. . . .

Tell the children that God promised the chosen people a land with enough food for everyone. It was called a land flowing with milk and honey. Jesus, the Good Shepherd, guides us to green pastures. That means he sees that we have food to eat.

. . . .

Point out that when we pray the Our Father, we ask God to give us our daily bread. In other words, we ask God to give us food to stay alive.

. . . .

Explain that the parable in the gospel is about a man who had such a good harvest that his barns couldn't hold it all. He decided to make bigger barns. Ask the children what the man could have done with the leftover grain instead. (He could have given it to the poor.)

. . . .

Tell the children that if food was passed out equally on the earth, no one would be hungry. There is enough food for all, but not everyone receives enough. Ask the children to tell of programs or organizations that help distribute food. Mention that many of the saints we honor during the year worked to see that those who were hungry were fed, saints such as St. Francis, St. Martin de Porres, St. Elizabeth of Hungary, and St. Frances of Rome.

• • •

Remind the children to pray prayers before and after meals to thank and praise God for our food.

Those who do not have this practice at home might suggest it to their families.

• • •

Tell the story of St. Isidore who spent his life working the land as a farmer. He and his wife often brought food to hungry people and prayed with them.

• • •

Point out that one way we celebrate events is by eating food together. Our greatest act of worship is also a meal: the Eucharist.

For Refugees and Exiles

(PAGE W365) HEBREWS 13:1–3, 14–16 • LUKE 10:25–37

Jesus' law of love tells us to show love for everyone, including strangers and even enemies. People who are forced to leave their homeland and go to another country need our help. Today at this Eucharist we pray for the refugees and exiles of the world. May they find people who will welcome them and help them begin a new life. May our love reach out to refugees and make them feel at home.

Universal Prayer

The response is *"Lord, hear our prayer."*

That the Church may offer shelter to refugees and exiles, we pray to the Lord.

That nations may have peace and justice so that their people do not have to be refugees, we pray to the Lord.

That refugees and exiles may find what they need to live safely and happily, we pray to the Lord.

That our country may respect foreigners and make them welcome, we pray to the Lord.

That we may treat people from other countries with compassion and love, we pray to the Lord.

Special Features

• Display a globe or world map.
• Have students pantomime the parable of the good samaritan as it is read.
• In the Prayer of the Faithful include prayers for specific groups of refugees.

Songs

Blest Be the Lord; Christians, Let Us Love One Another; Each Time That You Love; God of the Hungry; Here I Am, Lord; Service; We Are the Family; Whatsoever You Do; Yahweh, the Faithful One

Homily Ideas

Visual: A candle

Show a candle and tell the children that at Christmas time some people set a candle in the window as a sign that anyone is welcome in the home. Ask the children if they know what the Statue of Liberty holds in her hand (a torch). Explain that the torch is like a candle that welcomes people into the land. On the base of the statue is a poem that says, "Give me your tired, your poor, your huddled masses yearning to breathe free….I lift my lamp beside the golden door." The United States is a land of immigrants, people who have come from other countries. Many of these people have come because they were no longer able or allowed to live in their own countries. They are called refugees because they look for refuge or shelter in another land.

• • •

Ask the children what hardships refugees suffer (leaving their homes, friends, and relatives; not having a job; not knowing the language of the new country; being teased or looked down on by some people).

• • •

Have the children recall a time when they were in a new place, perhaps the first day of school, or after moving into a new neighborhood. Ask how they felt.

• • •

Point out that according to the Bible, Jesus, Mary, and Joseph were once refugees. After Jesus was born and King Herod was seeking to kill him, the Holy Family fled from the Holy Land into Egypt, a foreign country.

• • •

Mention, or ask the children to name, groups of people who are refugees today.

• • •

Refer to the first reading in which we are told, "Be sure to welcome strangers into your home." Tell the story of Abraham who welcomed three strange men to his house, let them rest and bathe their feet, and served them a good meal. The men turned out to be two angels and the Lord. The Jewish people highly valued hospitality, that is, making guests welcome.

• • •

Mention that sheltering the homeless is one of the seven corporal works of mercy. The good that we do to refugees Jesus sees as done to him. Remind the children of Jesus' story in which the good Samaritan showed great kindness to a stranger who was in trouble. He interrupted his own journey to take the stranger to a shelter and care for him.

• • •

Explain that the children probably won't have strangers knocking on their doors asking for shelter. They can, however, be kind and helpful to people who come from another country. They should have a candle burning in their hearts that says, "Welcome."

For the Sick

(*PAGE W368*) JAMES 5:13-16 • MATTHEW 8:14-17

Jesus is a healer. As he went from town to town teaching about God, he healed many people who were sick and suffering. He made them whole again and able to enjoy life. At the end of his life, Jesus healed the human race from sin and death by his dying and rising. During this Eucharist we pray for the sick, especially for (Name). May Jesus heal them, comfort them, or give them strength to suffer their sickness peacefully.

Universal Prayer

The response is *"Lord, hear our prayer."*

For the holy people of God, that they may heal and comfort the sick, let us pray to the Lord.

For governments, that they may work to improve the lives of the sick people in their countries, let us pray to the Lord.

For those who are physically or mentally ill, that they may be healed or sense the closeness of Christ in their suffering, let us pray to the Lord.

For doctors, nurses, and other people who care for the sick, that they may have compassion for their patients, let us pray to the Lord.

For ourselves, that we may show love and concern for those who are sick, let us pray to the Lord.

Special Features

- In the Prayer of the Faithful pray by name for parishioners who are sick.
- As part of the homily, invite someone who has experienced the anointing of the sick to tell about how it felt.
- Take up a collection of money and donate it to a group that does research to combat a particular disease.

Songs

Because of Jesus; Gather Us In; Jesus, Heal Us; Lay Your Hands; Only a Shadow; Peace Is Flowing like a River; Service; Son of David; The King of Glory; We Cannot Measure How You Heal; You Are the Healing

Homily Ideas

Visual: A thermometer or bottle of aspirin

Show a thermometer or a bottle of aspirin. Ask the children to tell what they feel like when they are sick. Ask them what makes them feel better.

• • •

Explain that God doesn't want us to be sick. God made us to be healthy. When someone is sick, we can pray that God will cure him or her. When we ourselves are sick, we can pray to get better.

• • •

Point out that the gospel tells the story of Jesus curing Peter's mother-in-law one day. That night Jesus healed every sick person who came to him. Ask the children to recall other stories of Jesus healing people. Comment that these stories show that Jesus is stronger than sickness and other evils.

• • •

Ask the children why they think God does not always cure people when we pray. Tell them that sick people can unite their pain to the pain Jesus suffered on earth. They can become holy through their suffering. They can become patient, loving, gentle, and wise. They can also offer their suffering to God. Then it can be used to help other people in the Church.

• • •

Comment that sick people give us a chance to practice love. Ask the children what they can do to show love for the sick (write to them, send cards, visit them, run errands for them, serve them, pray for them).

• • •

Tell the children that the Church carries out Jesus' work of healing people today. There is a sacrament especially for the sick called the anointing of the sick. Just as the first reading says to do, sick people can call on the church leaders to pray for them and anoint them with oil. Through this sacrament Jesus sometimes heals people. He also can forgive their sins. This, too, is a way of healing people, because sin is like a disease.

• • •

Tell the story of someone who was healed after praying, such as Patrick Peyton, St. Thérèse of Lisieux, St. Julie Billiart, or a person you know. Or mention places of healing, such as Lourdes, and people who had the gift of healing, such as St. André Bessette.

For the Dead

(PAGE W372) ISAIAH 25:6A, 7–9 or EPHESIANS 1:3–5 or 1 THESSALONIANS 4:13–14, 18 or
1 JOHN 3:1–2 or REVELATION 14:13 • MATTHEW 11:25–26, 28–30 or LUKE 7:11–17 or JOHN 11:21–27

A world exists beyond this life on earth. We have Jesus' word on it. Those who die will be brought to life just as Jesus died and rose to a new life. Each of us too will have new life someday. This is the wondrous truth that we celebrate at every Eucharist. It is the truth that we celebrate today.

Universal Prayer

The response is *"Lord, hear our prayer."*

For the Church, that it may offer the Good News of eternal life to the world, we pray to the Lord.

For people who will die today, that they may have a happy death, we pray to the Lord.

For those who work with the dying, that they may hope in Christ and convey this hope to the people they tend.

For our loved ones who have died, that they may enjoy lasting peace in glory, we pray to the Lord.

For ourselves, that we may live well and be ready when the Lord calls us home to heaven, we pray to the Lord.

Special Features

- Display a banner with a large butterfly on it.
- Before Mass invite the children to write in a special book the names of friends, relatives, and people who have died. Then pray for these people in a special intercession at Mass.
- As the response in the Prayer of the Faithful pray *"Kyrie eleison,"* the Greek for "Lord have mercy."

Songs

Journeys Ended, Journeys Begun; Only a Shadow; Peace Is Flowing like a River; Psalm 42 (As the Deer Longs); Song of Farewell; Soon and Very Soon; You Are the Healing

Homily Ideas

Visual: An obituary page

Show an obituary page and read a few entries. Explain that every person someday will be written up in the newspaper on this page that announces deaths. No one gets through life without dying.

· · ·

Tell the children that because Jesus died and saved us, we do not have to fear death. It is not the end of everything for us. Jesus has made us God's adopted children. We can inherit God's kingdom of heaven. If we have faith and live good lives, someday we will live with God in glory in heaven. We will be united to Christ forever. Death is like a doorway through which we walk into the next world.

· · ·

Explain that at a funeral Mass we are sad because we will never see the person who died on earth again. But we also rejoice and the priest wears white vestments because we believe that the person who died was born into a new, everlasting life. Death is just like falling asleep and waking up in a whole new world.

· · ·

Point out that Scripture tells us that people who have had faith in Jesus will be able to rest and will receive a reward in the next life.

· · ·

Ask the children to name people Jesus brought back to life on earth (the son of the widow of Nain, Jairus' daughter, Lazarus). Explain that by these miracles Jesus showed us he had power over death. By rising from the tomb with new life himself after he was crucified, Jesus proved that he conquered death.

. . .

Comment that we can pray for the dead that they may enter heaven soon. Explain that some people who die without having enough love yet to enter heaven must suffer in purgatory until they are ready. We can help them by our prayers.

. . .

Tell the children that we visit cemeteries, keep the graves tidy, and place flowers on the graves to show our love for the people who have gone before us into the next world. At the end of this world we will all be together again.

. . .

Ask the children what will be wonderful about heaven. Make sure someone points out that we will be with Jesus our Lord forever.

. . .

Refer to the transformations of caterpillars into a butterflies and seeds into plants to illustrate how different our next life will be compared to this one. Point out that our bodies that were made temples of God through baptism and that received Christ in the Eucharist will someday be glorified in heaven.

. . .

Tell the parable below:

> *A loved one who dies is like a ship setting out into the ocean. Standing on the shore, we see the ship spread its white sails to the breeze. We watch it until it is only a speck where the sea and sky meet. Someone says, "There! She's gone." The ship is only gone from our sight. It is as large, as beautiful, and as strong as when it left. At the moment someone says, "There! She's gone," other people are watching the ship coming. Other voices are ready to shout with joy, "Here she comes!"*

Resources

Church Documents

Lectionary for Masses with Children

Catechism of the Catholic Church, Book Two

General Instruction of the Roman Missal
(in the Sacramentary)

Constitution on the Sacred Liturgy

Directory for Masses with Children

Built of Living Stones: Art, Architecture, and Worship

Sing to the Lord: Music in Divine Worship

Books

Bartley, Barbara, and Carol Wilson. *Children's Liturgies Made Easy*, Books 1 and 2. Dubuque, IA: Brown/ROA, 1989, 1992.

Fearon, Sr. Mary, RSM. *Practical Liturgies for the School Year*. Dubuque, IA: Brown/ROA, 1991.

The Weekday Book of Readings Adapted for Children. Loveland, OH: Treehaus Communications, 2003.

Glavich, Mary Kathleen, SND. *Gospel Theater for the Whole Community*. New London, CT: Twenty-Third Publications, 2006.

Jeep, Elizabeth McMahon. *Blessings and Prayers through the Year: A Resource for School and Parish*. Chicago: Liturgy Training Publications, 2007.

Kodner, Diana. *Sing God a Simple Song: Music for Celebrating the Word with Children*. Loveland, OH: Treehaus, 1995.

Mazar, Peter, and Robert Piercy. *A Guide to the Lectionary for Masses with Children*. Chicago: Liturgy Training Publications, 1994.

Miller, Les. *25 Questions about the Mass*. Mystic: CT: Twenty-Third Publications, 2010.

Pottebaum, Gerard A. *To Walk with a Child*. Loveland, OH: Treehaus Communications, 1993.

Pottebaum, Gerard A., Paule Freeburg, and Joyce M. Kelleher. *A Child Shall Lead Them*. Loveland, OH: Treehaus, 1992.

Staudacher, Joseph M. *Lector's Guide to Biblical Pronunciations*. Huntington, IN: Our Sunday Visitor, 2001.

Vos, Joan Patano, and Timothy Vos, eds. *Celebrating School Liturgies: Guidelines for Planning*. Collegeville, MN: Liturgical Press, 1991.

Audiovisuals

The Angel's Advent Lesson; *The Angel's Lenten Lesson*; and *The Angel's Mass Lesson* (three videos), Gwen Costello, Mystic, CT: Twenty-Third Publications.

Celebrating the Church Year for Children series (seven videos), Gaynell Cronin and Jack Rathschmidt, OFM Cap., Paulist Press.

The Mass for Children and Young People (DVD). Gaynell Cronin and Jack Rathschmidt, OFM, Cap. Ikonographics.

Following Jesus through the Church Year (eight videos) Gwen Costello. Mystic, CT: Twenty-Third Publications.

Come On In (Church Tour for Children, two videos), Fredric Hang, Mystic, CT: Twenty-Third Publications.

We Go to Church: A Child's Guide to the Mass. (Interactive CD-ROM) Ken Meltz. JLP International, Inc, and Paulist Press.

Music

Child of God: by the Dameans. GIA Publications.

Rise Up and Sing: Children's Music Resource. Oregon Catholic Press.

Sing for Joy: Psalm Settings for Children. Julie Howard. World Library Publications.

Singing Our Faith: Hymnal for Young Catholics. GIA Publications.

Sing Out! A Children's Psalter. World Library Publications.

Singing the Psalms, Vol. 1 and 2. Oregon Catholic Press.

We Are God's People: Psalms for the Family of God. Jeanne Cotter. GIA Publications.

Liturgy Planning Sheets

(to be duplicated and cut apart)

GROUP 1	ENTRANCE PROCESSION
What	*Who*
Cross	
Candles	
Lectionary	
Extraordinary ministers of the Eucharist	
Other:	

Special features: _____

_____

GROUP 2	READINGS	
	What	*Who*
First reading		
Responsorial psalm		
Gospel acclamation		
Gospel		

Special features: _____

_____

GROUP 3	UNIVERSAL PRAYER

Response: _____ *Read by:* _____

1. _____

2. _____

3. _____

4. _____

5. _____

GROUP 4	PREPARATION OF GIFTS

Preparing the altar by: _____

Procession: _____

What	Who
Bread	
Water and wine	

Thanksgiving after communion: _____

_____

_____

GROUP 5	MUSIC	
What	**Who**	
Opening Song		
Presentation Song		
Communion Song		
Closing Song		

Other sung parts (Lord, have mercy; Holy, Holy; Acclamation; Our Father; Great Amen; Lamb of God):

_____

_____

_____

_____

Special accompaniment: _____

Special singers: _____

Eucharist Plan

Date: _____ Season/Theme: _____

Presider: _____ Homilist: _____

Introduction read by: _____

Entrance song: _____

First reading: _____ read by: _____

Responsorial psalm: _____ read by: _____

(Second reading: _____ read by: _____)

Gospel acclamation: _____

Gospel: _____

Universal Prayer read by: _____

Presentation of gifts of: _____

    by: _____

Presentation song: _____

Holy, Holy	☐ Sung	☐ Recited
Memorial acclamation	☐ Sung	☐ Recited
Great Amen	☐ Sung	☐ Recited
Our Father	☐ Sung	☐ Recited
Lamb of God	☐ Sung	☐ Recited

Communion song: _____

Thanksgiving/reflection: _____

Closing song: _____

Special features (Decorations, mementos): _____

_____

_____

_____

_____

Index of
Readings for Weekdays

Index of Solemnities, Feasts, and Memorials

OF RELATED INTEREST

Also from SR. KATHLEEN GLAVICH

Leading Young Catholics into Scripture
Fun and Creative Ways to Bring the Bible to Life

Children remember what they hear, see, and say, but they remember best what they do. That is what this resource is all about. It's a how-to book for teaching Scripture that is packed with exciting classroom ideas for helping children meet God through Scripture in fun and creative ways.　**144 pp | $16.95 | 978-1-58595-800-9**

Liturgical Resources from KATIE THOMPSON

The Liturgy of the Word with Children
A Complete Three-Year Program following the Lectionary

This perfectly delightful and all-inclusive resource covers Years A, B, and C of the liturgical cycle. It is geared to ages five-eight, and for each week of the lectionary cycle there are creative hand-out activity sheets that involve children in the scriptural message.　**392 pp | $39.95 | 978-1-58595-700-2**

The Complete Children's Liturgy Book
Liturgies of the Word for Years A, B, C

Here's a resource that provides a complete and flexible format for celebrating the Liturgy of the Word with children (ages five-eight). It offers a framework for every Sunday of the year and the major feast days and can be adapted to suit the needs of any particular group.　**352 pp | $39.95 | 978-0-89622-695-1**

Step by Step
Lectionary Activities for Kids Ages 4-7 for Every Sunday of the Three-Year Cycle

Introduce young children to God's Word with this wonderfully illustrated and fun-to-use resource. Each easy-to-duplicate, double-sided activity sheet reinforces the Sunday gospel message with pictures to color and complete, drawing activities, and puzzles.　**368 pp | $39.95 | 978-0-89622-987-7**

Footprints in Faith
Lectionary Activities for Kids Ages 7-12 for Every Sunday of the Three-Year Cycle

This invaluable resource offers older children ways to fully enter the gospel stories and their teachings. Each easy-to-duplicate, double-sided activity sheet reinforces the Sunday gospel message with age-appropriate questions and activities.　**368 pp | $39.95 | 978-0-89622-986-0**

1-800-321-0411
www.23rdpublications.com